Published by
Rajneesh Foundation International
Rajneeshpuram, Oregon 97741 U.S.A.

Bhagwan Shree Rajneesh

TAO
THE GOLDEN
GATE

Volume 1

Discourses on Ko Hsuan's **The Classic of Purity**

Editor: Ma Prem Asha
Design: Ma Puja Abhar
        Swami Dhyan Abhudaya
Direction: Ma Yoga Pratima, D.Phil.M. (RIMU), Arihanta
Copyright: ©1984 Rajneesh Foundation International
Published by:
  Ma Anand Sheela, D.Litt.M. (RIMU), Acharya
  Rajneesh Foundation International, President
  P.O. Box 9, Rajneeshpuram
  Oregon 97741 U.S.A.

First Edition: March 1984—10,000 copies

The sutras of Ko Hsuan's *The Classic of Purity* are taken from the
Shrine of Wisdom Manual No. 14 (1934), published by the Shrine of
Wisdom, Fintry, Brook, Nr. Godalming, Surrey, England and are
used with kind permission.

ISBN 0-88050-646-6
Library of Congress Catalog Card Number 84-42615

Printed in U.S.A.

CONTENTS

INTRODUCTION

EAT, DRINK AND BE MERRY. This is Tao. This is Bhagwan. Bhagwan Shree Rajneesh is a living, enlightened 20th century Master. He belongs totally, wholeheartedly to today, to this moment, to this mad, crazy time of tremendous scientific discovery, rebellious kids, great wealth, great poverty, fast food, starvation, disposable diapers, TV—this time of increased violence and crime, high taxes, the breakdown of the family and a stockpile of nuclear weapons that can destroy the world 700 times over.

Into this chaos Bhagwan brings the pure insight of Tao—the no-nonsense, down-to-earth art of being.

Bhagwan has said "Truth is a gift" and He giftwraps it as only a Master can. Wrapped in love and tied with laughter, the gift is offered, a rare champagne that will transform your life. Enjoy this opportunity of being non-serious, of laughing, of dancing. And if you think there is no fun to have, then Tao is for you.

The magic of the Master is in every word. Sit back, take a sip and allow Bhagwan to warm your heart. He is the Master of Masters. His is the magical touch. "Life consists of small things, but if you learn how to enjoy these small things the ordinary becomes extraordinary, the mundane becomes sacred, the profane becomes profound."

CHEERS!

Ma Shanti Bhadra,
D.M. (RIMU), Arihanta

These ten discourses were
given by
Bhagwan Shree Rajneesh,
based on Ko Hsuan's
The Classic of Purity
and responses to questions
from visitors and disciples
between June 11 and 20, 1980
at the Shree Rajneesh Ashram, Poona, India.

The Supreme Tao is formless,
yet It produces and nurtures Heaven and Earth.
The Supreme Tao has no desires, yet by Its power
the Sun and Moon revolve in their orbits.
The Supreme Tao is nameless,
yet It ever supports all things.
I do not know Its name
but for title call It Tao.

JUST
AN
EMPTY
PASSAGE

THE CLASSIC OF PURITY is one of the most profound insights into nature. I call it an insight, not a doctrine, not a philosophy, not a religion, because it is not intellectual at all; it is existential. The man who is speaking in it is not speaking as a mind, he is not

1

speaking as himself either; he is just an empty passage for existence itself to say something through him.

That's how the great mystics have always lived and spoken. These are not their own words—they are no more, they have disappeared long before; it is the whole pouring through them. Their expressions may be different, but the source is the same. The words of Jesus, Zarathustra, Buddha, Lao Tzu, Krishna, Mohammed are not ordinary words; they are not coming from their memory, they are coming from their experience. They have touched the divine, and the moment you touch the divine you evaporate, you cannot exist anymore. You have to die for God to be.

This is a Taoist insight. Tao is another name for God, far more beautiful than God because God, the word "God", has been exploited too much by the priests. They have exploited in the name of God for so long that even the word has become contaminated—it has become disgusting. Any man of intelligence is bound to avoid it because it reminds him of all the nonsense that has happened on the earth down the ages in the name of God, in the name of religion. More mischief has happened in the name of God than in any other name.

Tao in that sense is tremendously beautiful. You cannot worship Tao because Tao does not give you the idea of a person. It is simply a principle, not a person. You cannot worship a principle—you cannot pray to Tao. It will look ridiculous, it will be utterly absurd, praying to a principle. You don't pray to gravitation, you cannot pray to the theory of relativity.

Tao simply means the ultimate principle that binds the whole existence together. The existence is not a chaos, that much is certain; it is a cosmos. There is immense order in it, intrinsic order in it, and the name of that order is Tao. Tao simply means the harmony of the whole. No temples have been built for Tao; no statues, no prayers, no priests, no rituals—that's the beauty of it. Hence I don't call it a doctrine, nor do I call it a religion, it is a pure insight. You can call it Dharma; that is Buddha's word for Tao. The word in English that comes closer or closest to Tao is "Nature" with a capital N.

This profound insight is also one of the smallest treatises ever written. It is so condensed—it is as if millions of roses have been condensed in a drop of perfume. That's the ancient way of expressing truth: because books were not in existence, people had to remember it.

It is said that this is the first mystic treatise ever written down as a book. It is not much of a book, not more than one and a half pages, but it existed for thousands of years before it was written. It existed through private and personal communion. That has been always the most significant way to transmit truth. To write it down makes it more difficult because then one never knows who will be reading it; it loses all personal contact and touch.

In Egypt, in India, in China, in all the ancient civilizations, for thousands of years the mystic message was carried from one person to another, from the Master to the disciple. And the Master would say these things only when the disciple was ready, or he would say only as much as the disciple could digest. Otherwise words can also produce diarrhea; they certainly do produce it—our century suffers very much from it. All the mystics for centuries resisted writing down their insights.

This was the first treatise ever written; that's its significance. It marks a certain change in human consciousness, a change which was going to prove of great importance later on because even though it is beautiful to commune directly, person to person, the message cannot reach many people; many are bound to miss. Yes, it will not fall in the wrong hands, but many right hands will also remain empty. And one should think more of the right hands than of the wrong hands. The wrong people are going to be wrong whether some profound insight falls in their hands or not, but the right people will be missing something which can transform their being.

Ko Hsuan, who wrote this small treatise, marks a milestone in the consciousness of humanity. He understood the significance of the written word, knowing all its dangers. In the preface he writes: "Before writing down these words I contemplated ten thousand times whether to write or not, because I was taking a dangerous step." Nobody had gathered that much courage before.

Ko Hsuan was preceded by Lao Tzu, Chuang Tzu, Lieh Tzu. Even they had not written anything; their message was remembered by their disciples. It was only written after Ko Hsuan took the dangerous step. But he also says, "Ten thousand times I contemplated," because it is no ordinary matter. Up to that moment in history no Master had ever dared to write anything down, just to avoid the wrong people.

Even a man like Buddha comtemplated for seven days before uttering a single word. When he attained to enlightenment for seven days he remained utterly silent, wavering whether to say anything or not. The question was: Those who cannot understand, what is the point of saying to them such profound insights? They will misunderstand, they will misinterpret, they will do harm to the message. Rather than allowing the message to heal them they will wound the message itself—they will manipulate the message according to their minds, prejudices. Is it right to allow the message to be polluted by foolish people, by mediocre people, by stupid people?

Buddha was hesitant, very hesitant. Yes, he also thought of the few people who would be able to understand it, but then he could see that "Those people who will be able to understand my words will be able to find truth on their own because they cannot be ordinary people, they will be super-intelligent people, only then will they be able to understand what I am saying to them. If they can understand my words they will be able to find their own way, they will be able to reach the truth on their own, so why bother about them? Maybe it will take a little longer for them. So what?—because there is eternity, time is not short. But the message, once it gets into the wrong hands, will be corrupted forever." Even to utter he was hesitant.

I can understand Ko Hsuan's contemplating over the matter ten thousand times—whether to write it down or not—because when you say something to people, if they are stupid people, they are bound to forget it very soon. If they are mediocre people they will not bother even to listen; they won't care. But once it is written down then they will read it, study it; then it will become part of their schools, colleges and universities, and stupid scholars will ponder over it and they will write great scholarly treatises on it. People who know nothing will be talking about it for centuries and the truth will be lost in all that noise that scholars make—they will argue for and against.

It is said that once a disciple of the devil came running to him and he said, "What are you doing sitting here under this tree? Have you not heard?—one man has found truth! We have to do something, and

5

urgently, because if this man has found truth our very existence is in danger, our very profession is in danger. He can cut our very roots!"

The old devil laughed. He said, "Calm down, please. You are new, that's why you are so disturbed by it. Don't be worried. I have got my people, they have already started working."

The disciple asked, "But I have not seen any of our people there."

The devil said, "I work in many ways. Scholars are there, pundits are there, philosophers are there, theologians are there. Don't be worried. They will make so much noise for and against, they will create so much argumentation that the still small voice of truth will be silenced by them. We need not worry. These scholars and pundits and these professors are my people: I work through them—they are in my service, they are my secret agents. Don't be worried. You may not have seen my well-known disciples there because I cannot go directly, I have to go in disguise. And I have arrived there and my people have started working—they have surrounded the person. He cannot do any harm. And soon he will be dead—he is old—and then my people will be his apostles, his priests, and they will manage the whole affair."

Priests are in the service of the devil, not in the service of God. The so-called great scholars who go on and on with logic-chopping, hair-splitting arguments are in the service of the devil, not in the service of God.

Once you write down something you are giving a chance to these people; they will jump upon the opportunity, they won't miss the opportunity. They will mess the whole thing up, they will create great confusion around it. That is their expertise.

Hence I can understand Ko Hsuan contemplating ten thousand times whether to write it or not. But finally he decided to write and I think he did the right thing. One should never be afraid of darkness. Light, howsoever small, is far more powerful than darkness, howsoever big, howsoever old. In fact, darkness has no power, light has power.

These words are powerful words. And the way mystics speak the truth, it is almost beyond the scholars; they really cannot destroy its beauty. In fact, they cannot even touch its truth; it is impossible for them for the simple reason that the mystics speak in a paradoxical language, they don't speak logically. Hence they are beyond the grasp of the scholars. The scholars can only see contradictions in them because the scholar functions through logic and all the mystic expressions are paradoxical—illogical or supralogical. And particularly Taoist sayings are superb in that way—nobody has been able to transcend their paradoxes. Even in this small treatise you will come across paradoxes almost in every sentence, in every utterance.

That, too, has to be understood. Why do mystics speak in paradoxes? To remain unavailable to the scholars. The paradox can be understood only by a meditator; it can never be understood by a person who lives in the head, in the mind. Unless you have tasted something of the no-mind, you cannot understand a paradox. That is a safeguard, that is an inbuilt safeguard: speak paradoxically, speak as if you are almost mad.

Once a journalist came to see George Gurdjieff. He was drinking his morning tea. He always avoided journalists because they are the most stupid people around, and his way of avoiding them was unique. He asked the woman disciple who was pouring tea for him, as the journalist sat by his side, "What day is it today?"

And the woman said, "Today is Saturday."

And Gurdjieff became so angry that he went into a rage and threw the cup on the floor. The cup was shattered into thousands of pieces. The journalist became very much afraid . . . because it *was* Saturday.

And Gurdjieff said, "You always go on talking nonsense to me! Just the other day you were telling me that it was Friday and now today it is Saturday? How can it be? How can Saturday come after Friday?"

The journalist thought this man was mad. He simply escaped without even saying goodbye, and Gurdjieff had a good laugh. The woman was very much shocked. She was new; she did not know that this was his way of avoiding wrong people. She said, "But why did you become so angry?"

He said, "You will understand if you remain here a little longer. Now this man will never come back; for his whole life I have put him off. And he will go and spread rumors about me to his professional colleagues, so not only has he been thrown out, many more who may have bothered me will never come here."

He was thought to be a madman, utterly mad.

The paradoxical statements of the mystics have a purpose. The purpose is: the scholars avoid them. The moment they come across a mystic, deep down they know this man is mad—they won't bother about such a man. Secondly: the paradox is the only way to indicate something that is really true. Logic is always half, it never takes in the whole, it cannot take in the whole. Life consists of polarities: just as electricity consists of positive and negative poles, the whole of life consists of polarities. And polarities are only apparently opposite to each other; deep down they are not opposite to each other. Deep down, for those who understand, for those who have the intelligence to see that deeply, they are not opposites, they are complementaries.

But for that you will need a deep experience of meditation; mind only won't help. Mind will say, "These are contradictory statements. This man is saying one thing at the beginning of the sentence and by the time he ends the sentence he has uttered just the opposite." But the mystic knows what he is doing: he is trying to put the whole truth in it. But the whole truth can be understood only by a person who has tasted something of the whole.

Mind always splits things: it divides, it separates, it functions like a prism. When a white sunray passes through the prism it becomes divided into seven colors. That's how a rainbow is created: it is created by very small drops of water hanging in the air; those drops of water function like prisms and the sunrays passing through them become divided into seven colors. The mind is a prism: it divides everything into *many*. The truth is one, but if you look through the mind everything appears to be many. And the mystic's way of saying things is such that he wants to put all the colors of the rainbow again back together as they were in the very beginning before passing through the prism.

Because of this paradoxical way of expression scholars avoid them. People who live in the mind cannot comprehend them; it is a safeguard. That's how such beautiful treatises have survived for centuries.

Ko Hsuan is simply writing it, remember it; he is not the creator of the treatise. He has also experienced the same truth because the truth is always the same whoever experiences it. Whenever one experiences it it is always the same, it does not change; time makes no difference. But what he is saying has been transferred by word of mouth for centuries, maybe for thousands of years. That's why we don't exactly know whose words they are.

He simply says:

The venerable Master said . . .

WHO IS THIS MASTER? Nothing is said about him. Perhaps the Master simply represents all the Masters of the past and all the Masters of the present and all the Masters of the future. Maybe it simply represents the essential wisdom—not any particular person, but simply the principle.

Nothing is known about Ko Hsuan, nothing at all. Hence for at least a few centuries it had been thought that these words belonged to Lao Tzu. But Lao Tzu has a different way of speaking, a totally different way; these words can't be coming from Lao Tzu. We have gone into the words of Lao Tzu; he is even more mad than Ko Hsuan, he is even more mystical. And it is a well known fact that he never wrote anything other than *Tao Te Ching*, and that too he wrote under pressure, at the last moment, when he was leaving China to die in the Himalayas.

He had decided to die in the mountains, and one cannot find a more beautiful place to die than the Himalayas—the silence of the Himalayas, the virgin silence, the beauty, nature in its most profound splendor. So when he became very old he said to his disciples, "I am going to the Himalayas to find a place where I can disappear into nature, where nobody will know about me, where no monument will be made in honor of me, no temple, not even a grave. I simply want to disappear as if I had never existed."

When he was passing through the country he was stopped at the border because the king had alerted all the borders and ordered that "If Lao Tzu passes out of the country through any gate he should be prevented unless he writes down whatsoever he has experienced." His whole life he had avoided it. In the end, it is said, because he was caught on the border and they wouldn't allow him to go to the Himalayas, he stayed in a guard's hut for three days and just wrote down the small treatise, *Tao Te Ching.*

So this cannot be that *The Classic of Purity* belongs to Lao Tzu. But because nothing much is known about Ko Hsuan, people used to think that they must be words of Lao Tzu and Ko Hsuan must be a disciple of Lao Tzu who has simply written them down—the notes of a disciple. That's not so. Ko Hsuan himself is a Master in his own right.

In his preface to this small treatise he says a few things which have to be remembered. First he says: "When I attained to union with Tao I meditated upon this insight ten thousand times before writing it down." He says, "When I attained to union with Tao. . . " He is not just a disciple, he is an enlightened man. He has attained to union with Tao. He is not writing notes heard from somebody else, he has experienced it himself. He has attained to the ultimate union with Tao: he has become one with nature.

He says in the preface, "It is only for the seekers of the beyond; the worldly cannot understand it." He makes it clear in the preface that if you are a worldly man it is better not to bother about it. Don't waste your time, it is not meant for you, it will not be of any use to you. It may even confuse you, it may even distract you from your wordly affairs. It is better not to get involved with things in which you are not really interested. It is better not to be accidental.

There are many people who are accidental, just by the way. They will meet somebody and they will become interested.

Just the other day I received a letter from Amritsar. From the International Hotel in Amritsar a man writes . . . You will be surprised to know that when I was talking about *The Dhammapada*, the last series, I mentioned a man, Michael Tomato, who had written to me from a hotel in Bangalore because he came across a sannyasin who told him that in my ashram, in Sufi dancing, his president, Reverend Canon Banana, was being laughed at. He became angry. He wrote a very angry letter to me saying: "This is not good that you should allow such things in your ashram, because it is insulting to our great nation of Zimbabwe."

The nation was born just seven days before that and this man, Reverend Banana, had become president just two days before Michael Tomato met this sannyasin—just two days before that—and we have been using the word "banana" in Sufi dancing for years! In fact, it may be because of our prayers that one of the bananas has become the president, because prayers have their own ways of working miracles.

That time I told you that this man was angry and that his name was Michael Tomato, and just jokingly I mentioned that soon another letter would be coming to me from a certain Michael Potato. It has come! This letter comes from the Amritsar International Hotel. Two sannyasins are staying there and this man saw them. This man comes from the West, but he has become a converted Sikh. Seeing two orange people he became interested; he introduced himself. And those sannyasins must have wondered when they heard his name, Michael Potato Singh, because now he has become a Sikh. They said, "Wait, we've got the tape—you listen to it!"

He listened to the tape and he thought, "This is a miracle! How did Bhagwan know about me?" So he has dropped his new religion. He is coming here! Soon he will be here.

Now these are accidental people. I was just joking, in a way knowing perfectly well that in this big earth

there must be someone who is known as Michael
Potato, but I was not hoping that so soon, just after
one month, we would find him! Now, he had become
a Sikh, so he dropped Sikhism. He writes: "I have cut
my hair and I am coming, and I want to be a sannyasin
because you are the right man I have been searching
for my whole life."

These are accidental people. This is not the way to
grow. These people are like driftwood: they simply go
on moving with any wave, they are just at the mercy
of the winds, having no sense of direction.

Ko Hsuan says: "It is only for the seekers of the
beyond." He makes it clear that if you are a seeker of
the beyond, if you are ready to risk . . . because the
search for the beyond is risky. It is the greatest adventure, tremendously ecstatic, but not easy at all; it is arduous too. It has its ecstasy, it has its agonies—it has
its own cross. Of course, resurrection comes through
it, but it cannot happen unless you are crucified. So he
makes it clear that it is only for the seekers.

One has to be very certain about oneself whether
one is a seeker or not. Are you really interested in
truth?—because every child is distracted from the
very beginning. No child seems to be interested in
God, but parents go on forcing the idea of God on
every child. If by chance you happen to be born in a
family of atheists, then they impose the idea of
atheism on you. If you are born in a communist country, then of course communism will be imposed upon
you. If not the Bible, then *Das Kapital*. If not the holy
trinity, then the unholy trinity of Marx, Engels and
Lenin, but something is bound to be imposed upon
you.

No parent is loving enough to leave you alone to
yourself to grow, to help you, to nourish you and to
give you total freedom to be yourself, authentically
yourself. Hence there are many people who think

they are seekers of God—they are not. Their whole seeking is an imposed phenomenon, a conditioning. And if you are only searching for God because you have been told, you have been continuously told again and again, then the word has become a reality in you but it is not part of you, it is not intrinsic; it has come from the outside. You are just like a parrot—or maybe even parrots are more intelligent than you are.

An overly enthusiastic Italian communist finds a parrot who can sing the popular communist song "Bandiera Rosa". He buys it and takes it home, but after a few days the wife can no longer stand it. The parrot keeps singing the song the whole day long.

In a moment of rage she knocks the parrot over and then covers it with a cloth. When the husband comes back she tells him everything.

In despair the man lifts the cloth to see how the parrot is.

Opening one eye the parrot whispers, "Hey, comrade, are those dirty fascists gone-a?"

Even parrots are far more intelligent than so-called human beings. They go on simply repeating cliches that have been handed over to them by their parents and the priests and the teachers, schools, colleges, universities. This whole society goes on conditioning you in a certain way, and after twenty-five years of conditioning, if you forget what you really want to do, what you really want to be, it is natural.

The first thing to be decisive about is whether there is a deep longing to know the truth. Are you ready to risk everything for it, even your life if the need arises? If it is so, "Then," Ko Hsuan says, "These words are for you." If you are only a worldly person—by "worldly" he means one who is interested in money, power, prestige—then it would be better if you don't bother about such great things; they are not for you —at least not yet.

You have to become fed up with all your so-called worldly desires. First go into those desires. Unless you become tremendously frustrated, unless you see that they are all futile: that whether you succeed or fail you always fail; that whether you have money or you are poor you are always poor; that whether you are a beggar or an emperor you are always a beggar . . . When that insight dawns on you, then only you can really become a seeker of the beyond. Otherwise, if you pretend to be a seeker of the beyond, you will bring your whole world with you, you will bring all your desires with you.

That's why people think of God, of heaven. It is not that they are interested in God and heaven, they are only interested in power, prestige. Maybe they are afraid of death and out of fear and out of greed they start praying to God. But a prayer that arises out of fear and greed is not prayer at all.

A real prayer arises out of gratitude, never out of fear and greed. A real prayer arises out of love for truth, whatsoever it is. Otherwise your worldly desires will again be projected onto God, onto heaven.

If you look into the descriptions of paradise of different religions and different countries you will be surprised: what they desire is projected. For example, the Tibetan paradise is described as warm—obviously, because Tibetans suffer from cold so much that they would like heaven to be full of sun and warmth so that they can at least take a bath every day. In Tibet the scriptures say that it is your duty to take one bath at least every year!

The Indian paradise is cool, in fact, air-conditioned. They did not know the word at that time so it is "air-cooled". It is bound to be so—India has suffered so much from heat. And you know through your own experience now that all that the Indian mind wants is a little shade and coolness. So the Indian paradise is always full of cool breezes and there are big trees, so big that a thousand bullock carts can rest under a single tree. The Indian idea of shade and coolness . . .

The Tibetan hell is absolutely icy and the Indian hell is full of fire.

Now, there cannot be so many hells and so many paradises; these are our projections. Whatsoever we desire we project onto heaven and whatsoever we are afraid of we project onto hell. Hell is for others, for those who don't believe in our ideology, and paradise is a reward for those who believe in our ideology—the same worldly things. These are not religious people.

In the Mohammedan heaven there are streams of wine. This is very strange: here you condemn wine—it is a sin—and there you reward your saints with wine!

All the paradises of all countries are full of beautiful women because they are all created by men, so I have never come across a description of beautiful men. If women . . . and, of course, sooner or later the Lib women are going to write about their own paradise. They won't talk about beautiful women, they will talk about beautiful men—henpecked husbands, always following the women like shadows, obedient, etcetera, etcetera, just like servants. That's how women have been painted by men in their heaven. And they are always young, they never grow old. This is strange!

If you look at the idea of God, all the religions think of God as a very very old man. Have you ever thought of God as a young man? No country has ever thought of God as a young man because you cannot trust young people: they are dangerous and they are a little foolish, too. A wise man has to be very old, so God is very old. But the women he is surrounded with are all very young, in fact, stuck at the age of eighteen; they don't grow beyond that. Very stagnant! They must be getting tired of remaining eighteen for millions of years!

But this is man's idea: here the saints renounce women, they renounce sex; they condemn sex, they praise celibacy—and, of course, they are hoping they will be paid well, they will be rewarded. These are our worldly desires again coming back from the unconscious; you cannot push them away. Unless you have encountered them, unless you have watched them, you cannot just repress them.

Ko Hsuan is right: he says, "The worldly cannot understand it." They are bound to misunderstand.

The new patient comes into the analyst's office. He is a theologian, a great scholar, and a philosopher. He says, "Doctor, I came here because everybody says I think too much of myself."

"Let's get into this," says the doctor. "To analyze your problem it is necessary that you tell me your story; it is necessary that you tell me your problem from the very beginning."

"Okay," says the professor, and sitting down continues. "In the beginning all was darkness."

You see? And he has come to tell the analyst, "People think I think too much of myself." And he really begins from the very beginning! His understanding is bound to remain with him wherever he goes, whatsoever he does. Whatsoever he chooses is going to be out of his mind and mentality.

A jealous Italian husband comes home early one night. He finds his wife in bed, smoke hanging in the bedroom. Suspicious, he starts beating his wife.

"I swear-a I'm alone!" cries the wife. "Don't-a beat-a me! You might-a be punished. Remember, up-a there, there is-a someone who knows-a everything!"

From the top of the closet a male voice says, "Yes, but the one under the bed knows even more!"

How long can you repress? How long can you hide? It is going to come up, if not from the front door then from the back door.

Two madmen looked at the clock: it is twelve o'clock.

One says, "It is midday."

The other says, "It's midnight."
The discussion becomes so heated that they decide to ask the director. "Is it midday or midnight, sir?" they ask him.

The director looks at his watch and says, "Well, I don't know—it's stopped."

In a madhouse you can't expect the director to be less mad than the other madmen. In fact, he may be the director because he is more mad! He may be the oldest inmate, hence he has been chosen to be the director.

The father calls his son and asks him, "Is it true that you are planning to leave home as Mother tells me?"

"Well, yes," the boy firmly replies.

"Well," says the father in serious voice, "when you decide to go, tell me—I'll come with you!"

Ko Hsuan says in his preface: "I received it from the divine ruler of the Golden Gate."

Truth is always a gift, it is not an achievement because all achievements belong to the ego and truth cannot be part of your ego trip. Truth happens only when the ego is dropped, so you cannot say, "I have achieved it," you can only say, "It has been given." It is a gift. Ko Hsuan is right: he says, "I received it . . ." Hence, remember it, you have to be at the receiving end. You are not to be aggressive about truth. The real seeker is not an achiever, he is not aggressive, he is not masculine, he becomes feminine. He is just like a womb—he receives. He empties himself totally so that space is created to receive.

And that's the whole art of meditation. That's what we are doing here, and that's what for centuries mystics have been doing and Masters have been telling their disciples to do: Empty yourself totally, become a nothingness. And the moment you are totally nothing, at that very moment, truth descends in you; you become full of it. First you have to be empty of yourself and then you become full of God, Tao, Dharma, or whatsoever name you would like to choose for it.

He says: "I received it from the divine ruler of the Golden Gate." This is a mysterious saying, "the Golden Gate." That is Taoist way of saying that God is not really a person but a gate, an opening into existence, and if you are empty, the door opens *within you*. It is your ego that is blocking the door, it is you who are blocking the door; except you there is no hindrance. Remove yourself, don't come in between, and suddenly the Golden Gate opens. And it is called golden because the moment *you* pass through it you are pure gold. The dust disappears, is transmuted, is transformed; it becomes divine.

This is the definition of alchemy: transforming dust into the divine, transforming base metal into gold.

And it happens simply by becoming a receiver. You have to be utterly a non-entity.

Ko Hsuan says: "It has been previously only transmitted by word of mouth. Those who will be able to comprehend the meaning will become ambassadors of the divine and enter the Golden Gate."

This small preface says: "Those who will be able to comprehend it, understand it, will become ambassadors of the divine . . ." Not that they *have* to become, they *will* become so naturally, without any effort, effortlessly. They will start radiating God, they will start radiating light, they will become luminous. Miracles will start happening through them without any effort.

It is said that many miracles happened in Ko Hsuan's life. They are the same miracles which have been happening to many mystics. For example, it is said he was able to walk on water. The same is said about Jesus. It is not a fact, remember—Jesus is not so foolish, neither is Ko Hsuan so foolish as to walk on water. There is no need to walk on water. Then what does it mean? It is a poetic expression, it is a metaphor. It simply means they were able to do the impossible.

And what is the most impossible thing in the world? The most impossible thing in the world is to transcend the world. The most impossible thing in the world is to know oneself. The most impossible thing in the world is to become utterly empty.

These are just metaphors, "walking on water"; don't take them as facts. They are poetic ways of saying certain things.

The second thing said about him is that he knew the secret of the elixir of life, that is the secret of alchemy. One who knows his consciousness, the consciousness which is just a witness to his thoughts, one who comes to know his state of no-mind, knows absolutely that there is no death for him—no birth, no death—that he has never been born and will never die, he has gone beyond both. This is the secret of life, this is the secret science of alchemy.

And the third thing said about him is that he ascended to the beyond in the full light of the day. That is said about Mohammed also and about many others. These are all beautiful ways of expressing the inexpressible. These people have ascended to the ultimate, not by any back door; they have achieved to the ultimate in the full light of the day. Those who had eyes have seen them ascending. Those who had ears have heard the music when they were ascending. Those who had hearts to feel have felt it, their transformation. These people lived on the earth and yet they belonged not to the earth. They were not earthly people, they were utterly unearthly.

Don't be misguided by religious fanatics who go on emphasizing that these metaphors are not metaphors but facts, that these poetic expressions are not poetic expressions but part of history. Be a little more poetic if you really want to understand the mystic way of life.

The perfection of the paradise was such that Peter got bored. One day, when everyone was sitting all together, he said to God, "I am so bored . . . I'd love to visit earth now and then, wouldn't you?"

"Not at my age," replies God.

Says Jesus, "Once has been enough for me."

Says the Holy Ghost, "Not until they stop shooting at doves!"

Jesus is called by his father who tells him that he has to sacrifice himself once more for the redemption of mankind.

21

Though rather unwillingly, Jesus says okay.

He goes around heaven saying goodbye to all his friends and promising to come back in thirty-three years. Then, followed by all the angels, he comes down to earth.

Thirty-three years go by, but there is no sign of Jesus. Finally, after eighty years, an old lean man comes to heaven saying that he is Jesus. He is taken to God who recognizes him immediately and exclaims in astonishment, "What happened? Why did you take so long?"

"Well, you see, Father," replies Jesus, "there is no more capital punishment on earth. I was condemned to a life sentence!"

Jesus is walking amongst the people and performing miracles. Suddenly a man falls at his feet and says, "Lord, Lord, cure me, cure me!"

"Calm down, son. Have faith and you will be cured."

Jesus moves closer to the man and looks into his eyes, then backs away and signals to Peter to come over. As Peter draws near, Jesus whispers to him, "It's not going to work, Peter. Pretend we have to go—he's got cancer!"

Reality is reality!

Either these miracles are metaphors or some coincidences. For example, Lazarus coming back to life: he may just have been in a coma or it is just a beautiful metaphor, because every Master calls his disciple to come back to life from his grave, because ordinarily you are dead; you have not tasted of life at all. You are all Lazaruses! And he was dead for only four days; you have been dead for millions of lives. It would certainly be a miracle to call you forth! And if you listen and come back to life it would be just as much a miracle done by you as it would be a miracle done by the

Master. In fact, you will be doing a greater miracle than the Master!

The same miracles are described in all the lives of the saints; there are not many differences for the simple reason that every mystic lives such a life that he is in the world and yet not in the world. How to express it? How to say something significant about him? It can be said only through miracles. The language of miracles is the only possible way to express something, at least to hint at something, that is indescribable.

But there are foolish people who cling to these things and then they start creating a history. They are not helpful in spreading the divine message; they create obstacles, hindrances. In fact, many more intelligent people would be with Jesus if all these miracles and the nonsense attached to them were dropped. Yes, fools would desert him because they are only with him because of the miracles, but intelligent people would be with him.

And that's my effort here. I want you to be aware, intelligent, conscious. And if you choose to be with me it should not be for any foolish reason.

Just three, four days ago I received a letter from Australia from a new sannyasin, a young woman who had read only one of my books; it must have been because of the title, *Be Realistic: Plan for a Miracle*. So she read that book and she started planning for a miracle: she became a sannyasin and then she started planning to come to India. Her friends laughed, her family laughed. They said, "You are mad!" But she was so convinced that she didn't listen to anybody. She had been out of work for many months so she had no money, and because for many months she had been unemployed she had borrowed from almost everybody she knew; she could not get any more money from anybody else. So there was no possibility of her coming to India, but she started planning.

And one day at a friend's house she saw a magazine with an advertisement for a ninety-day trip to India. She looked into it and she said, "It must be Bhagwan who is doing the miracle!" You had to read a book . . . you had to purchase the book and read the book and then answer a few questions in only twenty lines. She had only six dollars left but she purchased the book—that was the price of the book. She read the book because the last date was coming so close that day and night she had to read the book. It was one thousand pages long! And then she answered.

She writes to me: "I don't know who was answering. You must have been answering!" Now, I have no idea what she is talking about. I have not answered at all—I must say it before it is too late! But she says, "You must have answered because," she says, "*I* don't have any idea what I wrote—I don't even remember what I wrote." Naturally, because if for three days she was reading day and night, how could she know what she was writing? And how could she remember some stupid book, one thousand pages long? And the book must be stupid, because this is not the way to sell a book of any value; this is the way to sell stupid books.

And she was determined that it was going to happen. But this is a series of coincidences! She went, handed over the answer because it was the closing date. She was not in her senses about what was happening and who was doing it. The next day while she was going to some friend's house, on the way suddenly she had the idea that she had to run back home—the telegram had come! She rushed back. Yes, there was a telegram. Now, even if I tell her that I had nothing to do with all these things she won't listen to me. She won't believe me, she will believe in her own

JUST AN EMPTY PASSAGE

experience, obviously. And the telegram said, "Come immediately and contact us." She rushed there—she had won the first prize! Now she is coming for ninety days. She says, "Bhagwan, you have done it. You promised and you have done it!" Now, I am not guilty at all!

Sometimes coincidences and sometimes a series of coincidences is possible which can make a person believe. And when these things happen—and these things can happen, it is such a vast world—people are bound to believe. People are gullible.

But my effort here is to make you intelligent, not believers. There are no miracles. There is only one miracle—*the* miracle I call it—and that is your being utterly empty. The death of the ego is the only miracle; if that happens you have attained the Golden Gate, you have passed through the Golden Gate. You have known what eternity is; you have gone beyond time.

Now these small sutras:

THE VENERABLE MASTER SAID:
The supreme Tao is formless . . .

FROM THE VERY BEGNNING Ko Hsuan wants you to know that Tao has no form. So you cannot make a statue of Tao, you cannot create a temple around Tao, you cannot create rituals; no priesthood is possible.

The supreme Tao is formless . . .

It is the universal law of existence. You cannot worship, you cannot pray. All your worship is foolish and all your prayers are unheard and will remain unheard. There is nobody to hear your prayers or to fulfill your prayers. Your prayers are your desires in a new form. Watch your prayers—what they are. The garb is religious, the jargon is religious, but nothing has changed; the desires are the same. People are asking

25

for money, power, prestige. Whatsoever you are asking for you are asking for something wrong because there is nobody to give you anything. The very idea of getting by asking is absurd. Be utterly silent.

Tao is not the path of prayer, it is the path of meditation.

> . . . *Tao is formless,*
> *yet it produces and nurtures*
> *heaven and earth.*

It does not mean that Tao is indifferent to you; it simply means you cannot worship it, you cannot pray to it. But it goes on nourishing you, you are nourished by it; it nurtures you. The whole breathes it. It is the heartbeat of the cosmos, but not a person.

> *The supreme Tao has no desires . . .*

So if you want to have a communion with Tao you will have to drop all desires. People simply go on changing their desires, but they basically remain the same. People go on changing their outer structures of life; they call it character. Somebody smokes, you may not smoke; then you start chewing gum. It is the same stupidity. Or you may stop chewing gum, then you start doing something else. But because *you* are the same, nothing is going to change. If you go to the moon you will do the same stupid things that you are doing here. Everything will be different and nothing will be different.

A couple has been captured by a flying saucer from Mars and are taken to the living room of the space-craft. There they are received by a Martian couple, are offered green drinks, and begin chatting. After several drinks, everyone relaxes. The man from earth asks the Martians, "How do you procreate?"

"My wife and I will demonstrate for you," answers the Martian.

They go over to a refrigerator-like closet and the female picks up a bottle containing brown liquid and the husband picks up a bottle containing white liquid. They go over to a table where there is an empty jar. Each pours the liquid into the empty jar.

"Now we put the jar in this closet," explains the Martian, "and in nine months we will have another baby. How do you do it on Earth?"

So the earth couple demonstrates for the Martians. They take off their clothes and lie down on the floor with the man on top of the woman. As they are coming and going, they notice the Martians are laughing at them.

"What are you laughing at?" they ask.

"Excuse us," they answer, "but we find it very funny because that is the same way we make coffee!"

You can be here, you can be on the moon, you can be on Mars, you can change outer things—it makes no difference. Either you will make love in a stupid way or you will make coffee in a stupid way, but you will do something stupid!

Unless intelligence arises in you, unless your unconsciousness is transformed into consciousness, unless your darkness disappears and becomes light . . .

> *The supreme Tao has no desires,*
> *yet by its power the*
> *sun and moon revolve in their orbits.*
> *The supreme Tao is nameless,*
> *yet it ever supports all things.*
> *I do not know its name . . .*

THESE ARE IMMENSELY VALUABLE WORDS: *I do not know* . . . That's how the people who know speak.

27

The people who claim that they know are utterly ignorant. The real knower functions out of a state of not-knowing.

Ko Hsuan says:

> *I do not know even its name*
> *but for title call it Tao.*

But we have to call it something. See the non-fanatic attitude. You can call it anything—XYZ. Tao simply means XYZ. Just because we have to call it something, we call it Tao. If you choose some other name there is no problem.

So when Buddhists reached China they were surprised because Taoist mystics simply agreed with them. They said, "Perfectly right! We call it Tao, you call it Dharma. It is the same thing, because we define Tao as nameless, you define Dharma as nameless. We say Tao is formless, you say Dharma is formless, so there is no problem. We are only speaking different langauges, but we are indicating towards the same truth."

That is one of the most beautiful things that has ever happened in history. When Buddhism reached China there was no conflict, no argumentation, no conversion, and yet Buddhists and Taoists met and mingled and became one, absolutely one. It has not happened in the history of Christianity or in the history of Judaism or in the history of Mohammedanism; their history is full of ugliness. It has happened only in the tradition of Buddha and Lao Tzu: a very rare phenomenon—no argumentation. They simply tried to understand each other and they laughed and they hugged and they said, "Perfectly true!"

A Christian missionary went to see a Zen Master and he started reading the beatitudes from the Bible. And he said, "Blessed are the meek for theirs is the kingdom of God."

The Master said, "Stop! That's enough. Whoever has said it is a Buddha!"

The missionary was utterly dumb. He had come to argue, he had come to convert. He had come to convince the Zen Master that Buddha is wrong and Jesus is right. And this man said, "Whosoever has said it—I don't know who has said it—but whosoever has said it is a Buddha. There is no need to read more; that one sentence is enough. You can taste the ocean from anywhere, it tastes the same—it is salty. This one sentence will do!"

The same happened in China. Buddhists went there and the whole of China became Buddhist without anybody converting anybody else. Because Taoism was so generous and Buddhism was so understanding; there was no question of converting. The whole idea of converting anybody is ugly, is violent. They never argued—yes, they communed, they nodded at each other's understanding and they said, "Yes, that's true. That's what Lao Tzu also says. That's what Buddha has said in his own words."

And out of this meeting—which is the rarest in the whole of humanity—Zen was born. Out of the meeting of Buddha and Lao Tzu, out of the meeting of Buddha's insight and Taoist insight, out of the meeting of Dharma and Tao, Zen was born. Hence Zen is a rare flowering. Nowhere else has it happened that way—so silently, without bloodshed, without a single argument. There was no question of argument; the difference was only of language.

This is how a truly religious person is. He is not a fanatic—he cannot be.

Ko Hsuan says:

> *I do not know its name*
> *but for title call it Tao.*

It is a nameless experience, but we have to call it something so we will call it Tao. That is arbitrary. If you have some other name—God, *logos*, *Dharma*, truth, *nirvana*—you can choose from those names; they are all beautiful because it has no name of its own so any name will do.

My sannyasins have also to be in this attitude, this should be our approach. You should not be part of any dogma—Christian, Mohammedan, Hindu. You should not belong to any church; that is all childish, political. A religious person is absolutely free from all dogma. Only in freedom understanding grows.

My sannyasins have to understand this approach towards life; this is very fundamental. Once you are rooted in it you will start growing. Great foliage will happen to you and great flowering and fulfillment.

EXISTENCE IS GOD'S EXPRESSION

The first question:

Bhagwan,
Could you say something about discipline and
repression?

Anudeya,

THEY ARE AS DISTINCT as the earth and the sky. The distance is so great between the two, that it is unbridgeable. Repression is just the opposite of discipline, but for thousands of years repression has been misunderstood and thought of as if it were discipline. It gives a pseudo appearance of it.

And remember one very fundamental thing: that the real is never in danger from the unreal; the real is always in danger from the pseudo. The unreal cannot harm it, but the pseudo can harm it because the pseudo looks like it. It is not it and yet it has the mask of it, the appearance of it.

Repression is cheap. Any stupid person can do it—it needs no intelligence to repress. Discipline needs great intelligence. Discipline means awareness. Discipline comes from your innermost core; it is not an imposition from the outside. Nobody can discipline you.

The very word "discipline" is beautiful: it means the art of learning. Hence the word "disciple": one who is ready to learn, one who is capable of learning. Learning is an inner process. One has to be always alert, only then can one learn. One has to be awake, only then can one learn. One has to watch all that goes on happening around you and one has to deepen this watchfulness so that you can see even the inner processes of your body, mind and heart. You have to become a mirror. You have to witness everything within yourself, then only do you learn from it, and that learning brings discipline. Then a deep harmony arises in you, because whatsoever is wrong starts falling away from you of its own accord. You are not to drop it. If you have to drop it through effort, then it is repression; if it falls like dry leaves falling from the tree, then it is discipline.

Discipline has to be effortless; it has to be out of sheer understanding. Repression has nothing to do with understanding, with learning. Others tell you what to do and what not to do; others give you the Ten Commandments. You have simply to follow, you have to be obedient. And who are these others? They are the powerful people—politically powerful, religiously powerful. They may be the rich people, the people who own the state or the church, the dominant people. They have their vested interests; to safeguard their vested interests they create a certain kind of slavery, a mental slavery. They want people to be obedient, they don't want people to be rebellious; hence they cannot allow intelligence.

Intelligence is basically rebellious; it is radical, it is revolutionary. To be intelligent is the most dangerous thing for those who are in power. Hence every child has to be crippled and paralyzed; no child can be allowed to live his life according to *his* light. Every child is born intelligent, but twenty-five years of conditioning from the primary school to the university creates a stupid person out of an intelligent child—so much conditioning that the intelligence disappears. He becomes so afraid to say no to anything, he becomes so afraid, so frightened of the crowd that he simply follows like a sheep; he is no more a man. The only way to do it is to teach him how to repress himself. First he has to repress his intelligence, then he has to repress all that can be a danger to the status quo.

For example, every society talks about peace but lives for war. Hence sex has to be repressed because sexually repressed people can be changed into soldiers very easily; there is no problem about it. The sexually repressed person is always ready to fight, he is always on the verge of violence. His sex becomes violence, he loses all tenderness, all loving qualities, and the instinct for love becomes perverted; it becomes the instinct for hatred. Up to now all societies have basically been warring societies, always preparing for war; they cannot allow sexual freedom. If a society is sexually free and a person is allowed to live his sexuality totally, then his violence will appear. Then he will not be ready to do such utterly stupid things as killing people for no reason at all; it will be impossible for him even to conceive. He will ask, "Why? Why should I kill? There seems to be no reason. Just because a few power manaics want to dominate the whole world we have to be victims and we have to turn the whole world into a chaos?"

The sexually free person will be loving, tender; war will become impossible. Unless sex is free, war cannot disappear from the earth.

All psychological research shows one thing very conclusively: that weapons are nothing but phallic symbols. Hence societies which are preparing for war are bound to be repressive. Intelligence has to be crippled, sex has to be repressed. All that can make you capable of being an individual has to be discarded. You have to be forced to be a Christian or a Hindu or a Mohammedan or a Jaina or a Buddhist for the simple reason that if you are part of a crowd you lose your individuality, you start functioning according to the collective mind—and the collective mind means the lowest mind. The collective mind functions through the lowest common demoninator.

It is said that the best teacher in the schools, in the colleges, in the universities, is one who can make himself understood, who can help the students understand him in such a way that the most mediocre student is also capable of understanding him. If only the first grade students understand him he is not a good teacher. The third-rate should be capable of understanding him, then he is a good teacher. But to make himself understood by the third-rate he has to fall that low. He has to speak the language of the mob, of the crowd. And the crowd consists of the mediocre people.

It is because of centuries of conditioning, otherwise it would not have been so; it is a man-made calamity. So many people need not be so mediocre and stupid. They are not born that way, they are manufactured. Individuality has to be effaced, completely effaced, because individuals seem to be dangerous to the power-holders because individuals will think, and they will say yes only if they agree with it, otherwise they will say no.

I have heard:

It happened in the Second World War. Many people were needed in the army so all kinds of people were being recruited. Everybody was asked to sacrifice for the country, for the motherland, for the fatherland and all that nonsense. A professor of philosophy was also recruited.

The first day the corporal calls the newly enlisted men for their first training and starts shouting, "Platoon, attention! Platoon, halt! Platoon, attention! Platoon, about face! Platoon, halt! Platoon, right face!"

The professor steps out of formation and starts to walk away.

"Hey, you!" shouts the corporal. "Where are you going?"

"To the pub," says the professor, "I'll come back when you've made up your mind."

Naturally, a man who thinks will see the whole nonsense of it. What is the point of it? Why should one do all these things? But they have a certain reasoning behind it: this is how your intelligence is killed, this is how you are slowly transformed into a robot, into a machine. The man is slowly killed; then you start functioning like a machine. "Right turn!" and you need not think, you simply turn right. Not that you think why—there is no question of why—no question arises in you. In fact, your body functions almost mechanically. Just as you push a button and the light goes on or off or the machine starts functioning. So when the soldier hears "Right turn!" he simply turns right without paying any attention to what is being done by him; it simply happens.

I have heard about William James—one of the most significant psychologists that America has contributed to the world. He was sitting with a friend in a restaurant talking about conditioning. It was the talk all over the world because just recently the Russian psychologist Pavlov had discovered the conditioned reflex: that a man can be conditioned so deeply that he starts functioning like a machine.

And Pavlov has become the father of Russian psychology and communists have been following his ideas for all these sixty years.

William James was talking to his friend, but the friend was not willing to accept the idea so easily—it was so new.

At that very moment a retired soldier was passing along the street with a bucket full of eggs. To demonstrate, William James shouted, "Attention!" and the poor old soldier simply went into the attitude of attention. The bucket fell; all the eggs were destroyed. He was very angry. He said, "Who has done this?"

William James said, "But we didn't say that *you* had to follow!"

He said, "It is no longer a question of following, it has become my nature. Attention means attention! I was in the army for twenty-five years: attention means attention; it does not mean anything else. And it is not a question of my deciding whether to follow or not; it has become automatic."

This is what all the societies have been doing and all the so-called religions have been doing: they have been automatizing you. And this is done through the process of repression—repress everything that can be dangerous to the establishment.

That's why Jesus is crucified and Socrates is poisoned and Al-Hillaj Mansoor is killed, for the simple reason that these people were bringing rebellion, these people were releasing others from their bondage, from their mental slavery. They were telling people to be intelligent, to be individuals, to be a light unto themselves. That's the message of Gautam the Buddha: Be a light unto yourself. Follow your own light, follow your own intelligence. Don't listen to those with vested interests because they are working for their own purposes. They have nothing to do with your welfare, they are not concerned about it.

And once you repress anything, the energy that is being repressed starts turning sour in you. The same energy that would have become a flower becomes a thorn. The same energy that would have helped you to grow becomes stagnant, starts stinking. Energy needs to remain in a flowing state; repression makes your life stagnant.

People's mental age is not more than twelve years. That means at the age of twelve they stopped growing psychologically. They may be eighty years old, but their minds are childish—remember, not childlike but just childish. It is beautiful to be childlike but it is ugly to be childish.

And why have they stopped at the age of twelve? For what reason? How does it happen? And this is the average all over the world. It is the same in the East, in the West; it is the same for the Hindu and for the Christian. All the societies in their own ways have been able to repress everybody before the age of twelve—why? Because the age of thirteen is the dangerous age. At that time a person becomes sexually mature; before then all his growth has to be stopped. Once he becomes sexually mature then it will be very difficult to repress him. He will have so much energy that all your measures for repression are bound to fail. So repression has to happen before thirteen.

All kind of nonsense has to be put in people's minds before they are thirteen; by the time they reach twelve the work should be finished. Then they will only be growing old but not growing up.

In an oral exam in biology the teacher asks a student, "Which organ of man's body once stimulated can grow up to three hundred times its size?"

The girl replies, "I am not going to answer such questions!" and she walks out.

So the teacher asks the same question of another student who answers, "The pupil of the eye."

"Very good!" replies the teacher. "Now go and tell your friend that she's going to be disillusioned!"

This is the work of repression: if you repress something your mind slowly slowly becomes colored by it; everything becomes colored by it. A sexually repressed person is constantly concerned with sex. He may talk of celibacy, he may try to be a celibate, but his whole mind is full of sexuality; he dreams of sex and nothing else. And it is not so only when you are young . . .

Mahatma Gandhi writes in his autobiography that even at the age of seventy he was suffering from sexual dreams. That is bound to happen—it is a seventy-years-old repression; otherwise, by the time one is seventy one should be mature enough to drop all these toys. Repression keeps things hanging in the air. The repressed person, even when he is dying, will be thinking of the thing that he has repressed his whole life.

I am against repression, I am all for expression.

Express yourself. Existence is God's expression— that's what creativity is all about. Express yourself, and don't condemn anything. Nothing is wrong with you; all that is is beautiful. It may need transformation, but it is not wrong. It has not to be dropped, it has to be transformed. And transformation happens through discipline; discipline comes through meditation. Become more aware, watchful. But don't carry conclusions, *a priori* conclusions.

If you are already convinced that sex is wrong then you cannot watch your mind. How can you watch if you have already concluded? Whenever a sexual thought arises you will shrink back; you will want to throw that idea out of your being. You will immediately jump upon it, you will start struggling and fighting. You cannot be simply watching; you will start evaluating.

A meditator has to be absolutely unprejudiced, with no conclusions. He has to be an utterly scientific observer. He simply observes, takes note of whatsoever happens in his mind. Notice, don't let anything go unnoticed, that's all. And the beauty of watchfulness is that whatsoever is meaningless starts disappearing of its own accord and whatsoever is meaningful starts growing. Your energies start gathering around the meaningful and they start deserting the meaningless. Then a certain discipline is born, not imposed by anybody from the outside.

Many people, particularly Indians, write to me asking why I am not giving a certain discipline to my sannyasins. I cannot—I am not their enemy. I am not in any way here to dominate anybody, I am not here to dictate. I can help you to understand, then it is up to you. Out of your understanding if something happens in your life, good, but if it happens because I have said it then it is ugly. Then sooner or later you will repent, then sooner or later you will take revenge on me.

I am your friend. I can help you to be more alert; that's my whole function. And then whatsoever is good follows so silently, just like your shadow. It makes no noise and it does not give any ego to you. As you become more aware, all ego disappears. You become more and more humble, more and more simple, more and more ordinary. And that ordinariness is divine, that simplicity is sacred. But discipline has to arise in you. I can commune with you my understanding, I can share with you my experience, that's all; then it is for you to decide what to do and what not to do.

My sannyasins have to learn how to live in freedom. I know it is very difficult for you, too—even my sannyasins ask: "If you give us definite rules it will be easier for us to follow them." I know it will be easier because that's what you have been doing your whole life. Somebody has been giving you orders and you have been following; that has become your habit. You would like me also to be a father figure, just to tell you that this has to be done and this has not to be done. That makes things cheap and simple; you need not bother, you can simply depend on me. But that creates dependence and you lose something immensely valuable: you lose your freedom, you lose your independence, you lose your individuality, you lose yourself. And that is not my purpose here.

My purpose here is to make you more and more unique individuals, more and more authentic individuals. I would like you to take the responsibility of your life upon your own shoulders totally so that you become completely free of all kinds of father figures. That brings great blessing and great benediction.

The second question:

Bhagwan,
Please say something to us about Swami Prem
Chinmaya's death yesterday.

Prem Samadhi,

THE FIRST THING about Prem Chinmaya's death is that it was not a death at all. He died very consciously. He died so beautifully! It was rare. Ten years ago when he came to me I was afraid that he might die before he could taste something of deathlessness, because he was suffering from such a disease . . . it was incurable.

But he was a rare individual. He lived for these ten years by the simple strength of his individuality. His body was not capable of living. The doctors were puzzled, the physicians were unbelieving, but I knew the secret. He was not afraid of death, but he wanted to grow to a certain point before death happened. And he managed it!

And the moment he was ready I allowed him to go. I had to tell him, "Now you can drop your body."

A deep communion had started between me and him. Because of illness he was not able to come to see me—and that's how sometimes blessings come in disguise. Because he was not able to physically see me, slowly slowly an inner communion was established.

The day before yesterday I called Sheela to my room just to tell her, "Now it is time. Chinmaya can go—he is ready. Now there is no need for him to suffer anymore in the body. He has done whatsoever was needful, he has attained to a certain integrity. Yes, he will be born once more, but that is a great achievement.''

He died from his sixth center. To attain to the seventh would have been almost impossible in such a condition; even this was almost a miracle to achieve—to die from such a height.

The moment Sheela reached Chinmaya's room he immediately said, ''Did Bhagwan call you to his room?'' She was surprised because it is very rare that I call anybody into my room. In these six years I may have called Sheela only thrice, so it was not an everyday thing. And Sheela may be the only one besides Vivek and Laxmi who has ever been called to my room. But immediately he asked, ''Did Bhagwan call you to his room? What did he say? What is his message?''

A deep communion had started happening lately. And when Sheela told him, ''Now Bhagwan has said that you must rest, relax, go deep into yourself and forget about the body'' . . . It was very difficult to forget the body because his body was in immense pain; it was not an ordinary pain. No pain-killer was of any help. Great doses of pain-killers were being given to him, but nothing was helping him. It was even impossible to help him to go to sleep; the pain was so great that it was keeping him awake.

He laughed and he said, ''Yes, I will do it!''

Thrice in the night, again and again he asked Sheela, ''Please tell me again what is the message of my Master? I don't want to forget his message at the last moment.''

And whenever she said, ''He has said only three words: 'Rest, relax, go deep into yourself,' '' he would say, ''Yes, now I remember,'' and fall asleep again.

He told Sheela that he wanted to listen to this series—that he hoped at least he would be able to listen to the first lecture. And he managed! Yesterday he listened to the whole lecture—and fully conscious. With all that pain he listened to the lecture. Then he asked for the last time about the message, and then he closed his eyes and disappeared.

This is not death, this is something far more beautiful. This is let-go. This is surrender. This is love! He trusted me so totally. He died beautifully, silently, in utter relaxation. I am happy about him.

I was afraid that he may not be able to survive even these years, but it was through his sheer determination, his sheer will power that he survived. The body would have died at least six years ago; for six years he lived a kind of posthumous existence. He would have still lived—he could have still managed at least for three months—but I saw no point in it because it was not possible to attain more in this body than whatsoever he had attained. The body was getting rotten, absolutely rotten, and he was in such a good space that I did not want him to get disturbed as far as his inner space was concerned; I wanted him to leave. There are moments when one should depart. He was in such a positive mood in such a negative body, he was in such a healthy mood in such an unhealthy body.

Just the other day when I was telling you a joke about Jesus and the man who was suffering from cancer I was remembering Chinmaya and he was listening! And he must have laughed because he loved jokes.

The angels who must have carried him must be puzzled because he is at least six years late.

Three Italians arrive in paradise. St. Peter asked the first one, ''Who are you?''

"I am-a Carletto from Milano."

"Very well, you are on time—come in," says St. Peter. Then he asks the second one, "And you, who are you?"

"I am-a Genaro from Roma."

"You are six hours late. How come?" asked St. Peter.

"Well-a, San Pietro, from Roma to here it is-a a long-a journey. I stop-a to rest-a a little on the way."

"And you, who are you?" asked St. Peter to the third man.

"I am-a Pasquale from Napoli."

"Pasquale," says St. Peter, "this is too much! You are two months late!"

"Don't-a get-a angry, San Pietro. I have-a been-a in bed-a sick."

I don't know what Chinmaya is going to say because six years is really too much! They may have completely forgotten about him. They will have to look in the files—it will take days for them to find out who this man is! But I think by now they must be becoming acquainted with orange people—that these are not reliable people. They come at all kinds of odd hours, they don't bother about time, they don't follow any rules, they don't know anything of discipline!

He used to love jokes. He used to write me beautiful jokes. In his memory I will tell a few jokes to you.

A man enters a police station and says that his wife has disappeared.

"When did she disappear?" asked the policeman.

"Five or six years ago," he answers.

"Five or six years ago!" exclaims the policeman. "Why didn't you come earlier?"

"Well, you see," says the man, "I just couldn't believe it!"

In Moscow a communist chief sees an old man kneeling in front of an icon. He stops and asks him, "Are you praying, old man?"

"Yes, I am praying," answers the old man.

"You are praying for us, aren't you?"

"Of course."

"And you pray now for us just as in the old times you were praying for the Czar?"

"That's true," replies the old man.

"Now tell me, were your old prayers of any use?"

"Well, yes, they killed the Czar, didn't they?"

And this one he would like the most:

It is a bank meeting. The president, heated by the discussion, gets up and starts pacing up and down. His secretary notices that his fly is open so she whispers to him, "Mr. President, the garage is open. One can see everything."

"Ah yes, and what can you see?—my new Mercedes?"

"No," replies the secretary, "a Fiat with flat tires!"

Samadhi, yesterday you celebrated his departure. Always remember him. He should be a light to you all. He loved deeply, he laughed deeply. He was a man who knew how to celebrate. Of course the body was not willing at all, but he never bothered about the body.

Yesterday he wanted to come to the discourse. I had to stop him, but still he heard the whole discourse. And he said to Sheela, "I wanted to hear the whole series, but when Bhagwan says that I have to go then I have to go. Then this is the time, then this is the right time, and I don't want to miss it." He never wanted to let me down. He loved me tremendously.

His name, Prem Chinmaya, means love and consciousness. He was both. He was love and he became consciousness. He died with great love and with great consciousness.

It is not death at all, Samadhi—it is transcendence of death.

Soon he will be back, and whenever he comes you will know because whenever I see that he is back in the womb of some sannyasin of mine I will call him Ko Hsuan in memory of this series of which he wanted to hear the whole but could only manage to hear the first lecture. So whenever I call any child Ko Hsuan you will know that Prem Chinmaya is back to fool around!

The third question:

Bhagwan,
My husband loves me so totally that he has never thought of another woman in his life, and we have lived together almost twenty-five years. I cannot believe it although it is true. What do you say about it?

Niharika,

I CANNOT BELIEVE IT EITHER!

ONCE THERE WAS A MAN whose name was Unbelievable. He was married to a very nice woman and the two of them were a very contented couple.

One day Unbelievable was so sick that he knew he was dying, so he called his wife and said to her, "Darling, I have spent my whole life being called by this idiotic name. Now that I am dying, please promise me one thing—not to put this name Unbelievable on my gravestone. You can put a saying or a picture, anything, but not my name. I do not want to carry it into eternity."

So the wife agreed. When he died she put a saying on his gravestone which read "Here lies a faithful husband who never betrayed his wife."

From that day people would pass by and read the gravestone and say, "It's unbelievable!"

Niharika, either your husband is dead or insane—or maybe you have stumbled upon a Buddha! But what is a guy like Buddha doing with you?

At a beach resort two friends are talking. "Of course, all these young, almost-naked girls are a constant temptation for our husbands . . ." says one.

"Maybe," replies the other, "but I trust mine absolutely. He is madly in love with me."

"Oh," replies the first one, "and doesn't he ever have some sane moments?"

If a man loves a woman he is bound to love many other people too, or if a woman loves a man she is bound to love many people too, because love cannot be confined to one person. If it exists at all it cannot be confined; if it does not exist at all, then there is no question.

Love is like breathing. If a person says, "I breathe only when I am with you and the remaining time I never breathe," you will not trust him. How can you trust him? He will be dead if he does not breathe when he is not with you. Love is the breath of your soul.

But that's what we have done: for centuries we have conditioned people with such stupid ideas and created so much misery in the world and so much jealousy and so much possessiveness and so much hatred for no reason at all. We have conditioned people with this stupid idea that love can only be between one person and another, one to one: if it is true then it is one to one, otherwise it is untrue. Just the opposite is the truth: if it is one to one it cannot be true. Then it is false, pseudo; then it is only a make-believe. Then the persons are pretending and they are being untrue to themselves—not only to the other person but to themselves, too.

If a man is interested in beauty how can he avoid not seeing beautiful women and how can he avoid not being interested in them? The only way is to kill his interest in beauty totally—but then he will no longer be interested even in his own wife. That's what has happened: because of this idiotic idea that love has to be one to one, love has disappeared from the earth. The only possible way to manage it is that the husband should not love the wife. He should kill the very instinct of love, he should repress the very idea of beauty, he should forget that beauty exists in the world. But then, remember, he cannot love his wife either. Then he will pretend, then he will go on acting—empty gestures with no content. If a woman is told, "You have to be only in love with your husband and you cannot even feel interested in other people," she is bound to lose interest in the husband.

That's why husbands and wives lose interest in each other. They are constantly quarrelling; they go on finding excuses to quarrel. The real phenomenon is that they are quarrelling because their love energies are not being allowed to flower, but they have forgotten about it because the conditioning is so ancient. Their parents were conditioned the same way and their parents' parents; it comes from Adam and Eve's time. It has become so much part of us, almost part of our blood, bones and marrow, that we are not even aware of it; it has gone deep into the unconscious.

So husbands and wives are constantly angry at each other—sometimes more, sometimes less—and always finding excuses to be angry. And they look sad. They are bound to be sad, they are bound to be angry, for this simple reason. All other excuses are false. I am not saying that they are falsifying knowingly—they are unaware of the whole phenomenon.

The simple truth is that a man who is interested in beauty will remain interested in many women; a woman who is interested in beauty will remain interested in many men. Maybe she is more interested in one person—that is possible—maybe she is so interested in one person that she would like to live with that person, but that does not mean that her interest in other people simply disappears; it remains. But if you are going with your husband or with your wife for a morning walk and your husband says to you, "Look at that woman. How beautiful she is!" immediately there is trouble—he cannot say it! There is nothing wrong in it; in fact you should be happy that your husband is still alive and sane, that his tires are not flat yet! You should be happy that he is lively, young, that his eyes can still see beauty, that he can still be sensitive to all that is beautiful. There is no need to feel jealous.

But the husband cannot say it; in fact he will pretend that he has not looked at the other woman at all. He *has* looked, he *is* looking—he may be using sunglasses only for that purpose! He will find excuses to look at the woman: he may start talking about the beautiful tree. He is not concerned with the tree but with the woman sitting under the tree! And the wife knows perfectly well why he is suddenly interested in the tree; otherwise he is never interested in the tree.

The wife cannot say to the husband, "This man looks so beautiful!" The husband will feel offended—

51

his ego is hurt. Everybody carries this idea that "Nobody is more beautiful than me." Now everybody knows that this is sheer nonsense. Everybody is unique, that is true, but everybody has a few things that nobody else has. Maybe this man has more beautiful eyes than you have; you may have a beautiful nose and his nose is ugly, but what about the eyes? You may have a beautiful face, but what about his whole proportionate body?

People should be more intelligent and they should appreciate; they should help each other to appreciate. They should say to each other, "You are right. That woman looks beautiful, that man looks beautiful." And there is nothing wrong in it. And it is not going to destroy your love; it is, really, enhancing it, strengthening it. To communicate with each other so authentically is always a nourishment for love. Whenever you start pretending, whenever you are forced to pretend, whenever you are forced to say something which you don't want to say and you are not allowed to say something which you wanted to say then love starts disappearing, then distance is created.

Niharika, please help your husband to be alive again, help him to be sane again, help him to be sensitive again. You must have contributed much towards his dullness. This is not good, this is not healthy. This is a state of pathology. If he says that he has never thought of another woman in his life, then remember perfectly well that you are also a woman— nothing more, nothing less. Just by becoming a wife you are not more than a woman. And if he has no more interest in any woman—and this earth is full of beautiful women—then he has nothing to do with you either; then he is finished with you—or maybe you have forced him to be finished with you.

That's why you say: *I cannot believe it although it is true.*

You cannot believe it because you must be thinking of other men—how can you believe it? If you are still thinking of other men, how can you believe that your husband is not thinking of other women?

In fact whenever a man and a woman, particularly husband and wife, are making love, then in the bed there are never only two people, there are always four. He is thinking of some other woman and the woman is thinking of some other man. The woman is thinking of Mohammed Ali, he is thinking of Sophia Loren, and then things go well!

It is always good for wives and husbands not to make love in the daytime and even in the night to always put the light out so you can have free imagination; you can think of whomsoever you want to think. In fact, there is not much difference—basically there is not much difference. Different models, little differences in the bonnets, et cetera, but basically there is not much difference. When you come to the fundamentals it is the same—and when you are making love to a woman or a man you have come to the fundamentals, you have come to the very rock bottom; now there is no further to go. And this is good about nature: that about fundamentals it is very communist; there are not many differences. All differences are superficial.

But nothing is wrong in being interested. Help him—he needs your help, because my own experience of thousands of couples is that it is always the woman who destroys the man. The man pretends to be the master, but he is not. And women are so utterly confident of their mastery that they allow him to talk about his mastery, but they don't bother about it.

They say, "You can say it. That's a good division: you talk about it—that freedom is given to you—but we are the real masters."

One day I went to see Mulla Nasruddin. He was sitting under his bed. I asked Nasruddin, "What is the matter? Why are you sitting under your bed?"

He said, "Why not? I am the master of the house, I can sit anywhere!"

And then his wife came and she said "You coward! You come out and I will show you who is the master!"

He said, "Nobody can force me to come out! I am the master so I can sit anywhere I like!"

Now the wife is very fat and she cannot go under the bed, so I asked the wife, "What are you going to do now?"

She said, "You wait! Lunch time is coming closer—he will have to come out! And under the bed he can go on talking about his mastery; above the bed I know who is the master!"

Help your poor husband. You must have destroyed him—not knowingly, unknowingly; feminine strategies are very subtle. Revive him, bring him back from his grave. And only then will he be interested in you. And he will be grateful to you.

All couples should remember it: that by becoming a couple you are not becoming masters of each other—just companions, friends. And don't take your relationship for granted; it has nothing to do with possessiveness. Men or women are not things to possess, they are people; they have to be respected. They are not means to be used. Husbands are using wives as means, wives are using husbands as means, and that's why the whole world seems to be so ugly and so insane and everybody seems to be so miserable.

There is no need for so much misery—ninety-nine percent of it is our creation. One percent will of course remain because there are the limitations of the body. The body has to become old, sometimes it will be ill, some day it has to die, but that is only one percent. And if ninety-nine percent of misery can disappear, that one percent can be accepted, joyously accepted; there is no problem about it.

The last question:

Bhagwan,
I have heard from many sannyasins that we need to do nothing at all; "Let Bhagwan do it." Gurdjieff has taught that only through one's own efforts, stemming from a deep wish, does an awareness of being grow.
Please speak on this for a sannyasin suffering growing pains.

Anubhuti,

I KNOW YOU are not suffering growing pains, not at all, because you are not growing!

Anubhuti has been in Gurdjieff's work for many years—not with Gurdjieff himself but with somebody who had been with Gurdjieff. Now, to be with a Master is a totally different matter. If you had been with Gurdjieff your understanding about Gurdjieff would have been totally different. But you have never been with a living Gurdjieff, you have been with somebody who has been with Gurdjieff—and that somebody is not yet enlightened, that somebody is in the same boat as you are. But she—the person Anubhuti has been with—has conditioned your mind in a certain way: her own understanding of Gurdjieff.

Gurdjieff used to say that even the people who understood him the most had not understood him—even a man like P.D. Ouspensky was rejected by Gurdjieff. In fact, the whole credit goes to P.D. Ouspensky for making Gurdjieff world-famous; nobody would have known about him without Ouspensky. It is through Ouspensky's books that Gurdjieff became well-known—he might have died an obscure mystic. It was Ouspensky and his great capacity to philosophize, to argue, to write, that made Gurdjieff one of the greatest known Masters of the world.

But Gurdjieff was not happy even with Ouspensky's understanding of him: he used to say that Ouspensky had misunderstood him totally. Ouspensky was of course very angry, and finally he departed from Gurdjieff and became antagonistic. Even to mention Gurdjieff's name in Ouspensky's presence was an offense. No disciple of Ouspensky was allowed to mention Gurdjieff's name although what Ouspensky was teaching was Gurdjieff's teaching according to him. And if you read Ouspensky and Gurdjieff you will be more convinced by Ouspensky than by Gurdjieff because Gurdjieff is not a philosopher. He is not a good writer either—his writing is so tedious, so boring that if you can finish his whole book that will show great will power. I have come across many people who have been deeply interested in Gurdjieff, but they have not read his books; they all have read Ouspensky, Nicoll and others.

Anubhuti, whatsoever you know about Gurdjieff is not about Gurdjieff; you don't know anything about him. Even the people who lived with him for many years were not capable of understanding him—he was a very mysterious man. And to each disciple he was saying different things because each disciple's need was different. He said one thing to Ouspensky and another thing to Nicoll, just the opposite of it because their needs were so different that the same thing could not be said to them.

To a few people he said, "Surrender everything to me . . ."

It happened once:

A very rich Russian woman came to him and the first thing he asked was: "You surrender all your valuable ornaments to me immediately. If you want to be my disciple give all your diamonds and jewels." And she had really beautiful things with her; she was one of the richest women of those days. She became very afraid—naturally. She went in her room to think over it, "What to do? Is it right to surrender everything?"

She was sharing the room with another woman, one of her old acquaintances; she was also rich. She asked about the matter—what to do.

The other woman said, "There is no problem—the same thing happened with me. When I came he asked me, 'Give all your valuables to me first. If you cannot sacrifice that much then forget all about me and my work; then your search is not authentic. You have to pay for it.' And I immediately surrendered then and there all my ornaments. And do you know what happened?" the woman said. "The next morning he came to my room and gave everything back to me!"

So the new woman was very happy. She went and surrendered everything—and Gurdjieff never came back! She waited and waited, and she asked the other woman, "What is the matter? He has not come back!"

The woman said, "I don't know what the matter is, but that was what happened with me. I don't know why he is not coming."

The woman became very distrustful, left Gurdjieff, and started spreading rumors about him: "That man is a charlatan. He is exploiting people."

The other woman asked Gurdjieff, "Why did you return everything to me and not to her?"

Gurdjieff said, "You surrendered so immediately, without a thought, that there was no need to keep it. She thought over it, she asked you about it. Only when she was certain that her things would be returned to her did she give them to me. That was not surrender at all, that was calculation. And I don't want calculative people around me. If I had returned those things to her she would have stayed here. So I have killed two birds with one stone: we have that money—we needed it for the work—and we got rid of that stupid woman. And now she is spreading rumors about me, so other stupid people won't come to me."

Anubhuti, you are not going through growing pains, you are simply in a confusion because my work is totally different from Gurdjieff's work; it is bound to be so. Your problem now is what to do?

Anubhuti has entered many groups and left every group because they do not fit with her understanding of work; they are below her. She knows far better —she has worked for years. But my work is totally different.

Gurdjieff depended on crystallization and my work is of dissolution; you have to dissolve, not to crystallize. Both are valid means; through both doors you can enter the ultimate. Either you have to enter through will power—and that was Gurdjieff's work, or you have to enter through surrender—that is my work.

You ask:
Please speak on this for a sannyasin suffering growing pains.

You are just trying to understand me with your Gurdjieffian jargon. That won't work. If you want to understand me you will have to put Gurdjieff aside. I love the man, I love him immensely, I respect the man, but my ways are totally different.

But old habits die hard . . .

An American teacher is tired of seeing her white students fight with the black ones who are forbidden to use the school bus. So one day she calls them together and says, "Boys, what are all these discriminations? I won't have any more of this! Remember, we are all equal. Everybody is equal, black or white! So from now on we can think of ourselves as blue! Have you understood? We are all blue!

"And now, the light blues will go on the bus and the dark blues will go home on foot!"

Old habits . . .

Heaven is in a havoc. God asks St. Peter the reason for it and St. Peter replies, "Well, it's that man, Adolf Hitler. He is impossible. He keeps shouting at everyone, 'Jew! Jew!' But don't worry, I'll tackle him myself!"

After a while peace and harmony reign in Heaven again. Curious, God asks St. Peter, "How did you do it?"

"Well, it was easy," says St. Peter. "I just gave him a brush and now, instead of shouting, 'Jew! Jew!' he is busy writing 'Jew' on all the clouds!"

Old habits . . .

You have come here, you have waited to come here for months, you have longed to be here, you have disappointed your so-called teacher, you have disappointed your whole group, but you are not here either. You are neither there nor here; you are in a limbo.

If you want to work according to Gurdjieff, escape from here as quickly as possible. If you want to work according to me then you will have to learn different ways.

You ask:
I have heard from many sannyasins that we need to do nothing at all . . .

That is the most difficult thing in the world—to do nothing at all. Don't think it is the easier way; it is the most difficult thing, to do nothing. You can do anything; the problem arises when you are told *not* to do anything.

> *Sitting silently,*
> *doing nothing,*
> *the spring comes,*
> *and the grass grows by itself.*

Gurdjieff's work is work; my work is not work, it is play. And there is a great difference between the two. Gurdjieff wanted you to force yourself to the extreme; he was a hard taskmaster. I don't want you to be extremist, I want you to be exactly in the middle. I want you to be exactly in the middle, remember it, because only through that is balance possible, is equilibrium possible. You are not asked to do anything at all.

You say: And your sannyasins say, "*Let Bhagwan do it.*" I don't do anything at all—that is just a way of speaking. I don't do anything and I want my sannyasins not to do anything either. But their old habits are there so I tell them, "Leave it to me. I will do it!" I don't do anything at all—I have never done anything in my life. I am the laziest man you can find in the world! Can't you see?—I don't even walk a hundred yards! And I have told Laxmi, "In the new place the car has to come on top of the stage!" I am the laziest person in the world—why bother with these steps? I don't do anything.

But my sannyasins are accustomed to doing, so just to help them I say, "Don't be worried, I will do it. Leave it to me." That is just an excuse for them to leave doing—and then things start happening on their own. I want you to be natural.

Gurdjieff's work is extremist: it creates tension in you. It depends on friction: it creates friction in you. My work is not work; it is relaxation, it is rest, it is becoming more and more silent, utterly silent. Even if you are doing something you are not to be the doer of it; you have not to take it seriously. Gurdjieff's work is serious. My work is not serious at all; it is playfulness, it is fun, it is dance, it is song. I don't call it work. Work is a dirty word, a four-letter dirty word here!

But you are misunderstanding me for the simple reason that you have your own understanding. Either you will have to drop the understanding that you are carrying with you or you will have to drop me. You will have to choose. You cannot ride on these two horses.

A beautiful looking tomcat is strolling down the road. On the way to the park, he meets a little white tomcat.

"Hey, Tommy, where are you going?" asks the little cat.

"I'm going to the park to fuck around!" answers big Tommy.

"What's that? Something like fish?" asks the little one.

"Come with me and you'll find out!" says Tommy.

Soon the two tomcats come to the big fountain in the park, and there sits Jolly, the most beautiful cat in town, her golden fur shining in the sun. She sees the big tomcat coming closer with a mischievous smile on his cat face. "I'm in trouble!" she exclaims, jumps up, and starts running around the fountain.

"Come on, boy!" cries Tommy and he starts running after her. One round, two rounds, three rounds. "Come on, faster!" Tommy screams. Round and round the fountain they run.

The little white cat, hardly keeping up with Tommy, exhausted, gasping for air, trembling on his little legs, cries: "Hey, Tommy, listen—I'll fuck one more round and that's enough for me!"

You say: *Gurdjieff has taught that only through one's own efforts, stemming from a deep wish, does an awareness of being grow.*

That is true, but then you have to follow the whole Gurdjieffian method, and for that you will need a Gurdjieff; without a Gurdjieff it is impossible to do it. Without a living Master no method, howsoever beautiful it is, works. In fact it is the *Master*, his *presence*, that is the real thing, not the methods. With an alive Master everything works; with a dead Master nothing works. Let it be settled forever in your consciousness.

That's why beautiful methods later on are found to be bogus. It is not the methods, it is the Master, it is the man behind them, it is the golden touch, the magical touch of the Master, it is his charisma that works.

When I am gone, then Sufi Dancing will continue and there will be Kundalini and there will be Chaotic Meditation, and all the things will continue in the same routine way, but something will be missing —something which was the very soul of them. Then they will be just rituals.

That is how the Christian Church goes on, Hindus go on, Mohammedans go on, Buddhists go on. And these methods did work once. They worked when Jesus was alive, they worked when Krishna was alive, they worked when Buddha was alive. Being with a living Master is what works; it is not the method.

That's the difference between science and religion: religion is magic. Science depends on method; religion depends on Masters, on the presence of those who have become awakened.

Only if you can get attuned with me here is something possible—even the impossible is possible. But you will have to get attuned with me. Gurdjieff will be a hindrance.

If you choose Gurdjieff, choose Gurdjieff, but remember you are choosing a dead Master. You can go on repeating his methods your whole life—nothing is going to happen through them.

GROW REAL ROSES

The first question:

Bhagwan,
What is the secret of remaining happy and
married?

Sarjan,

IT IS IMPOSSIBLE! It has never happened—it cannot happen in the very nature of things. Marriage is something against nature. Marriage is an imposition, an invention of man—certainly out of necessity, but now even that necessity is out of date. It was a necessary evil in the past, but now it can be dropped. And it should be dropped: man has suffered enough for it, more than enough. It is an ugly institution for the simple reason that love cannot be legalized. Love and law are contradictory phenomena.

Marriage is an effort to legalize love. It is out of fear. It is thinking about the future, about the tomorrows. Man always thinks of the past and the future, and because of this constant thinking about past and future, he destroys the present. And the present is the only reality there is. One has to live in the present. The past has to die and has to be allowed to die.

The really intelligent person never looks back; he never bothers about the past—that which is finished is finished forever. And he never thinks of the future either because that which has not come yet has not come yet. And he knows that whenever it comes, he will be capable of responding to it, so why ponder over it? Why make ready-made answers to questions which have not even arisen? And all your ready-made answers are going to be irrelevant because life goes on changing. Life remains always a surprise; it is unpredictable.

But man thinks that he is being very clever by preparing for the future. You love a woman, you love a man, but what about the future? Tomorrow the woman may fall in love with somebody else. If she can fall in love even with you, Sarjan, why can she not fall in love with somebody else? You know it, you are aware of it: "She has fallen in love even with me so there is every possibility she can fall in love with somebody else." So something has to be done to prevent her from falling in love with somebody else so that your tomorrow is safe and secure, so that you can use her tomorrow, too. Whether love remains or not, at least you will have the physiology of the woman.

You are not much concerned with her soul— because law cannot restrain the soul, but law can create barriers for the body; the body is not beyond its reach. Law can control her; law can condemn her, can punish her in many ways.

And another thing: not only are you afraid of the woman, you are afraid of yourself too. If you can fall in love with this woman, you can fall in love with somebody else. You know that your mind is constantly thinking of other women. You know there is every possibility that tomorrow you may lose interest in this woman; in fact it is almost a certainty, not just a possibility, not just a probability. And then you are afraid of yourself. You may escape, you may run.

And you want to cling because this woman is taking care of you. She has been a comfort to you, she has been a consolation in your life, she has been in many ways a mother to you, a nourishment. You are afraid to betray her. You are afraid of your own mind, of your own unconscious; it can take you anywhere.

And you have promised her that you will never leave her, that you will always love her, that you will love her forever, life after life. You are afraid of breaking your promises. Your ego feels that to break those promises will mean only one thing: that you will never be able to forgive yourself. It will remain a heavy weight on you, it will create guilt for you.

And the same is the situation from the side of the woman. Hence it has been a necessary evil, and men and women have agreed to plan for the future. Afraid of themselves they have taken support from the law, from the society, from conventions, from respectability. They have created a thousand and one barriers around themselves so that they remain together.

But if—and that "if" is not a small "if", it is a big "if"—something happens tomorrow, then your life will become miserable. And something is going to happen tomorrow; tomorrow is not going to remain the same. Life never remains the same, not even for two consecutive moments. Nothing can be said about the future; it remains unknown, unknowable, unpredictable. No astrology can help, no palmistry can help, no tarot card reading can help, no *I-Ching* can help—nothing can help. Man has tried every possible way to make something certain out of the uncertain future, but nothing can be done. The nature of the future is unknown, and it remains unknown and open.

So you close yourself to all possibilities. You close all the doors, all the windows. But then you will feel suffocated and you will feel angry and you will feel constantly in conflict. With the woman you had loved once you will feel angry for the simple reason that now it is difficult to get out of this prison. You have imprisoned yourself; now the only way to go on living in it is to make yourself as insensitive as possible, to become as unloving as possible, to become as false as possible, to be as dead as possible.

Hence people die very soon. They may be buried after forty years, fifty years, but they die nearabout thirty. By the time their love starts dying they die, because life is love. But love is not law, life is not law. Life is not logic, love is not logic. Life is basically insecure, and that is the beauty of it.

Hence I don't see that with the coming age, with the new maturity that man is attaining, marriage can exist anymore in the same old way. It has to become more fluid; that means it can no longer be an institution. People will live together—they need each other . . . Men and women are halves of one whole; their need is intrinsic. Together they become one whole, together they are complementary to each other. But they will live together only because of love, not because of any law. And they will live together out of freedom, not out of bondage.

And with the disappearance of the institution of marriage the whole structure of society will change—it cannot change otherwise—because once marriage disappears many things will disappear automatically. The family will not be the same anymore; the family will be replaced by communes—that is inevitable. And children will not belong to persons but to the commune. Hence they will not be much of a problem—because children have been a big problem: what to do with the children when people separate? The children are left in a limbo; something has to be done about the children. And marriage has persisted for the simple reason that children have to be protected, they have to be helped; they are helpless. And it is your responsibility.

Love becomes duty, responsibility. And the moment it is duty and responsibility it loses all poetry, it becomes pure calculation. Then it is a compromise, then you have somehow to pull it, then you start dragging your life.

A great revolution is on the way, and with the disappearance of marriage that revolution will become possible. Once children no longer belong to persons they will have more generosity, they will be more human. They will not be Hindus and Mohammedans and Christians because they will not belong to certain parents and they will not be conditioned by the parents; they will belong to the commune. And once children belong to the commune they will have a larger experience of people. One child may come in contact with many women as mothers, aunts, with many men as fathers, as uncles, with many children as brothers, sisters.

Right now the experience of the child is very limited. Each child is brought up by a certain woman. The impact of that woman remains hanging on the child's consciousness for his whole life; it becomes an imprint. And he is always searching for the same woman: in every woman he falls in love with he is really looking for his mother, whom he cannot find. Where can he find his mother? There are no two persons alike. He will never find his mother anywhere, but he is looking for his mother in every wife, in every beloved. And the same is the case with the woman: she is looking for the father in every husband, in every lover. And they cannot find them, but that is their *idea*.

The woman's idea of a man is nothing but her idea of the father and the man's idea of a woman is nothing but his idea of the mother. They will never find them, hence there will be frustration, hence there will always be despair, misery, failure, anguish.

If a child is brought up by many women in the commune and comes in contact with many men and many women he will not have a certain idea, he will have a more vague vision. He will not have a certainty how a man should be or a woman should be, his idea of a woman will contain many pictures. And then there will be more possibility of finding a woman who can fulfill him or a man with whom life can be a contentment, because one of the greatest miseries is that you are looking for someone you cannot find, hence everybody will seem to be falling short; nothing will ever satisfy you.

And because you will not be confined to one family you will not carry the rotten heritage of the family. Otherwise the Hindu parents will make the child Hindu, and a Hindu child is bound to be against the Mohammedans, against the Christians, against everybody else. And so is the case with the Jews and with the Christians and the Mohammedans. If the child moves with many people in a commune and feels attuned with the whole commune . . .

For example, in this commune, you can look at Siddhartha. He lives absolutely freely. Such a little child, with such freedom! He has no attachment to the mother or to the father. He makes friendships with grown-up people, then he starts living with them. He has so many friends—men and women, and all kinds of friends—children, grown-ups. He is really getting the idea of so many people that his vision of humanity is bound to be vast.

He had asked me—he was living in a kids' house where only kids live—he asked me, "Bhagwan, I want to live with real men, not with kids. Enough is enough! I have lived with kids long enough." So I sent him to live with Govinddas and other sannyasins. And they complained: "Sometimes he comes at twelve o'clock in the night and sometimes at one o'clock, sometimes at two o'clock. This is too much! He goes to parties and to dramas and to the disco and he is disturbing us continuously! And he has possessed the whole room—as if the room belongs to him and we are just living in his room! He has put all his things all around the room—all his toys are everywhere! So please," they asked me, "remove him!"

I told him to go to his mother, Neerja, to live with her. He said, "That is the last place I want to go! But if you say so I will go." He has been forced to go and live with the mother at least for a few days. And he has been living with many families, with many couples. Wherever he goes he makes friendships, and there are so many friends that he is never out of money—he asks everybody!

Sattva was once Neerja's lover. Now that love relationship is broken, but the love that has grown between Sattva and Siddhartha has continued. They are still friends—Sattva still has to give him money! He comes every day: "Today I need five rupees, ten rupees."

One day Sattva said, "I don't have any money." Then he said "You can ask me!" And he brought five rupees from somewhere and gave it to Sattva! "Why don't you ask me? I have so many friends, I can bring as much money as you want!"

Now, this child will be a totally different child! He has lived with Jews and with Christians and with Hindus. He will not be conditioned by anything, he will not have any conditioning. He will have a vast territory of being available to him.

That's my idea how all children should grow. then there will be no ugly religious conflicts, wars, bloodshed, no ugly fanaticism, no fascist ideologies in the world. These are all byproducts of the family, and the family depends on marriage. In fact, if the family disappears, nations will have to disappear, religions will disappear, states will disappear, churches will disappear. That's why nations, churches, everybody is in favor of marriage and they all go on praising marriage as if it is something holy, something divine. It is the ugliest thing on the earth! And they go on telling people, "Without marriage, where will children get love?" They will get more love; nobody is going to prevent their parents from loving them, but they will be available to others, too. They will not be dependent, they will start learning independence. From the very beginning they will have a certain new feel of freedom. And that's what is needed.

The whole of human history has been full of religious wars for the simple reason that everybody becomes conditioned, and once you are conditioned it is very difficult to uncondition you. I know the difficulty because that's my whole work here—to uncondition you. It takes months, years; and you struggle hard, you resist in every possible way because your conditioning means your ego.

You ask me, Sarjan: *What is the secret of remaining happy and married?*

I don't know! Nobody has ever known. Why would Jesus have remained unmarried if he had known the secret? He knew the secret of the kingdom of God, but he did not know the secret of remaining happy in marriage. He remained unmarried. Mahavira, Lao Tzu, Chuang Tzu, they all remained unmarried for the simple reason that there *is* no secret; otherwise these people would have discovered it. They could discover the ultimate—marriage is not such a big thing, it is very shallow—they even fathomed God, but they could not fathom marriage.

Socrates got married and he suffered his whole life. He did not discover through marriage the secret of remaining happy; he simply discovered that it would have been better if he had not got married. But in Greece there had never been such incidents as Jesus, Lao Tzu—Jesus had yet to come, five hundred years after Socrates. Socrates was a contemporary of Lao Tzu, Mahavira, but he knew nothing about them because the world in those days had no communication. So whatsoever was conventional happened in his life.

Mohammed married not one woman, he married nine women! Many times I have been asked, "What about Mohammed?" I know the secret of Mohammed, but I don't know the secret of remaining happy in marriage. If you have nine women they will fight amongst themselves and you will be free! Mohammed managed it and he has said to his followers, "Marry at least four women." So Mohammedans are allowed to marry four women. Four women are enough to fight amongst themselves and the husband will be spared.

Krishna did the best: he married sixteen thousand women! Now it is very easy to get lost. Sixteen thousand women . . . who will notice Krishna, where he has gone, where he is? There will be so much noise and fight, and in that cloudy, smokey atmosphere Krishna can escape anywhere. He can even sit in the middle of it and meditate and nobody will bother about him! They will all be concerned about each other's saris and each other's ornaments.

Buddha got married, but then he escaped. He had a beautiful wife, Yashodhara, but he escaped. He came back home only when he became enlightened, after twelve years. Yes, if you are enlightened then you can be happy anywhere, even in marriage, but no enlightened person has been known to get married after enlightenment.

Two friends meet.
"Hello, Luisa, how is your great love?"
"It's over," she replied sadly.
"Over? How come?"
"We got married!"

Two friends were talking.
"I've placed an advertisement in the newspaper, looking for a wife," says one.
"Did lots of women write back?" asks the other.
"Just a few women . . . but lots of husbands!"

The wife left home for the fifth time and the husband rushed to place an advertisement in the newspaper.
It read: "Do not come back and all will be forgiven."

It was a wise old woman who, when people asked her why she never married, would answer: "Why marry? I have a dog who snores, a parrot who speaks only dirty words and a cat who stays out all night, what do I need a husband for?''

The jealous husband hires a detective to find out if his wife betrays him. After a few days the detective comes back with a movie showing his wife and his best friend swimming, dancing, making love, having fun.

While watching the movie the husband keeps saying, ''I can't believe it! I can't believe it!''

''But,'' says the detective, annoyed, ''I'm giving you proof of it!''

''No, it's not that,'' replies the husband, ''I just can't believe someone can have so much fun with my wife!''

In heaven everybody is quiet and silent except for Paolo who keeps saying, ''What peace here! What peace here!''

Even St. Peter gets tired of him and so one day he sends him to purgatory. Even there though, Paolo keeps muttering, ''What peace here! What peace here!''

Everybody gets so tired that they decide to send him down to hell. But even in hell, among the flames and the devils, he keeps uttering, ''What peace here! What peace here!''

So Beelzebub calls him and asks him the reason for his behavior.

''Well, Beelzebub,'' replies Paolo, ''you would say the same if you had lived for fifty years with my wife!''

Love is enough. Live only out of love. It may last long, it may not last, but don't be worried whether it lasts long or does not last long. Even if it is there for a single moment it will give you the taste of eternity.

And there is every possibility that if you are not afraid it may last longer, because fear is poison; it poisons everything. If you are not worried about tomorrow you may live today so totally that out of that totality a beautiful tomorrow will arise. But if you are afraid of tomorrow you may destroy today. And once today is destroyed, from where is tomorrow going to come?

Live fearlessly—that is one of my fundamental messages to my sannyasins—and live dangerously. Don't compromise for conveniences, for comforts. It is better to live in discomfort but to *live* rather than to be in comfort and dead. For that you can wait—in your grave you will be perfectly comfortable and out of danger. Nothing can happen there; there is no danger. You cannot die again, no illness can happen, nobody can leave you, you can't go bankrupt, nothing can be stolen from you. You will be perfectly at peace.

You must have come across gravestones—and it is written on almost all graves: "Rest in peace." What else is there?

One man died. He had made his own gravestone, a beautiful, artistic thing, because he did not rely on his wife—she was such a miser that she might put up some ordinary stone. So he had purchased the most costly marble, asked the best artist to make rose flowers on it, and he had written on it: "Rest in peace."

When he died his wife discovered that he had not left any money for her. When the will was opened there was only one sentence: "I was a wise man, hence I have spent all that I had. I have not left anything to anybody."

The wife was furious. She went to the grave with the artist and told the artist to add a few more words: "Rest in peace 'til I come!"

But don't be worried: even wives can't come in the same grave; they will have their own graves. And even if they come they won't recognize you, and you won't recognize them either.

You can rest in peace in the grave, in absolute security, but while you are alive *be* alive. Accept all insecurity. In that very acceptance, insecurity disappears, and without any compromise on your part. Love totally, but don't ask for permanence. Only fools ask for permanence. And remember one thing: if you ask for permanence you will get only false things; only false things are permanent.

Real roses are bound to wither sooner or later, but plastic roses are permanent; they don't wither away. But they don't have any fragrance either, they don't have any life; they have only the appearance of roses.

Marriage is a plastic rose; love is a real rose. Grow real roses in your life. Of course they will wither—so what? You can grow them again, you can go on growing them. You can go on creating more and more love, sharing more and more with more and more people.

And this is my experience—and whatsoever I am saying I am saying out of my own experience—that if you love totally without desiring any permanence, even the impossible is possible. Your love may remain for a long period, maybe your whole life. But don't *ask* for permanence; in that very asking you have disturbed the whole thing: you have moved from the real to the unreal. Live totally!

"Totality" is my keyword—and up to now "permanence" has been the keyword. You have been told that your love should be permanent, only then it is real; if it is not permanent it is not real. That is sheer bullshit! A real love has nothing to do with permanence; there is no necessary relationship. It may happen only for a moment, it may be just like lightning, but that does not mean that lightning is unreal because it happens only for a moment. The rose flower opens in the morning; by the evening the petals have dropped, withered away, gone back to rest in the earth. That does not mean that the rose flower was unreal.

But you have been told again and again by the priests that if you are really looking for reality then the touchstone is permanence. They have moved your mind from reality to permanence, and once you become attached to permanence you are bound to purchase something false and you lose track of the real. The real is changing, constantly changing; the unreal remains the same. And you have to be available to the constantly changing.

Even if for a single moment love happens, be total in it. If you are total in it, the next moment will come out of this totality. It is possible—I cannot tell you it is certain, I can only tell you it is possible—that the next moment will deepen your love. But it will not be the same: either it will deepen or it will disappear, but it will never be the same again. No two moments are the same, and they cannot be the same.

And that is the beauty of life, that is the incredible adventure of life: that it is always a surprise, it is always unexpected. If you live totally things may deepen, but remember, when things are deepening they are not the same. If you think of permanence you have missed the target.

So don't ask me: *What is the secret of remaining happy and married?*

I can only tell you the secret of being happy—marriage is irrelevant. If you live together with somebody out of love, out of gratitude, good; if it goes on happening your whole life, good. If it disappears one day, depart from each other in deep gratitude, in the remembrance of the love that was once there—it has enriched you. Rather than clinging to each other in anger, in frustration, in rage, and being violent to each other and destructive, it is better to depart with grace. One should know how to fall in love and one should also know how to fall out of it gracefully.

The second question:

Bhagwan,
My Jewish parents are not happy that I have become a sannyasin. What should I do?

Garimo,

JESUS HAS SAID: Unless you hate your parents you cannot follow me. Now, the words are very strange—and they come from a man like Jesus. They are shocking. One cannot expect them, at least from Jesus, because he says: Love your enemies as you love yourself. Not only that, he even says: Love thy neighbor as thyself —which is far more difficult than loving your enemies! But when it comes to parents he is very clear. He says: Unless you hate your parents you cannot follow me. Why is he so hard on parents?

But it is nothing if you think of Gautam the Buddha. He used to ask his *bhikkhus*—his sannyasins, his disciples: Have you killed your parents yet or not? A man like Buddha, who is absolutely non-violent! Jesus is not so non-violent; at least he eats meat, he is not averse to eating fish. Buddha is a vegetarian, absolutely vegetarian; he is the greatest propounder of non-violence on the earth. And he asks to his disciples again and again: Have you killed your parents yet or not?

Of course they don't mean it literally, neither Jesus nor Buddha, but their words are significant. What they really mean is a great message; it is metaphoric. You will have to understand the metaphor. They are not concerned with the *outer* parents, your father and mother, they are concerned with the inner imprints that your mother and father have created in you.

It is not the outer parents, Garimo, who are dominating you. What can they do? You here and they may be thousands of miles away somewhere in Germany. What can they do? They cannot dominate you. But you have something inner: you have inner ideas, inner reflections, imprints, impressions of your parents, and those ideas go on dominating you. If they don't like your being a sannyasin, then your conscience will feel guilt. You will feel that you are hurting your parents, that it is not good, that this should not be so, that something has to be done.

But parents are always against anything that is new. Buddha's father was not happy with him; he was very unhappy, he was angry at him. Buddha had to escape out of his kingdom because he was afraid that he would be caught, because detectives were sent to catch hold of him. He was the only son of his father and the father was getting old; the father was seventy when Buddha escaped from his home. The father was afraid—who was going to possess his kingdom? And stories were coming to him, rumors, gossip of all kinds: that he had become a monk, that he was begging, that he had become a beggar. And, of course, the old king was getting very angry: "What is this nonsense? The son of a king begging—for what? He has everything—why should he beg? And he is begging from house to house, walking barefoot and surrounded by other beggars like him. What is he doing? He has betrayed me in my old age!"

Naturally he was angry, but the real anger is somewhere else. The anger is because he has gone against his religion, his ideology. He has gone against all that the father represents—he has gone against the ego of the father.

Jesus' parents were not happy with Jesus either. They were orthodox Jews, how could they be happy with a son who was preaching strange things and who was talking in such a way as if he knew more than Moses?—because Jesus was saying again and again: "It has been said to you in the past . . . but I say unto you that that is wrong. It has been told to you that if somebody throws a brick at you, answer him by throwing a rock at him. But I say to you, if somebody hits one of your cheeks, give him the other cheek too."

Now this was absolutely against the Jewish idea of justice; this seemed almost anti-Jewish—because even the Jewish God declares in the Talmud: I am a very jealous God. If you go against me I will destroy you.

And he destroyed two cities completely. What happened in Hiroshima and Nagasaki, the Jewish God had done three thousand years before! He destroyed two cities for the simple reason that people were not behaving according to his idea of morality; they were becoming immoral. He destroyed two whole cities.

Now, all the people could not have been immoral and even if all the people had been immoral, they could not have been immoral to the same degree. There were small children also; they could not have been immoral. They didn't know anything of morality or immorality. There were very old people also; they could not have been immoral. There were ill people who could not even get out of their beds. What immoral acts could they have been doing? But he was so angry that he destroyed two whole cities just to teach a lesson to humanity.

And this young man Jesus is saying: Forgive . . . He was going against all the ideas of the Judaic religion completely. He was teaching people new concepts, new visions, new ways of approaching God. The parents were angry.

Once it happened Jesus was teaching, surrounded by his disciples and a crowd also. His mother came and somebody informed him from the crowd: "Your mother is waiting outside and she wants to see you urgently." Jesus is reported to have said, "Tell that woman"—not "my mother"—he says, "Tell that woman that nobody is my father and nobody is my mother and nobody is my relative. All my relatives are those who are with me; those who are not with me, I have nothing to do with them. Tell her to go away."

It seems hard, it seems cruel, but there is a reason in it. These are all symbolic stories, I don't think it really happened. I don't think Jesus would say, "Tell that woman . . ." But it says something. You have to drop the idea of your father, of your mother from your innermost core; only then do you become mature. If you carry that idea you remain childish, you never become mature. And no father, no mother ever wants you to become really mature because maturity will mean that you will become free.

All the relgions have taught you to respect your parents for the simple reason that if you respect your parents you will respect the past, you will respect traditions, you will respect conventions. If you respect your father you will respect God the Father. If you don't respect your parents then naturally you are cut off from tradition, and no church can afford it.

I will not say to you don't respect your father and mother, I will say to you that you can respect your father and mother only when you are completely free of your inner impressions of father and mother; otherwise your respect is false, pseudo. You can love your father and mother only when you are completely free of them, otherwise you cannot love them; you will remain angry with them. Nobody can love anybody unless one becomes free of that person. If there is dependence of any kind, love remains only a facade; deep down there is hatred. And every child hates his father and mother—every child, without any exception. But respect is imposed from the outside.

Just look within your unconscious, look deep down within yourself, and you will find a great revengeful fire. You want to take revenge on your parents. You are angry because they are responsible for the way you are. It is the way they have brought you up that is making you miserable. It is the way they have conditioned you that is making you crippled and paralyzed. Hence, naturally, there is hatred.

I would like you to become aware of it so that you can drop it, because whatsoever they have done they have done unconsciously. They need to be forgiven. Forgive them.

Jesus says: Hate your father and Mother; Buddha says: Kill them. I say to you: Forgive them—which is far more difficult. Forgive them because whatsoever they have done they have done unknowingly; they were conditioned by *their* parents and so on and so forth. Even Adam and Eve were conditioned by their father, God; conditioning begins there. God is responsible for conditioning Adam: "Don't eat the fruit from the Tree of Knowledge." That "don't" became an attraction; that is a negative way of conditioning. And if it is said emphatically that you shouldn't do a certain thing, a great urge arises in you to experiment, to experience it. Why? Why is God so interested?—because the Tree of Knowledge cannot be a bad thing, knowing cannot be bad. If you become wise, what is wrong? Wisdom is good, knowledge is good.

Certainly Adam must have thought within himself: "God is trying to keep me from becoming as knowing as he is so that I always remain dependent on him, so that I always have go to for his advice, so that I can never live on my own, so that I always have to be just a shadow to him. He does not want me to be free and independent." That is a simple logical conclusion.

And that's what the devil did—he argued the same thing. He told Eve . . . Why had he chosen Eve, not Adam?—because if you persuade the wife, if the wife is convinced, then you need not worry about the husband.

Every advertisement expert knows it, hence all advertisements are meant for women. Once they are convinced then nobody can unconvince them, at least not their husbands. They have to follow suit, they have to do it, because the woman will become a continuous torture if you don't do it.

The devil was the first advertisement expert. He was the pioneer, he was the founder of the whole art. He did not bother about Adam—he must have known that all husbands are henpecked, so why bother about them? Persuade the wife. He persuaded her, and of course she was convinced because the logic was so clear. He said, "God has prohibited it only because he does not want you to become like gods. Once you eat the fruit of the Tree of Knowledge you will be like gods. And he is jealous, he is afraid. And it will be foolish on your part if you don't eat. Be like gods!"

And who would not like to be like gods? Once the temptation was there it was impossible to resist. But the whole conditioning came from God himself; it was a negative kind of conditioning.

Your parents are not responsible really. An unconscious person cannot be held responsible: he functions unconsciously, he does not know what he is doing.

Garimo, you have to go within yourself and cleanse yourself of all the impressions that your parents have put upon you, both negative and positive. Then there will arise great compassion in you for your parents, great compassion and great gratitude also, because whatsoever they have done they have done—according to them at least—thinking that it is good. They have not deliberately done anything wrong to you. Even now, if they are against your sannyas, if they are not happy with your sannyas, it is because they think you have fallen into wrong hands, that you have fallen from their traditional heritage. They are afraid you may go astray, you may suffer later on, you may repent one day. They feel for you.

Their love is unconscious, hence you need not listen to them, but you are not to become angry with them; you have to understand them.

You say: *My Jewish parents are not happy that I have become a sannyasin.*

First, they are Jewish; that is one of the oldest religions in the world. There are only two old religions in the world, the Judaic religion and the Hindu. The older a tradition, the greater is its weight; it crushes people more. Anything new is light.

My sannyasins can walk light-footedly, almost dancingly. But a five thousand year-old tradition creates a great weight; it is a long past. They could not forgive Jesus, how can they forgive you? And Jesus has not become my sannyasin! If fact, he never went outside the tradition; he remained a Jew. He was not a Christian, remember, because there was no Christianity at that time. Christianity was born out of his death, out of his crucifixion. Hence I always call Christianity "Crossianity"; it has nothing to do with Christ, it has something to do with the cross. That's why the cross has become the symbol of Christianity—far more important than Christ.

They could not forgive Jesus, and he never went outside the tradition. Of course he was saying things which looked a little strange, a little new. He was bringing new light; he was clearing the mirror of the Jewish consciousness from the old dust. But they have not been able to forgive him, not even now. I have not come across a single book written by a Jew in favor of Jesus. They still think he was wrong, they still think that it was right to crucify him, they still think that he was a criminal.

And to become *my* sannyasin is certainly far more dangerous because it is going totally out of all traditions. It is not just changing one tradition for another, it is dropping the very traditional mind itself. It is dropping being traditional as such; it is becoming non-traditional, unconventional. It is pure revolution! And they are afraid, naturally; for many reasons Jews are afraid.

And there is some attraction between me and the Jews. I have attracted so many Jews here that sometimes I myself wonder—am I a Jew or what is the matter?—because Jews are not so easily attracted to anybody. They were not attracted to Jesus. They are not attracted to anybody else. Why have they come to me? I have touched something deep in them. In fact, they have suffered from tradition more than anybody else; that's the reason why they have become so interested in my vision, because I am anti-traditional. They would like to get rid of it.

A Jew and a black man are siting next to each other on the train. Suddenly the Jew realizes that the black is reading a Hebrew magazine. He keeps silent for a while, then whispers to him: "Listen, friend, is it not enough to be a black?"

Your parents, Garimo, may be afraid: "Is it not enough to be a Jew? Now you want to suffer more?" Because to be with me is going to be dangerous. Freedom is far more dangerous than anything else in the world. Freedom is fire: it burns your ego, and because it burns your ego it hurts many other people's egos and they all become enemies to you.

And then Jews are very worldly people. It is the only religion which is very worldly. There are two kinds of religions: the worldly religions—Jews represent the worldly religion—and there are the other-worldly religions, for example, Buddhism. Buddhists will be against me because to them I will look a little worldly, and to Jews I will look a little too other-worldly.

I am both: I am a bridge. My sannyas is a synthesis because I don't divide "this world" and "that world". To me both are beautiful. And one has to live in both worlds together because they are not separate, they are inseparable. The very idea of dividing them has been a great calamity.

Jews are more interested in money than in meditation. Now, thinking that you have become a meditator they will be afraid. "What are you doing? This is the time to earn money. This is the time to get rooted in the world. Don't waste this precious time!" According to them, when you are young you can do something; as you become old you will be less and less able to make money, to have power, prestige, to make a name in the world. You are wasting your time here.

Even with those who are here, if they are Jewish, the hangover continues. One of the sannyasins went to the office a few days ago, in a euphoria—must have touched something intangible in meditation, may have been silent here in the discourse, may have had a glimpse of something unknown. In those moments even if you are a Jew your Jewishness disappears. She went to the office and said that she wanted to donate one hundred thousand dollars to the new commune. After five minutes she went back and said that she wanted to cancel it! She was asked, "What happened? Yes, we will cancel it. It was you, nobody had asked you for anything. You came on your own; now, just after five minutes . . . what has happened?"

She said, "I went to see Amitabh, one of my friends, and he said, 'Are you a fool or something? Go immediately and cancel it!' He scolded me!"

Now, Amitabh is a Polack Jew! That is the most dangerous combination you can find—Polack and Jew! Of course, he loves me and loves me tremendously—he is here, he is one of my topmost therapists, he lives in my house, in Lao Tzu—but hangovers are hangovers!

Very excited, Isaac calls David, "Come immediately, David, I have an incredible bargain. Three hundred trousers for only fifty dollars!"

David runs to Isaac, where he finds the pile of three hundred trousers. He looks them over and then says to Isaac, "But Isaac, these trousers have only one leg! No one can wear them!"

"Listen, David," replies Isaac, "Besides the fact that there are people with only one leg, I already told you—we have to sell them, not to wear them.!"

A Jew arrives in Chicago from Israel; he is coming to America for the first time. It's raining, so he stops at a shop to buy a pair of shoes. Mindful of his father's advice, when the clerk asks twenty dollars for the shoes he starts bargaining: "Ten dollars!"

"That's impossible!" replies the clerk.

"Ten or nothing!" is the Jew's reply.

So the clerk consults the manager, then says, "Okay, ten."

"No," replies the Jew, "five!"

Again the clerk consults the manager . . . "Okay, five."

"No, two!" replies the Jew.

"Listen," says the clerk, tired of him, "just take these shoes and get out!"

"No!" exclaims the Jew.

"No? You don't want them?" asks the clerk incredulously.

Says the Jew: "I want two pairs!"

Garimo, your parents must be worried about what you are doing here. Such an intelligent guy like you wasting his time meditating? Have you gone crazy or something, sitting silently doing nothing? Is this a way a Jew is supposed to behave? Time is money—don't waste it!

And, moreover, whether your parents are Jewish or not, parents are parents; they feel offended—they feel offended by the very idea that you think you know more than they know, that you are trying new ways, that you are trying to be wiser than your parents.

A Jew arrives in heaven and God, in a very compassionate voice, asks, "What happened to you?"

He says, "I was brokenhearted. When my only son, my pride and my joy, announced that he had become Catholic, I felt this terrible pain in my chest . . ."

"You should not have despaired so much. Even *my* only son did the same!"

"And what did you do, my Lord?"

"I made a new will and testament!"

So, Garimo, what can they do? They will make a new will and a new testament—let them make it! Learn to forgive them. I will not tell you to hate them, because hate is not freedom—if you hate somebody you remain attached. Hate is a relationship; love is freedom. Love is not a relationship; hate is a relationship. That's why those who live in relationship live in hate, not in love. Love is freedom. Love them, then you are free. But to love them you will have to cleanse yourself totally. I will not tell you, like Guatam the Buddha, to kill them, because killing is not going to help. Understand them. Be compassionate. Killing will be doing something in a hurry; there is no need to be in a hurry. And parents have gone so deep in you; they are not only in your blood and bones, they have entered in your very marrow. You cannot kill them easily—it is impossible. You will have to commit suicide if you want to kill them because only then will they be killed. They have entered your being: you are part of them, they are part of you. But through deep understanding you can be free of them.

A lawyer has succeeded in acquitting a Jew who has killed his mother, his wife and his sister. Before separating he says to the man, "As you still have a father I'll just say 'See you soon!'"

I will not suggest that; my methods are far more subtle. What Jesus said and what Buddha said are very primitive methods; what I am saying is far more sophisticated—it has to be, it is the twentieth century! Forgive them. Understand them. And the whole question is within you; it has nothing to do with the outer parents. If you can relax within yourself and if you can feel compassion for them—because they have suffered in their own way . . . They have wasted their whole life, now they want to waste your life, because that is the only way they know how to live. Great compassion is bound to arise in you, and out of that compassion maybe you can be of some help to them because compassion functions in a very subtle way. Love is the greatest magic in the world.

I will not tell you to go and listen to them and follow them to satisfy them; that will be wrong. That will be destroying your life and it will not help them either. You have to remain yourself and yet be compassionate and forgiving. And if you happen to go there, remain compassionate and forgiving. Let them feel your compassion, your love, your joy. Let them feel your celebration. Let them feel what has happened to you through sannyas. Let them see the difference.

Buddha's father remained angry till he came to see him. Even when he saw him, for a few moments he was so angry, his eyes were so full of anger, that he could not see. Buddha remained silent. The father went on insulting him, saying, "You have been a deep wound to me—you have almost killed me. Why have you come now after twelve years? I have waited so long! You have not been a son to me, you have been an enemy!"

Buddha listened, did not utter a single word. Then the father suddenly became aware that the son had not spoken even a single word. He asked, "Why are you not speaking?"

Buddha said, "First say everything that you have carried for all these twelve years. Cathart, unburden yourself! Only when you are unburdened will you be able to see me. One thing I would like to say to you:

that you are talking to somebody else, not to your son. The man who had left your palace has not come back—he has died. I am a totally new man. I have come with new consciousness, with new love, with new compassion. But first you unburden yourself, otherwise your eyes are so full of rage you cannot see me. Let your eyes be cleared."

The father was trembling with anger. Slowly he cooled down; this very answer cooled him. Tears of anger were coming to his eyes. He wiped his tears, looked again. "Yes, this is not the same man who left my palace; this is a totally different person. Of course, the face is the same, the figure is the same, but it is a totally new being—the vibe is new."

He fell at the feet of Buddha and he said, "Initiate me too, because now I am very old; death is coming closer. I would also like to taste something that you have tasted. And forgive me and forgive all my anger. I have not known what is happening to you and what has happened to you. It is good that you have come. It is good that you remembered me, that you have not forgotten me."

So whenever you go back, Garimo, let them first cathart. And remember, they are German parents so they will cathart longer than Buddha's parent! Listen silently. Don't get angry. Remain meditative, calm and quiet, and your coolness will transform them. If you really want to help them . . .

And each sannyasin *should* want to help his parents, because they have given you birth. They have brought you up in some way, the way they could; it was not possible for them to do otherwise. Whatsoever they could do they have done and they have done it for your good. Whether it proved good or not is another matter, but their intentions were good. So whenever you go back, remember to help them.

The last question:

Bhagwan,
Don't you ever get tired of us and our stupidity?

Gurudas,

I RATHER ENJOY IT! Moreover, I have to do something and this is the only thing that one can go on doing forever and forever.

Jesus was bored so he went to God his father and asked him, "Dad, give me something to do—I am bored!"
"Take a file and smooth the top of the Himalayas," said God.
After seven thousand years Jesus came back again.
"And now what can I do?" he asked God again.
God gave him a spoon and told him to empty the Indian Ocean. After seven thousand years, he was back again.
"It's done . . . and now?" he asked God.
Tired, God looked at him and said, "Listen, Jesus, go down to earth and convince the men down there to love each other—that will keep you busy for eternity!"

I am not a priest; it is not my duty. Otherwise one is bound to get bored and tired. It is my joy, it is my love!

The Pope is redecorating his summer residence of Castelgandolfo. When the work is finished he comes with the chief decorator to see the results. Everything is perfect.
When he arrives at his bedroom, the decorator, to give the final touch, hangs a beautiful antique twelfth-century cross just over the bed.

"Oh, no, no, no, my son!" exclaims the Pope. "I have already told you not to put anything here that reminds me of my office!"

This is not my work, this is my joy, this is my play. I am really enjoying it!

A Russian cosmonaut comes back from his space travel. Brezhnev receives him: "Tell me the truth, comrade. Did you meet God up there?"

"If you want the truth—yes, I found him!" replies the cosmonaut.

"I thought so," replies Brezhnev. "Now promise me never to reveal this to anyone."

After a few months the same cosmonaut is received by the Pope. When they are alone, the Pope whispers to him, "Now, my dear son, please tell me—did you meet God up there?"

Faithful to his promise, the cosmonaut replies, "No, unfortunately not, Your Sanctity."

And the Pope sadly replies, "I thought so. Now listen, promise me never to tell this to anyone!"

DISCOVER YOUR OWN GOD

The first question:

Bhagwan,
Please talk about people like Bertolt Brecht who
reject religion and spirituality and yet whose
powerful creative love shines like an angry light
in the twentieth century.

Tim Green,

RELIGION FOR CENTURIES has become associated
with a life-negative attitude, and obviously any life-
negative attitude cannot be creative; it becomes in-
trinsically impossible for it to be creative. Creativity

needs a life-affirmative philosophy, creativity needs a tremendous love for existence, and the so-called religions have been teaching people to renounce life, to escape from life; they have been against life.

Because of this, no creative person can be interested in such religions. If he becomes interested he will lose his creativity; if he wants to remain creative he will have to sacrifice his religiousness. Religions have not left any other choice. Because of this, only uncreative people became interested in religion.

I am not talking about Gautam the Buddha, Lao Tzu, Zarathustra, Jesus, Mohammed, Mahavira, Krishna, Kabir, Nanak; leave aside these few names. They are immensely creative, they are poets of existence. They are far greater poets than your so-called poets—their whole life is poetry. They are great musicians. They may never have played on any musical instrument, but their heart is full of harmony, music, melody. Their very heartbeat is that of rhythm, of music. Their life is a dance, it is a song, it is a celebration. Hence, please leave aside these few people.

But the religions have nothing to do with them. Christianity, Hinduism, Jainism, Buddhism, Mohammedanism, these organized religions have nothing to do with their own founders. If you look deep, if you meditate over the matter, you will be surprised. This is *my* observation: that the people who call themselves Christians are not at all concerned with Christ and his message; in fact, they are against everything which Christ stood for and sacrificed his life. The people who call themselves Hindus have nothing to do with Krishna; although they worship him, worshipping makes no difference in their lives. They have not learned the art that Krishna represents; in fact, they have interpreted Krishna according to their own ideas. And the same is the case with the

Buddhists and the Jainas and other religions: they have all gone against the original founders. They have fallen victims of priests—and priests have nothing to do with religion at all.

Priests and politicians are in a conspiracy to exploit people, and the best way to exploit people is to destroy their intelligence. Of course, people like Bertolt Brecht cannot support such religions. These religions have enslaved humanity. They have not helped people to be free, to be independent, to be their own selves; on the contrary, they have reduced them to slaves; in the name of religion they have created great prisons. And the strategy is subtle—very subtle, very cunning. The basic strategy is the same one used all over the world by all the religions.

The first and the most fundamental principle of that strategy is: destroy people's love for life, love for joy, love for celebration. Once people's roots are cut away from existence they start shrinking in themselves, they start losing the sources of nourishment. Their whole being becomes poisoned.

They cannot really escape from life—nobody can really escape from life. Even the people who escape to the mountains have to depend on people who work in the marketplace. Nobody can really escape from life. The people who have gone into the monasteries are dependent on people who live outside; they depend on their support.

If all the world, if the whole of humanity renounces life, it will be committing a global suicide. The Buddhist monk has to beg from those who are not yet monks. The Christian monk has to live on the donations of the people who are still in the world. Nobody can really escape from life while he is alive; it is impossible. But your sources can be poisoned. You cannot escape from life and you cannot live your life totally. You start feeling guilty about being alive: you start feeling as if to be alive is a sin. You start cutting your life as much as you can; you start living at the minimum. That too you accept only as a necessary evil.

That's why laughter has disappeared, wholeness has disappeared. People look sad; their existence has become meaningless. They are uncreative; they are in a kind of limbo, neither here nor there. This is what your religions have done.

I am in agreement with people like Bertolt Brecht. I am also not in support of the so-called religion and spirituality. But I cannot agree totally with Bertolt Brecht for the simple reason that whatsoever religions have done, that is not the work of true religion. The true religion has yet to arrive, the true religion has yet to be born. Be against Christianity, be against Hinduism, be against Mohammedanism, be against Buddhism—I can agree—but don't be against religiousness as such because that means you have made organized religion synonymous with religiousness; it is not so. Condemn the priests, condemn the Pope, condemn the Shankaracharya, but don't condemn Buddha and Lao Tzu and Jesus and Mohammed. They have contributed immensely to man's inner growth; they are absolutely creative. Of course, they have been interpreted by wrong people, but what can they do about it? They need people like Bertolt Brecht to interpret them.

So I can agree with Bertolt Brecht up to a certain point and then we part. The so-called religion has to be eradicated from the earth because that is the only way for the real religion to arrive, for the authentic to arrive, but the authentic religiousness cannot be condemned. If you condemn it, then the result will be this . . . Tim Green himself says in his question:

. . . yet whose powerful creative love shines like an angry light in the twentieth century.

Now, love cannot be angry. Anger is destructive, love is creative. Anger is part of hatred; it is never part of love. That's where Bertolt Brecht has missed the point. If you are against religiousness then you will be creative, but your creativity will be pathological. It will be ill at ease, it will not be beautiful.

And you can see it. The whole of modern art is ugly for the simple reason that it has no spiritual origins, it has no meditative quality in it. You can look at Picasso's paintings: they show something insane in the man. Picasso *is* a genius—with just a little spirituality he would have surpassed Michelangelo. He has the capacity, he has the talents, he has the intelligence, but something is missing. He is in a chaos, he has no inner discipline.

That's why while Michelangelo creates beautiful art Picasso creates ugly art. Looking at Picasso's paintings one is bound to be struck by the fact that there is some insane note in it.

There are so many stories about Picasso . . .

An American millionaire came to Picasso. He wanted two paintings and he wanted them immediately. And he was ready to pay any price—money was not the question. Picasso was a little puzzled because he had only one painting left. He asked such a price that he thought the millionaire would say, "I will purchase only one. "

But he said, "Okay, I will pay the price. Where are the paintings? Bring the paintings, and here is the cheque!"

He went in, cut his painting in two and he gave the millionaire two paintings.

In fact, you can even cut his paintings in four; it will not make much difference.

I have heard another story:

One rich woman wanted him to paint her portrait; he did it. When she came, she looked at it and she said, "Everything is okay, only I don't like the nose. You will have to repaint the nose."

Picasso said, "That is impossible."

She said, "Why is it impossible? I am ready to pay for it. If you need more money for it I am ready to pay for it."

He said, "Money is not the question. I don't know where the nose is!"

A man was looking for a wife. He asked an agent. The agent said, "I have a beautiful woman just for you, a very rich widow. Of course, she is a little older than you, but with so much money that I don't think you would like to miss the opportunity. And she is beautiful! Come along with me. I will show you the woman."

The man went to see the woman. Looking at her he could not believe his eyes—he had never seen such an ugly woman. One eye was looking in one direction, the other eye was looking in another direction. Her nose was crooked, her teeth were coming out, her hair was false, one leg was longer than the other. It was just disgusting to see her!

He whispered in the agent's ear, "You call this woman beautiful?"

The agent said, "There is no need to whisper—she is deaf also! You can say out loud whatsoever you want to say. And I can't help it if you don't like Picasso. That's not my fault!"

DISCOVER YOUR OWN GOD

Modern art is ugly for the simple reason that it has
no spirituality in it. Modern poetry is ugly. Modern
music is just noise—very sexual, because when
spirituality is not present, all that is left is sexuality.
Spirituality is the same energy as sex but at the highest
peak, at the most refined peak. Sex is also the same
energy but very rough, at the lowest point. Sex is
animal energy; the same energy passing through the
art of spirituality becomes spirituality, becomes
samadhi, becomes superconsciousness; it becomes
divine energy.

Hence Bertolt Brecht is angry. That anger can be
understood. But anger cannot be creative; even if it
creates, that creativity will carry something destructive in it.

You will be surprised to know that Adolf Hitler,
when he was young, wanted to become a painter. He
was refused admission to an art academy. Then he
wanted to become an architect, but again he was
refused. And the same man became the most destructive man this century has known—not only that the
century has known but the whole of history. If he had
been admitted to the art academy he would have
become another Picasso; his paintings would have
been destructive.

He painted a few things—those paintings still survive. They say much about him. He uses the blood-red
color out of all proportion. His most loved colors are
blood-red and black; with these two colors he worked,
he painted. He has left a few drawings, his architec-
tural ideas; they don't look like the Taj Mahal, they
look like madhouses! But the man became powerful,
he became a politician, and he really did his painting
and his architecture and his artwork with living
humanity, on the vast canvas of humanity. But those

two colors remained his colors: dark black, the color of death, and blood-red, the color of murder, anger and rage.

Bertolt Brecht would have been a Buddha, just as Friedrich Nietzsche would have been a Buddha. But they became too obsessed with so-called religion. And going against so-called religion, they went against religion as such. That's where they missed, they went wrong.

I am against so-called religion, but I am all for religion as such. In fact, I am against so-called religion because I am in favor of, because I am *for*, true religion.

The real religion is in danger not because of ir-religion, remember. The real is never in danger from the unreal; it is always in danger from the pseudo-real because the pseudo gives the appearance of being the real. We have to change this whole pattern that has dominated humanity for centuries.

My approach is that of life-affirmation. I teach my sannyasins to be loving, to be joyous, to be creative, to be aesthetic. The old so-called religions have all been sad and serious. I teach my sannyasins to love and to laugh and to celebrate. Celebration is the only true prayer; it is the only way we can show our gratitude to God. Renouncing life is complaining against God. God gives you life as a gift and you renounce it! Life is a great gift; you have to be thankful for it. And that thankfulness brings spirituality.

People like Bertolt Brecht are beautiful people. They would have become of tremendous value if they had been able to see what is pseudo in religion and what is real, if they had been able to discriminate. They condemned without any discrimination.

That's where the whole western mind is wrong. For one hundred years after Friedrich Nietzsche, all Western intellectuals have been condemning religion.

Nietzsche declared; "God is dead and man is free," and since that moment this has been the constant slogan of all the intellectuals. And I can understand why. But Nietzsche should have said, "The God of the priests . . ." Even if he had put it in brackets "[of the priests]" things wold have been absolutely clear— because the God of the priests is not the God of the mystics. And the God of the priests need not be dead —he has always been dead! The God of the priests has never been alive. The alive God is that of the mystics.

I teach you the God of the mystics.

The God of the mystics can be found not by belief but by a deep going inward. It has nothing to do with theology; it has something to do with an inner search, an insight into your own being. The moment you know who you are you have found God, and in that very finding you find freedom. It is good that the God of the priests should be dead, should be thrown away, so that you can discover your own God. Your own God is your freedom, your truth.

Without your truth you are bound to remain angry and your life is bound to remain empty, meaningless. And whatsoever you create will not be beautiful creation; it will not be like roses and the song of the birds and the sunset and the stars, it will be something out of a mad mind. It may help you in a certain way because your own madness will be thrown onto the canvas or on the stone and you will be relieved of it—it will be something like catharsis—but it will not be good for others. Those who will see your work of art will get infected; it will be contagious.

Look at the statue of a Buddha. Just sit in front of the statue of a Buddha, silently watching it, and you will be surprised: something in you also starts settling; something in you also becomes quiet, still, silent.

Gurdjieff used to call this "objective art", because the person who has created the statue has created it out of his own meditation; it is a work of meditation. It may not represent exactly the physiology of Gautam the Buddha—it does not really represent it; it is symbolic. It represents his meditation, not his body; not his mind but his very being. It represents his stillness.

"Sitting silently, doing nothing, spring comes and the grass grows by itself." It represents that silence. He is not doing anything. Sitting in front of a Buddha statue you will fall into a deep silence. Sitting in front of a Picasso painting you will be in a turmoil; you will start getting angry, you will start getting restless. You cannot move into meditation; it is impossible. If you keep Picasso paintings in your bedroom you will have nightmares!

The second question:

Bhagwan,
Why is it that I cannot understand your philo-
sophy?

Virama,

WHAT PHILOSOPHY are you talking about? It is not philosophy at all, it is living truth! I am not teaching you any doctrine; I am simply sharing my joy, my insight, my love, my light with you. A philosophy is something of the mind and I've dropped the mind long ago. It is a *communion* that is happening here; it is a communion of hearts. I am using words because you won't understand silence, but all my words are to help you to understand one day my silence. The words are just fingers pointing to the moon. Look at the moon; don't start biting my finger!

It is not a philosophy at all. Philosophy is a very ordinary thing; it is thinking about truth. It is like a blind man thinking about light: he can go on thinking, but do you think he will ever come to any conclusion about light? Will he have any experience of light through thinking for a long, long time about light? He may come to know everything about light, but to know about light is not to know light; to know light is a totally different phenomenon. It needs eyes, not thinking.

I am not a philosopher, I am a physician. I would like to help you to open your eyes. You have kept them closed for many many lives and you have become addicted to closed eyes; you have forgotten that you can open them. I am here just to remind you that nothing is wrong with your eyes—just open them! And whatsoever you will come to know, that is God. God is not a belief but an experience.

Philosophers have spent their lives defining their philosophies.

Jean-Paul Sartre says, "To be is to do."
Albert Camus says, "To do is to be."
And then comes Frank Sinatra who says, "Do-be-do-be-do."
This is my no-philosophy: "To be is just to be."

There is nothing to be done about it. There is no question of doing, it is a question of *being*. You need not try to understand it.

That's where you are going wrong, Virama. If you try to understand it you are bound to misunderstand it because understanding means an effort of the mind.

And your mind is a confusion, your mind is a chaos. Your mind is full of a thousand and one ideologies. Your mind is utterly fucked up!

Two hippies, having shared a joint, are walking down the street. Suddenly a police car goes by at sixty miles per hour with its red light flashing and siren screaming.

One hippie slowly turns to the other and says, "Man, I thought that fuzz would never leave!"

The mind is a kind of drug; it keeps you drugged. You have to get rid of the mind; you have to put it aside. Then there is no question of understanding; you simply see the truth of it. It is a question of *seeing*, not of understanding.

I am leading you towards the state of no-mind and you are trying to understand it *through* the mind; that is impossible. Mind has no capacity to understand the no-mind—the no-mind is incomprehensible, obviously, the mind cannot grasp it, it can only deny it.

Put the mind aside. While listening to me, don't try to understand, just listen silently. Don't figure out whether what I am saying is true or not true. Don't be bothered with its truth or untruth. I am not asking you to believe in it so there is no need to think about its truth or untruth. Listen to me just as you listen to the birds singing or the wind passing through the pine trees or the sound of running water.

But you remain hung up in the head. The head keeps you almost drunk with thoughts, ideas, interpretations.

Every time he got drunk, Mario could not find his house, so his friend told him to put a lantern outside his door. Mario did so and that night, when he came back drunk, he saw the lantern and said, "This must be my house!"

Then taking the lantern with him, he climbed the stairs, entered the bedroom and said, "Right—this is my bed, that is my wife and there I am sleeping next to her! But who the hell is this guy with the lantern in his hand?"

Beware of your mind! You have never thought about it as a drug—it is a very subtle drug. And the society goes on drugging you from your very childhood. It becomes part and parcel of your life and it colors everything. Whatsoever you see, you see through it; whatsoever you listen to, you listen to through it—and it is quick at interpreting for or against.

Listening to me, if you are thinking about for or against, you will go on missing me.

A drunkard accidentally found his way into a luxurious swimming club and was standing by the pool when he was approached by the manager.

"Excuse me, sir, but we are forced to ask you to leave," the manager told him.

"Why should I leave?" asked the drunkard.

"Because you are pissing in the pool!" exclaimed the manager.

"Are you telling me that I am the only person in this club who has been pissing in the pool?" asked the drunkard.

"From the diving board, yes!" answered the manager.

You don't know where you are standing, what you are doing, who you are. My whole effort here is to bring you to your senses—from your mind to your senses.

Mind keeps you in a kind of madness. Mind *is* madness; the difference is only of degree. The mad people have gone a little ahead of you, that's all.

Maybe you are in the mind to ninety degrees, somebody else to ninety-nine degrees, and somebody else has crossed the borderline of a hundred degrees; then he is mad.

But the only sane man is one who has come out of the mind because then your vision is clear, unclouded; your consciousness is pure, like a mirror without any dust on it.

Two madmen are crouching on the branch of a tree when suddenly one falls down.

"But what are you doing?" exclaims the one sitting on the tree branch.

"Well, I had to fall—I was ripe!"

A man is strolling in a park. Suddenly a man comes up to him and without saying one word slaps him on the face.

"Why!" exclaims the man. "You are mad!"

Says the other very quietly, "Yes—do you mind?"

Your mind keeps dreaming—day in, day out, it goes on dreaming. In the day, the dreams are known as thoughts; they are verbal dreams. In the night, thoughts are known as dreams; they are pictorial thoughts. But there is no difference. And even while you are awake, if you just close your eyes and look inside, you will find a subtle stream of pictorial dreams continuously going on like an undercurrent.

Meditation means dropping out of this stream: neither thinking nor dreaming, just being. And then, suddenly you will see what I am saying. It will not be a question of being convinced of its truth; it will be a realization. And truth is never a conclusion; it is always a realization, a revelation.

"Every night I have the same awful nightmare," says one man to his friend. "I dream that Sophia Loren enters my room . . . stark naked!"

"What! You call this a nightmare?"

"Of course I do! Every time she comes in she slams the door so violently that I wake up!".

An American Indian and a hippie are sitting next to each other in a bar. After a few moments the hippie turns to the Indian and says, "Listen, man—you've been staring at me for more than an hour! Mind your own business!"

And the Indian replies, "Many moons ago I lay with a skunk . . . I keep thinking you may be my son!"

When you are with me, stop all this kind of nonsense! I am not here to help you to think more clearly, to think more logically, to think in a more sophisticated and philosophic way. My whole effort is to make you aware of the stupidity of all thinking as such. Then silence comes, and with silence comes seeing. When all is still within you, when nothing stirs within you, you will be able to know what I am saying, what Buddha said twenty-five centuries ago, what Ko Hsuan said two thousand years ago. You will not only understand me, you will understand all the awakened ones of all the ages, past, present and future, too, because you will have been able to realize yourself, you will have been able to taste it yourself. It is a question of tasting it.

The third question:

Bhagwan,
Don't you have enough disciples? What is the need for videotapes of you and your commune?

Devesh,

I HAVE GOT only one hundred fifty thousand san-nyasins in the world—that is just a drop in the ocean of humanity. And if you want to transform the consciousness of man it is nothing; it is just the begin-ning, it is just a seed. We have to go on spreading this new message—new in a sense, because of the so-called religions, and yet the ancientmost, because whenever anybody has known he has known the same truth.

Truth never changes; it is always the same. Who knows it makes no difference, when one knows it makes no difference. Time and space don't matter.

And this is a very special moment in the history of humanity: either man will destroy himself totally or a new man will be born. It has never been so important to transform the consciousness of man, to bring a radical change in the very vision of man as it is today. And we have to do it quickly because time is short. The politicians are piling up atom bombs, hydrogen bombs and whatnot. Just within ten years the power to destroy man has increased seven hundred times. Ten years ago it was enough to destroy humanity; now it is enough to destroy seven hundred earths of the same size. It seems to be simply mad. What is the point?—because we don't know any other earths yet. Yes, scientists say there are fifty thousand planets with life, but that is only a hypothesis. We may never reach them—we have only reached the moon.

And those planets are far, far away. The nearest is four light years away; that means if a spaceship goes at the speed of light—which is impossible or next to im-possible because the speed of light is immense . . . Light moves at the speed of one hundred and eighty-six thousand miles per second. If we can create a spaceship which can move at this speed, then it will take four years to get there and four years to come back. But it seems not possible to create such a spaceship because when anything moves at such a speed it becomes light; it melts and becomes light. The spaceship will melt and become light and the people traveling in it will become light; they will disappear. At such speed such heat is created that everything becomes light. We don't know of any metal, not yet, which can resist heat at such a speed.

And those planets which the scientists think have life are thousands of light years away so there seems to be no possibility to destroy them. Then why go on piling up more and more atom bombs, hydrogen bombs, super bombs, death rays? For what? Do you want to kill each human being seven hundred times? Human beings die only one time. They are not Jesus Christs who will resurrect so you have to kill them again and they will resurrect and you have to kill them again—seven hundred times. But politicians make arrangements just in case!

In such a mad world where mad politicians are so powerful, meditation can be the only way to defend life on earth.

Devesh, the inner revolution has to be spread as quickly and as fast as possible. Moreover, I am a twentieth-century man—I don't believe in bullock carts. You can see my Rolls Royce!

But even Buddha tried every possible way in order to reach as many people as he could. Of course, there was no other way so he traveled from one village to another; that was the only possible way to reach people. But how many people could he reach? He could never go beyond one single province, Bihar. In fact, the name "Bihar" comes from the fact that he traveled there; the name "Bihar" means the place where a Buddha travels, where the awakened one has traveled. The boundaries of the province are the boundaries of his travels. But he could not reach all parts of Bihar either; he could reach only the important places and villages on the way.

Forty-two years he traveled; old, ill, but he traveled. He was so old—he died when he was eighty-two—and continuously traveling in the hot climate of Bihar, a physician had to continuously follow him to keep him healthy, to look after him. Why did he travel? For what?—to reach as many people as possible.

Mahavira did the same. They each tried in their own ways.

Two monks were talking to each other.

"Do you know why Jesus, after his resurrection, appeared to women?"

"No, I don't," replied the other.

"So that the news of his resurrection could spread more quickly!"

I don't go anywhere; there is no need now—that is out of date. I cannot reach many people by traveling, but now we have the media available. My word can go to the farthest corner of the earth—it is reaching already. Books are also old ways of reaching people; their days are also over. New methods have been evolved.

A videotape is a far better way to reach people because they can hear me the same way as you are hearing me. And just hearing the word without seeing the person is one thing; seeing the person also makes a lot of difference. It is totally different because when you are listening to me on a tape recording or on records you will not be able to see my hand, which says more than I can say with my words. You will not be looking at my eyes, which have much more to say than words can convey. Something will be missing, something of immense value—the person will be missing. You will be hearing only a ghostly voice.

I will use films, television, videotapes, tapes, every modern technique to spread the message. I belong to the twentieth century totally, wholeheartedly. And I love this century; I am not against it. I love science and its technology. It is in the wrong hands, but that always happens. Whenever something significant is discovered it always falls into the wrong hands first for the simple reason that they are very quick people, cunning people.

Even the discovery of atomic energy can be a blessing to the world. But it has fallen into the hands of the politicians. It should be in the hands of mystics; then there would be no need to be afraid of a Third World War. Then we could fill the whole earth with affluence; then poverty could disappear for the first time from the whole earth. Poverty could become a thing of the past. Much illness could disappear. Man's life could be prolonged to almost impossible limits. Three hundred years would not be a difficult target; each person could live three hundred years very easily because scientists say the body is capable of living far longer than it lives.

People die at the age of seventy just because they have always been dying at that age. It has become a fixed idea in the mind—in the collective mind it has become a fixed idea; it is a kind of auto-hypnosis. It can be changed.

Even the very program in your cells can be changed; they have the program. When a child is born his cells have the program how long he will live, but that program can be changed. If we can split the atom we can split the living cell and change its inner program; we can give it a new program, we can make it live three hundred, four hundred, five hundred years; we can give it a program which will keep it healthy forever, young forever. Old age can disappear. This is possible now.

Science has released tremendous power, but it has fallen into the wrong hands and the right hands are not there. We have to create the right hands; we have to create the right consciousness for that.

Hence, Devesh, I will go on working with all the modern media to reach as many people as possible. I am already reaching. You can see here people from almost every country. There is not a single country in the world now where my sannyasins are not. And they are creating a stir everywhere. They are bound to create a stir, they are bound to create a new kind of revolution—the real revolution.

Political revolutions are not revolutions; only spiritual revolutions are revolutions because unless the inner being changes, no outer change is going to help.

And, remember it, I am not an old type of saint: "Why bother about disciples and why bother about reaching many people?" It is not a question of bothering at all—I am enjoying it tremendously! It is not in any way work for me; it is play. And it is urgently needed, too.

I can understand Devesh's question because he works in the film department in the commune. He is sitting there just behind the video camera. He must be getting puzzled—why? He has written many questions of the same type.

Just two days ago when Prem Chinmaya left his body he immediately wrote a question to me: "Bhagwan, even Prem Chinmaya's departure and the celebration were videotaped. Can't a sannyasin die in peace?"

But he was already dead! Now you can do whatsoever you want—videotape him, film him . . . And K.B. was arranging his head for the right position—you can do anything now! Chinmaya must have been around laughing, enjoying. He must be saying to himself, "Gosh, had I known it before I would have died sooner! They are doing well!" He must have enjoyed it.

And he died in utter peace, he died in absolute peace. And your videotape cannot disturb him. His cancer was not disturbing him, how can your videotape disturb him? He was in immense pain, but he remained a witness. He died a beautiful death. That's the way a sannyasin should die.

Now Nartan has come. Just yesterday he wrote a letter to me: "I was fortunate to come and to see Chinmaya's departure and the celebration because I am also suffering from cancer; the doctors have said, 'You have only two years left.' And I have come to be forever here." Nartan was happy to see the way Chinmaya died and the way everybody celebrated his death.

I teach you not only to celebrate life but death too, because death is the climax of life, the crescendo. If you have lived your life really you will celebrate your death too.

And he died so beautifully, in such deep surrender. Even Nartan was immensely happy to be present. Now his fear of death is gone. In fact, he is looking forward to it.

So, Devesh, get ready!

The fourth question:

Bhagwan,
Why and how did God create the Italians?

Sanjayo,

ARE YOU IN LOVE with some Italian guy? Otherwise why this question? And this is really a great question! When I read your question I had to consult the Akashic records because neither the Bible says anything about it nor the Koran nor the Vedas! And really it is something very important. The keeper of the Akashic records is Master Kuthumi, well known to the Theosophists as Master K.H. He is the keeper—I had to ask his permission. "Let me see just a little thing, because I don't know the answer: Why and how did God create the Italians?"

He was also puzzled. He said, "Nobody has ever asked this, neither Blavatsky nor Annie Besant. Who is this Sanjayo? Seems to be very esoteric!"

I said, "My sannyasins are very esoteric, very metaphysical! They ask such questions that if they were to ask any other saint, either the saint would escape or they would be thrown out! But they can ask me each and every thing."

I had to look hard enough, then I came across a little passage. It says: "In the beginning there was darkness and spaghetti. And God loved spaghetti. One day, in the darkness, he was eating spaghetti and an idea occurred to him. He took a little spaghetti in one hand and a little spaghetti in the other and clapped both hands together and said, 'Wop!' and the first Italian appeared." That's why they are called wops.

The only question remains—please don't put it to me—who made the spaghetti in the beginning? I could not find the answer even in the Akashic records. And when I asked Kuthumi again and again, he said, "Shut up! Such questions are not written and such answers are not given. And God can do anything, he can do any miracle. Why can he not make spaghetti?"

I said, "That seems to be difficult. Without an Italian there in the first place who will make spaghetti?"

And you ask, "Why . . ."

In the Akashic records it says: The day God created Italy was a day of grace. Even God stopped to contemplate his work with great satisfaction.

"I outdid myself! What a wonder! Look at that beautiful scenery! It is a blessed country!" said God to himself.

And then, to balance things, God created the Italians.

One thing is certain: without the Italians the world would have never been so beautiful, would have never been so interesting. Italians have contributed much. Another thing is absolutely certain: without the Italians there would have been no commune here—impossible. I am dispensable, but Deeksha is not! Even if I am not here you can sit in silence, but without Deeksha how long can you sit in silence?

The lady was taking the census in a middle class Italian neighborhood. As she rang the bell, a naked man opened the door. She was a very professional type, so she made believe she had not noticed. But the guy explained himself.

"I hope you understand me—I belong to a nudist club."

"There is no problem," said the lady, "I just need some information, sir. Are you married?"

"Yes, for the third time."

"Do you have sons?"

"Yes," said the naked man. "I have seven from my first wife, twelve from the second and fifteen from the third."

"Well," said the lady, "it seems you are not a nudist, you just have no time to dress!"

Italians really have contributed great things to the world!

A very shy painter met a beautiful Italian woman in a bar and asked if she would pose for him. She agreed if he would pay her one hundred dollars.

So the painter borrowed money from all his friends and set up the appointment. Once they were together he said, "Miss, what I would really like to do is to paint your portrait with bare breasts."

She agreed for the price of two hundred dollars. So he sold everything he could and finally raised the money.

When she came to his studio and posed with her breast exposed, he became so excited that he couldn't resist asking her to pose entirely in the nude. She agreed, but asked for four hundred dollars.

Desperate, he sold his favorite paintings and even his art supplies in order to raise the enormous sum of money.

Finally she arrived at the studio and removed all of her clothes. The painter became so excited, he said, "Oh! The passion! I am dying with desire for you! What I really want is to make love with you! Say how much . . . how much?"

"Ai!" she exclaimed. "The same price as for everyone else—ten dollars."

Maria has six sons, all dark-haired. The seventh, however, is born redheaded.

Giovanni is furious.

"I know you have betrayed me!" he shouts in anger. "Confess that this is not my son!"

"I swear, Giovanni, he is your son. I swear it—I swear it!"

But Giovanni, in a blind rage, shoots her. Before dying, the woman asks him to come close and whispers, "I have to confess something to you, Giovanni. He is your son—it's the others that are not yours!"

Roberto left for America with the promise of sending for Maria once he had settled. Before leaving they made a fidelity pact with each other.

Two years later Roberto sent for Maria. On her arrival day he said to her, "Wow, you look lovely!"

"And you, Roberto, you are so handsome!" said Maria.

Soon they were sharing confidences of the past two years.

"Do you know, Maria," said Roberto, "these two years have been a great sacrifice, but I have been faithful to our pact. Every time I went with a woman I would remember our vow and would get up from on top of her. What about you? Did you fulfill our pact, too?"

And Maria answered, "You know, Roberto, to get out from underneath is much harder!"

Four men are in a bar talking about their professions.

The first, a German, says, "I'm a coke-sacker at the coal yard. I fill sacks with coke."

The second, a Frenchman, says, "I'm a sock-tucker at the clothing warehouse. I tuck socks into packages."

The third, a Dutchman, says, "I'm a cork-soaker at the barrel factory. I soak the corks so they'll make a good fit."

The fourth, an Italian, says, "I'm the real thing."

Without the Italians the world would not be the same; they are the most earthly people. And I love the earthly people; they are the most rooted in the earth. They are not abstract people, like Indians; they are not metaphysicians. That is their beauty.

And my work here is to create a synthesis of the sky people and the earth people. I would like my sannyasins to be as earthly as the Italians and as unearthly as the Indians, because unless your roots go deep in the earth your branches cannot reach to the stars. The deeper the roots go into the earth, the higher is the reach of your branches. Then you can whisper with the stars.

Up to now there has been a split. The earthly people have been condemned by the religious people as materialists and the materialists have been condemned by the spiritualist as hocus-pocus. Both are true in a way, but both are half. And a half-truth is far more dangerous than a lie because it looks like a truth.

The whole truth is that a real, authentic man, the whole man, will contain contradictions. He will be vast enough to contain contradictions. He will be a man and a woman together. He will be earthly and unearthly together. He will be materialist and spiritualist together, with no conflict. Unless this synthesis happens the world is going to remain schizophrenic.

My sannyasins are not to be unearthly, they are not only to be earthly either; they have to be both. I am giving them the hardest task ever: they have to be materialists *and* spiritualists, spiritualists *and* materialists. They have to drop the whole division of this world and that, of this shore and that, of *this* and *that*. They have to make a bridge between the two. And once that bridge is made, man will be whole for the first time. And a whole man is holy. Neither the spiritualist is holy nor is the worldly man holy because both are not yet whole. They are unholy because they are half, and any person who is half is bound to suffer. He cannot rejoice, he cannot celebrate, he cannot know what a blessing life is.

You have to know that even dust is divine, that your body is a temple. You have to become Zorba the Buddha!

THE VENERABLE MASTER SAID:

Tao manifests both as the pure and the turbid,
both as movement and stillness.
Heaven is pure, earth is turbid.
Heaven moves, earth is still.
The masculine is pure, the feminine is turbid.
The masculine is active, the feminine is passive.
Manifesting from its radical essence,
Tao flows forth even to the last of things,
bringing forth heaven and earth
and all that is in between.
The pure is the cause of the turbid,
and movement of stillness.

A
WORLD
INSIDE
YOU

TAOISM IS NOT A RELIGION in the ordinary sense of the term, it is not a so-called religion; it is *authentically* religious. But to be authentically religious it has to be basically scientific. Science and religion are

125

separate only as far as their direction is concerned, but not in their approach. Religion can be scientific without being a science; science can be religious without being a religion. Tao is scientific without being a science.

Science means trying to know the objective world without any prejudice, without any *a priori* conclusions. The same is true about the inner world, the subjective world. One should approach it also without any conclusions. A scientist cannot be a Hindu or a Mohammedan or a Christian; if he is then he is not scientific. At least in his scientific endeavor he should put aside all his prejudices.

If Galileo remains a Christian, then he cannot discover the truth that the sun does not move around the earth. If Copernicus remains a Christian even while he is doing his scientific research, then he cannot go beyond the Bible. And the Bible is many thousands of years old; it contains the science of those days. It is very primitive—it is bound to be so.

All religious scriptures contain certain facts which they should not contain. They are not religious facts; they are concerned with the objective world. But in the old days everything was compiled in religious scriptures—they were the only scriptures. Religious scriptures have functioned in the world for thousands of years as encyclopedias: everything that was known, was discovered, was theorized, was collected in them.

The Vedas in India are called *samhitas*; *samhita* means a compilation, a collection. Their function was exactly that of the Encyclopedia Britannica. All kinds of things are compiled in them: the literature of those days, the science of those days, the astronomy of those days, the geography, the history, the art; everything that it was possible to know was compiled.

As man has progressed, everything has become more and more specialized.

Science means the search for truth in the objective world; religion means the search for truth in the subjective world. Just as there is a world outside you there is a world inside you, too. And, of course, the inside world is far more significant because it is your inside, it is your very being, it is your subjectivity. But about the inner world we are still very unscientific— we still live through beliefs. About the outside world we have become a little more mature; we are ready to drop any belief. If a certain fact is discovered which goes against our older theories, we discard the older theories in favor of the new discovery. But the same is not true about the inner; to the inner we have a very deep clinging.

Tao is in that way a scientific approach to the inner —you can call it the science of the subjective, the science of being. This is one of the most significant things to remember while we will be meditating over these sutras of Ko Hsuan.

The second thing to remember is that Tao is the first revelation, realization, of the fact that existence is polar. No other religion has been so clear about this tremendously significant fact. "Existence is polar" means that existence is not logical, it is dialectical; it is not Aristotelian, it is Hegelian.

Logic is simple, logic is linear; dialectics is a little more complex. It is not simple because dialectics is possible only if the opposite is also involved in it; if the opposite is not there, there will be no dialectics. There can be no electricity without the two poles, the positive and the negative. Electricity is not logical, it is utterly illogical—it is dialectical. There can be no humanity without the masculine energy and the feminine energy. Just think of a humanity consisting only of men or women: it will die, it will not be able to live—it will not *have* any energy to live. Energy is created by the friction with the opposite.

The Hegelian formulation is: thesis needs antithesis. Unless there is a thesis opposed by an antithesis there is no dynamism; life becomes stagnant. Matter is possible only if there is consciousness, and vice versa. The sky and the earth, God and existence, the day and the night, summer and winter, birth and death, these are polarities opposed to each other. But the opposition is only apparent; deep down they are complementaries.

What Hegel discovered just two hundred years ago Taoists had discovered almost five thousand years before. They were the pioneers of dialectics; they were the first dialecticians of the world. They contributed one of the most important insights to existence: you will find it everywhere.

Life cannot exist even for a single moment without its opposite because it depends on the opposite. The opposition is only apparent; deep down they are complementaries. They have to be—they depend on each other. Man is not man without a woman, woman is not woman without a man; they depend on each other.

That's why there is something missing in a homosexual or a lesbian relationship—there is no dialectics. The homosexual relationship is far more logical, remember, and because it is logical it is simple; because it is logical there is less complexity about it, less conflict in it. It is not accidental that the homosexuals are called "gay" people—they *are* gay! They are happier than the heterosexual people because there is no conflict. A man can understand another man more easily than he can ever understand a woman. A woman can understand another woman more easily than she will be ever able to understand a man because man is a totally different existence. Their ways differ: they function from different centers. To each other they look absurd.

The man functions through the intellect; the woman functions through intuition. The man goes about everything through reasoning; the woman simply jumps on the conclusion without going through any reasoning. The man is simply amazed! He cannot find any clue. He may have lived with the woman his whole life, still the woman remains a mystery. And the same is true for the woman: the man remains a mystery. He cannot understand simple things which she can see clearly: that smoking can bring cancer. "Why do you go on smoking? Drinking alcohol will kill you sooner. Then why are you poisoning yourself?"

Mulla Nasruddin's wife was telling him . . . When he was drinking whisky one night, she told him, "I have told you a thousand and one times, stop all this nonsense! This is slow poisoning! This is slow suicide!"

Nasruddin looked at her and said, "Please don't exaggerate! You have not told me one thousand and one times—maybe a few dozen times. Don't exaggerate. Moreover, I am not in any hurry, so let it be slow poisoning! I am not in a hurry to die."

The man and the woman are constantly arguing about each and everything; they never agree about anything. They cannot agree: by their very natures agreement is not possible. There is always tension. Hence gay people are really gay. When you see two homosexuals hand in hand going for a morning walk you can see the joy! You never see that joy between a husband and wife—impossible. The gay relationship is simple; but because it is simple, because there is no tension in it, no conflict in it, there is no growth either. There is no pain in it, hence it is stagnant. There are no more surprises in it.

The woman remains always to be discovered by the man, and vice versa. You cannot exhaust discovering a man or a woman. If you belong to the opposite pole it is an endless discovery; you will never come to a conclusion.

Existence is not logical, and it is good, otherwise there would have been only death and no life. If God were Aristotelian there would have been no life at all. There would have been peace all over—nobody to know it, nobody to experience it. It is good that God is Hegelian, that he has created polarities.

Tao talks about *yin* and *yang*: that is its most fundamental approach to understanding existence. And you have to go deep into it.

There is a great attraction between man and woman for the simple reason that they are mysterious to each other. The same thing creates conflict and the same thing creates attraction. The farther away they are, the greater the distance between them, the more the attraction between them.

In modern societies, in advanced countries particularly, the attraction is disappearing for the simple reason that men and women are coming so close to each other, they are becoming almost similar. They dress alike, they both have started smoking, they both drink, they both behave in the same way, they both use the same language. The Liberation Movement has contributed much to this nonsense.

The Women's Liberation Movement is teaching women all over the world to be just like men—strong, rough, aggressive. They can be aggressive and they can be rough, but they will lose something immensely valuable: they will lose their feminineness. And the moment they become just like men they will not be mysteries anymore. This is something new happening in the world; it has never happened before.

The wise sages of the ancient days always made it clear to the old societies: make men and women as distinct as possible. Nature makes them distinct, but culture also should help them to be distinct. That does not mean that they are not equal; they are equal but they are different, they are unique. Equality need not mean similarity; equality should not be misunderstood as similarity. Similarity is not equality. And if women start becoming like men they will never be equal to men, remember.

The Women's Liberation Movement is going to do some very deep harm to the women's cause in the world, and this will be the harm: they will become carbon copies of men, they will have a secondary kind of existence. They will not be real men because they cannot be naturally so aggressive. They can pretend, they can cultivate aggression, they can be rough, but that will be just a facade; deep down they will remain soft. And that will create a split in their being, that will create a schizophrenia in their being. They will suffer from a dual personality and they will lose their mysteriousness. They will argue with men with the same logic. But they will be like men and they will become ugly. To be unnatural is to be ugly; to be natural is to be beautiful.

I would like them to be equal to men, but the idea of similarity should be dropped. In fact, they should become as dissimilar as possible; they should keep their uniqueness intact. They should become more and more feminine, then the mystery deepens. And that is the way of existence, the way of Tao.

Only one modern psychologist, Carl Gustav Jung, had some insight about this Taoist approach. He was the only one in the West who had pondered over and studied Taoism deeply; he introduced Taoism in his psychology, and he brought Taoism up to date. If you want to understand Taoism it will be good to understand Carl Gustav Jung and his understanding about Taoism; he was moving along the right lines. But after his death that work stopped. He had taken only a few steps—because Taoism is a vast ocean—he had moved in the right direction, but the work has stopped. It has to be deepened. Many more people have to work to make the insight modern because the language is old and sometimes the old language becomes a barrier.

For example, reading these sutras many women here will feel a little offended. But Ko Hsuan means no offense; he is simply using an old way. What could he do? That was the way in those days. There is no evaluation—he is not saying that the masculine is higher and the feminine is lower—that has to be remembered constantly, otherwise you will immediately become closed. Particularly women will become closed to the sutras; they will not be able to understand. And those women who have, unfortunately, been associated with the Women's Liberation Movement, will immediately become closed; they will not be able to understand the beauty of the sutras. So for them particularly I have to remind you that it is not biological masculinity and feminity that is meant, but psychological.

A man is not of necessity masculine, a woman is not of necessity feminine. A woman can be masculine, for example, Joan of Arc or, in India, Laxmibhai. These women were warriors, great soldiers; they were not feminine at all. Biologically, of course, they were feminine, their bodies were those of women, but their very souls were those of men. They have to be counted as masculine. And there have been men— poets, dancers, musicians, singers, painters—who were very feminine. So soft, so round was their being that psychologically they were women. They may have been able to reproduce children, they may have been able to become fathers and husbands, but deep down they were not masculine; their psychology can only be called feminine. It happens—in fact, it happens more often than you will ever think.

Secondly, every man and every woman is also the opposite. Every man, to be alive, carries in the unconscious the feminine principle, otherwise there will be no dynamism in his being, there will be no tension, not enough tension to keep him alive. He will simply die; there will be no reason for him to live. A certain tension is needed in his being. If the tension becomes too much he goes mad; if the tension becomes too little he will be dead.

There is a beautiful story in Buddha's life:

A great prince became initiated, became a sannyasin of Buddha. He had lived in great luxury his whole life, he had been a great sitarist, his name was known all over the country as that of a great musician. But he became impressed by Buddha's inner music—maybe his insight into music had helped him to understand Buddha.

When Buddha was visiting his capital he heard him for the first time, fell in love at first sight, renounced his kingdom. Even Buddha wanted him not to do such a great act so impulsively. He told him, "Wait. Think. I will be here for four months"—because during the whole rainy season Buddha never used to move; in the rainy season he would remain in one place. "So I am going to be here; there is no hurry. You think over it. Four months time and then you can take sannyas, you can become an initiate."

But the young man said, "The decision has happened; there is nothing more to think about. It is now

133

or never! And who knows about tomorrow? And you have been always saying, 'Live in the present,' so why are you telling me to wait for four months? I may die, you may die, something may happen. Who knows about the future? I don't want to wait even a single day!''

His insistence was such that Buddha had to concede; he was initiated. Buddha was a little uncertain about him, whether he would be able to live this life of a beggar. Buddha had known it from his own experience; he himself was a great prince once. He knew what it was to be in luxury, what it was to live in comfort, and what it was to be a beggar on the street. It was a great, arduous phenomenon, but Buddha had taken time. It took him six years to become enlightened, and slowly slowly he had become accustomed to being without shelter, sometimes without food, without friends, enemies all over for no reason at all, because he was not hurting anybody. But people are so stupid, they live in such lies, that whenever they see a man of truth they are wounded of their own accord—they feel hurt, insulted.

Buddha knew the whole thing was going to be too much for this young man. He felt sorry for him, but he initiated him. And he was surprised and all the other sannyasins were surprised, because the man simply moved to the other extreme. All Buddhist monks used to eat only once a day; that new monk, the ex-prince, started eating only once in two days. All Buddhist monks used to sleep under trees; he would sleep under the open sky. The monks used to walk on the roads; he would walk not on the roads but always on the sides where there were thorns, stones. He was a beautiful man; within months his body became black. He was very healthy; he became ill, he became lean and thin. His feet became wounded.

Many sannyasins came to Buddha and said, "Something has to be done. That man has gone to the opposite extreme: he is torturing himself! He has become self-destructive."

Buddha went to him one night and asked him, "Shrona"—Shrona was his name—"can I ask you a question?"

He said, "Of course, my Lord. You can ask any question. I am your disciple. I am here to tell you whatsoever you want to know about me."

Buddha said, "I have heard that when you were a prince you were a great musician, you used to play the sitar."

He said, "Yes, but that is finished. I have completely forgotten about it. But that is true, I used to play the sitar. That was my hobby, my only hobby. I used to practice at least eight hours per day and I had become famous all over the country for that."

Buddha said, "I have to ask one question. If the strings of your sitar are too tight, what will happen?"

He said, "What will happen? It is simple! You cannot play upon it—they will be broken."

Buddha said, "Another question: if they are too loose, what will happen?"

Shrona said, "That too is simple. If they are too loose no music will be produced on them because there will be no tension."

Buddha said, "You are an intelligent person—I need not say anything more to you. Remember, life is also a musical instrument. It needs a certain tension, but only a certain tension. Less than that and your life is too loose and there is no music. If the tension is too much you start breaking down, you start going mad. Remember it. First you lived a very loose life and you missed the inner music; now you are living a very tight, uptight life—you are still missing the music. Is there not a way to adjust the strings of the sitar in such a way that they are exactly in the middle, neither loose nor tight, with just the right amount of tension, so that music can arise?"

He said, "Yes, there is a way."

Buddha said, "That is what my teaching is: be exactly in the middle between the two poles. The tension has not to disappear completely, otherwise you will be dead; the tension has not to become too much, otherwise you will go mad."

And that's what has happened in the whole world. The East has become too loose, hence there is death, starvation. And the West has become too tight, hence there is madness, neurosis. The West is breaking down under its weight. The East has become so lazy and lousy out of its looseness.

A certain tension is needed, but there is a state of tension which is also a state of equilibrium. And that is the whole art of Tao. The equilibrating pulse of the mystical life, the secret . . .

The words in this sutra are not to be understood biologically, physiologically. Each man and each woman also have their opposite within them. If you are a man consciously, then unconsciously there is a woman in you; if you are a woman, then there is a man unconsciously in you. Your conscious and your unconscious are polar opposites and there is a tension between the two. That tension has to become neither too loose nor too tight. This is the whole art of religion, or the whole science of religion.

Tao does not believe in miracles; it believes in scientific methods to transform your life.

Lao Tzu, Chuang Tzu and Lieh Tzu were walking together along a forest path one day when they came upon a fast-flowing river which barred their way. Immediately Lieh Tzu sat down on the bank of the river and meditated upon the eternal Tao. Ten minutes later he stood up and proceeded to walk on the water to the other side.

Next, Chuang Tzu sat in the lotus posture for twenty minutes, whereupon he stood up and also walked across the river.

Lao Tzu, watching this in amazement, shrugged his shoulders, sat down on the river bank like the others and meditated for over an hour. Finally, with complete trust in the Tao, he closed his eyes, took one step into the river and fell in.

On the other shore, Chuang Tzu laughed, turned to Lieh Tzu and said, "Should we tell him where the rocks are?"

Tao does not believe in any nonsense. It is very pragmatic, practical, down to earth.

A street vendor was trying to sell his product. All day long he would call out, "Try a bottle of my elixir—long-life lotion!"

There was a boy helping him distribute the bottles and taking the money.

The vendor kept calling out, "Look! Long-life lotion! A wonder, gentlemen! A real miracle! Every morning I drink one bottle, and look at me—don't I look young? I am more than seven hundred years old!"

The people were amazed and sceptical. Finally one of the customers called the boy aside and asked, "Is your boss really over seven hundred years old?"

"I can't guarantee it," answered the boy.

Everyone turned to the boy to hear his answer.

"Why can't you guarantee it?" asked the customer.

"Because I have only worked with him for three hundred years," answered the boy.

All other religions are much more concerned with such stupidities—miracles, wonders. Not Tao. Tao is very straight, hence there is a great future for Tao. When all other religions have gone down the drain, Tao will still be around for the simple reason that it will fit in with the scientific climate that is growing every day on the earth. It will not only fit in with the scientific climate, it will help and nourish it. It will bring new visions to science because it does not ask you to believe in anything, it simply wants you to understand.

These sutras are not to be believed in. Please try to understand them, and try to understand them by putting aside all your prejudices as men and women.

THE VENERABLE MASTER SAID:

Tao manifests both as the pure and the turbid, both as movement and stillness.

Don't be offended by the "turbid"; it simply means muddy, not clear, vague. Both are manifestations of Tao.

Tao manifests both as the pure . . .

And the word "pure" does not mean anything moral, virtuous, et cetera; it has nothing to do with morality. "Pure" simply means clear, transparent; and "turbid" means muddy, not clear, vague. These are both manifestations of Tao.

The ordinary man is turbid; the Buddha is pure. The man who is sleepy is muddy, cloudy; he is surrounded by much smoke of his own creation. The man who has awakened out of all dreams and desires has a clarity; he has no smoke around him, no clouds. He is like a sunny day: the sun is there without any clouds.

Tao manifests both . . .

And remember, both are Tao. Never forget it. The asleep person is as divine as the awakened one, as godly as the awakened one. There is no intrinsic difference; the difference is only in manifestation. One is full of dreams, desires, hence one is turbid; and the other is finished with the dreams, has become tired of the dreams, has come to know that they *are* dreams, and in that very knowing those dreams have dropped of their own accord. Now his eyes are clear; he can see through and through.

> *Tao manifests . . .*
> *both as movement and stillness.*

So there is no need to insist that you should be still; even in movement you can experience Tao. You can experience Tao in stillness.

There are two possibilities. Buddha sat for years in silence and then he experienced Tao. He calls it *nirvana*; that is his name for Tao. And Jalaluddin Rumi danced for years, and then one day it happened while he was dancing: through dance he attained to Tao. He calls it God; that is his name for Tao. One can approach either through stillness or through movement.

It is because of this fact that in my commune both kinds of meditations are being used. People are dancing, people are singing, and meditating. People are sitting in silence—zazen, vipassana—and meditating. And one can move from one to the other because both are your possibilities: you can find it in dance and you can find it in silence, stillness.

In fact, your experience will be far more rich if you can find it in both ways. If you are capable of finding it in dancing and also capable of finding it while sitting silently doing nothing, your experience will be far more rich than the experience of Gautam the Buddha and Jalaluddin Rumi, both—naturally, because you will enter the temple of God from two opposite extremes, from two different paths. You will be more fluid and you will have known the beauties of both paths—because on one path you may come across a few things and on the other path you may come across a few other things. Both paths are full of different wonders. The dancer will come to know a few things which the person who is sitting silently will never know. He will reach to the ultimate peak, but he will not know a few things that happen on the way of dancing. And the same is true about the dancer: he will not know a few things which happen only on the way of stillness.

My emphasis is this: why miss any enrichment that is possible. Why not be multi dimensional? Why not experience God through as many ways as possible so that you know all the aspects of God? And in that very knowing you will know that all the religions are unnecessarily arguing against each other. Their arguments are absolutely meaningless—they are talking about the *same* God. But because they have known different aspects they are insisting on their own aspect: that "This is the truth." And the other is saying that just the opposite is the truth.

If you ask a Buddhist, "Can one become enlightened through dancing?" he will immediately say, "No," and his "no" will be categorical. He will say, "It is impossible, because if one can know through dancing, why did Buddha sit for years? Was he a fool? He would have danced!"

If you ask a whirling dervish, a follower of Jalaluddin Rumi, "Can one find God just by sitting silently doing nothing?" he will say, "No: Impossible—absolutely no. Otherwise, why should Jalaluddin have danced? Why should he have worked so hard dancing day in, day out?"

When the ultimate flowering happened he had danced for thirty-six hours continuously. Just as Buddha had sat for seven days continuously not moving, not even moving his eyelids, Jalaluddin had danced, not even waiting for a single moment, not even resting for a single moment—a mad dance for thirty-six hours till he fell down on the ground. But when he opened his eyes, the old man had disappeared, the new man was born. The new man was already there; he was a totally new person.

The Sufi will not agree that just by sitting you can find it.

But I say to you I have found him through both the ways: I have found him through movement and I have found him through stillness. And I perfectly agree with Ko Hsuan that:

Tao manifests . . .
both as movement and stillness.
Heaven is pure, earth is turbid.

Obviously. Heaven means absolute clarity. The sky is pure; there is nothing in it. Nothingness is the purest thing. The earth is full of many things, hence it is turbid.

And just the other day I was telling you that you have to be both earthly and unearthly. Because, in fact, you are made of both: something in you is contributed by the earth, by the turbid, and something in you is contributed by the sky, by the pure, by the clear. You are a synthesis of the earth and the sky.

Up to now, except Tao, all the religions have chosen. Either they have chosen to be very earthly . . . For example, Judaism is very earthly and Jainism is very unearthly. Jainism has chosen the sky component of your being and Judaism has chosen the earthly component of your being, but both are halves. They are not whole; something is missing in both. Tao is whole.

And in *my* understanding, in *my* realization, Tao is the only experience which is holy, because it is whole.

Heaven is pure, earth is turbid.

That's why I say to you be a Zorba—but not Zorba the Greek because then you are just turbid, just earth, just muddy. I say to you be Zorba the Buddha—not Gautam the Buddha because to be Gautam the Buddha means you are just sky, no earth, absolutely other-worldly, belonging to the farther shore. Why not be both? When it is possible to be both, why miss anything? Why not use all the opportunities to grow and to be?

Heaven moves, earth is still.

These are just metaphors.

The masculine is pure . . .

"Masculine" means, at the lowest, intellectuality, at the highest, intelligence. It is clear—intellect *is* clear. Two plus two is four; it is as clear as that. And the highest form is intelligence. *Buddha* means one who has attained to the highest form of intelligence. His words are very clear; his words are not at all in any way muddy. You cannot find more clear statements than Buddha's; his statements are not mystic, not esoteric.

In fact, he used to say to his disciples, "Please don't ask me any metaphysical questions because they are not needed, they are not going to help. Ask authentic, real questions, questions that are your problems in life, so that I can help you to solve them."

He used to tell this story again and again:

Once a man was hit by an arrow . . . He was a philosopher, a great metaphysician. People rushed to him; they wanted to take out the arrow, but he said, "Wait! First tell me whether the arrow is real or illusory."

Now, that has been one of the most important metaphysical questions, in India particularly: whether the world is real or illusory, real or *maya*, whether it exists or it only appears to.

The metaphysician was asking out of his old habit. "If it is unreal, why bother? If it only appears to be there, what is the point of taking it out? It does not exist. It is like a snake which does not exist. It is only a rope really, but in darkness you have misunderstood it as a snake. So there is no need to kill it. How can you kill a snake which does not exist in the first place?"

He puzzled people so much with all his metaphysical reasoning that they were at a loss what to do. It was difficult to prove . . .

In fact, it *is* difficult to prove: nobody has been able to prove conclusively that the world exists; there is no way to prove it. It may be all illusory.

For example, I am talking to you, but how can you prove that you are not dreaming? Many times you dream.

Asang writes to me, "Bhagwan, I am very grateful —you come in my dreams." Now it will be difficult for Asang to decide whether right now it is a dream or I am really here! There is no way to decide.

In western philosophy, the man who represents this philosophy is Berkeley. He says the whole world is your idea, it is just an idea. It is in your mind; it does not exist really. It is just like a dream phenomenon. It is made of the same stuff as dreams are made of.

He was going for a morning walk with his friend, Dr. Johnson. And Dr. Johnson was a very realistic type of person. When Berkeley told him that this whole world is just an idea, it does not really exist, Johnson got so mad—mad because he could not prove otherwise—that he simply took a big rock and threw it on Berkeley's foot. Berkeley shrieked in pain, screamed, blood started oozing out of his foot.

And Johnson said, "Now what do you say?"

And Berkeley laughed and he said, "This is all just an idea! My screaming, your throwing the rock, even *you*, Dr. Johnson, are just my idea. I am *your* idea, you are *my* idea. We are all ideas. Your rock cannot prove that it is real, because sometimes I have screamed in my dream. Sometimes rocks have been thrown at me in my dream, blood has come out in my dreams. So what? What is the difference?"

It is impossible to disprove such a philosophy. Shankara in India represents this kind of philosophy and Berkeley represents it in the West; they both remain as yet unrefuted. Nobody believes in them. I don't think that even they believed in themselves, otherwise they would have stopped eating, making love, sleeping, because if it is all dream stuff why bother? Berkeley continued to make love and produce children. What nonsense! He continued to eat, and when he used to fall ill he would take medicine. Now, killing one idea with another idea! I don't think they ever believed in themselves.

Shankara says that the world is illusory and yet he says: Renounce it. If it is illusory, why renounce it? What can you renounce? If it is not there in the first place, how can you renounce it? Something that is not can be renounced? And if the world is not, if the seen is not, then where is the seer? Without the seen the seer himself becomes illusory. If there is nothing to renounce, the renouncer himself becomes illusory.

They don't believe in their own philosophies but still they cannot be refuted; there is no way to refute them. Thousands of ways have been tried, but nothing can refute them. For example, Berkeley used to say when you go out of the room, your furniture in the room, your books in the room all disappear because there is nobody to project the idea. Obviously, if you take the projector out the film will disappear from the wall; there will be no pictures on the wall. Now how can you prove it? You can say, "I can look through the keyhole." He will say, "So you have come back through the keyhole. Again they will appear because the idea is projected through the keyhole."

One man worked for years to find out some way and he went on coming to Berkeley again and again. One day he went with the idea that "Now I don't think you can deny this. When you are sitting in a carriage you don't see the wheels of the carriage, but the carriage is moving—the wheels are there. You are not projecting them because you are not seeing them, but the carriage is moving. The movement of the carriage proves that the wheels are there."

Berkeley said, "You *don't* know. That will be God's idea. The world is not only *my* idea; ultimately it is God's idea, it is God's dream. In fact, he is dreaming us too—the driver and the passenger and the carriage and the wheels."

It is impossible to deny such philosophies. They are absurd, but they cannot be refuted.

Buddha used to say . . .

People, poor people, villagers gathered and they looked at each other. "What to do with this man?"

Buddha was passing by; he heard the whole story. He went to the philosopher and he said, "These questions can be answered later on, we can discuss them later on at our ease. First let us pull out the arrow because this arrow can kill you, and if you are alive we can discuss it later on. And whatsoever you decide later on, that the arrow is real or unreal, will be up to you. But right now you don't need philosophical discussion, you need a physician who can pull the arrow, who can take out the poison, who can give you some medicine as a protection. Right now no metaphysics is going to help you. Okay, if it is unreal, let it be unreal! But later on we can discuss it."

Buddha used to say that the same is the situation of man, every man. You are suffering, so the whole thing is how to pull out the arrow that is creating your suffering. It is not a metaphysical question. His words are very clear, rational, intelligent, comprehensible by the mind. He says only things which can be comprehended by any intelligent person. That's why Buddha has become very important today—because his approach seems to be so intellectual.

The masculine is pure . . .

That means the lowest form is intellect, intellectuality, and the highest form is intelligence.

. . . the feminine is turbid.

"Turbid" here will mean, at the lowest, instinct and, at the highest, intuition. Now the mystics, the Sufis talk in a totally different way. Their words are not so clear, their words are vague. Their words are not easily comprehensible; you have to figure out what their exact meaning is. And that is the state of the feminine mind. But remember, I don't mean it biologically. Of course, biologically also the woman functions more through instinct than through intellect . . .

Many people ask me, "Why have all the Buddhas you talk about been men? Why not women?" For the simple reason that the approach of the feminine mind will be totally different. They cannot be Buddhas. They can be Meeras, Magdalenes, Lallas, Rabias, but they cannot be Buddhas. Their approach is bound to be different. Meera will not talk in an intellectual way; she will sing. Her singing, her dancing has a totally different flavor. She will not argue—argument is not the way of the feminine mind; her argument will be her dance, her ecstatic dance. If you can see her dance, if you can *feel* her dance . . . I will not say if you can understand her dance because dancers cannot be understood, they can only be felt, they can only be experienced. Her words will be very instinctive.

For example, Freud has condemned very much all the women mystics he knew about. He never knew about Meera, otherwise he would have condemned her the most. He knew about St. Theresa; he has condemned her because she talks about being married to Christ. Now that is enough for Freud to bring his whole sexual theory in. That's enough—nothing more is needed. Married? That means this woman is suffering from some sexual perversion. She must have repressed her sexuality; and because she cannot have a sexual relationship with a real man, now she is contemplating an unreal man in the sky—somebody called Christ, the son of God. Now she is trying to create a love affair with Christ.

It is really a misfortune that Freud never knew about Meera. Had he known he himself would have danced out of joy! Because Meera uses such allegories: "My Lord, my beloved, when will you be coming? I have prepared the bed! I have prepared the bed with roses and I am waiting! And the night is passing and you have not come yet. And I am crying and weeping for you! When will you come and make love to me?"

Now, she is not even speaking in an indirect way, she is talking directly. Freud would have taken the whole thing literally; that is his technique. He can prove that all these mystics are perverts. In fact, he himself is a pervert because he cannot understand the feminine mind at all.

That is one of the reasons why Jung had to desert him, for the simple reason that his whole understanding was simply intellectual; there was nothing intuitive in it. And Jung had a more feminine mind, a deeper capacity to feel.

All men who have come in contact with women know it, that they function in a very different way. You cannot talk with a woman logically; it is impossible—it is as if she belongs to some other world, to some other planet. And the same must be the experience of women. They can't understand men—continuously in their heads, in their intellects, never understanding anything of the heart. Man tries to argue, tries to convince the woman logically, but she cannot be convinced. That is not her way; logic has no appeal for her.

Slowly slowly the husband learns that a rose flower is far more important than logic. If you bring a rose flower to your wife she will understand it more than all your arguments. You can argue for months, "I love you," and that won't convince her. Just bring a rose flower and that will be enough. Her approach is instinctive. Man cannot understand her because whatsoever she says seems illogical and absurd.

Slowly slowly husbands start remaining silent, they become deaf. They allow the woman to talk: "Whatsoever nonsense she wants to talk let her talk. Who listens?"

Do you know why God created first the man and then the woman?

To allow the poor guy to say at least two words!

148

Overheard at Vrindavan . . . One sannyasin was saying to another sannyasin, "It took a lot of will power, but I finally gave up trying to diet."

A lot of will power . . .

"Rob told me I was the eighth wonder of the world!" said Shirl.

"What did you say?" asked Pearl.

"Not to let me catch him with any of the other seven!"

"Can you operate a typewriter?" the boss asks the secretary.

"Yes, sir. I use the biblical system."

"I never heard of it."

"Seek and ye shall find," replies the secretary.

Why do husbands become henpecked? All husbands become henpecked. In fact, to be a husband means to be a henpecked husband; there are no other kinds for the simple reason that how long can one argue? And it makes no sense. You look foolish to yourself—you are talking to the walls! You argue and the woman cries! You tell her, "Cool down, and let us sit down and talk it over at the table," and she starts throwing things! She slams the door, she breaks cups and saucers. Now what is the point? You cannot argue. There is no possible way to connect, to relate with a woman coolly. That is not possible; it is always hot. Either you follow her or she will create trouble. And from her side all your arguments are just nonsense!

Then there was the guy so henpecked by his wife that when they were in the nudist colony she told him what not to wear.

The man says to the lawyer, "I'm going to ask for a divorce."

"Why?" asks the lawyer.

"Because my wife is always knitting!"

"But, for God's sake, that is no reason to ask for a divorce! Lots of women knit."

"While they are making love?"

The husband frequently traveled in his work. One day he returned home unexpectedly and found his wife in bed with another man. Enraged, he grabbed a gun and pointed it at the man.

The wife screamed, "Don't shoot! Are you going to kill the father of your sons?"

The young lady walks into a drugstore and asks, "Do you have intimate deodorants?"

"Yes, we do," answers the druggist. "Which kind would you like?"

"Chlorophyll."

"No, sorry, we will receive it tomorrow."

"Tomorrow I cannot come. Could you give it to my husband?"

"How am I going to know who your husband is?" enquires the druggist.

"Oh, it is very simple. He is a tall, dark-haired guy with a green moustache."

The masculine is active, the feminine is passive.
Manifesting from its radical essence,
Tao flows forth even to the last of things,
bringing forth heaven and earth
and all that is in between.
The pure is the cause of the turbid,
and movement of stillness.

But don't forget because of these anecdotes that Ko Hsuan does not mean that the biological masculine and feminine are *exactly* synonymous with the ultimate masculine and feminine. In a certain way, yes, they are related, but not totally synonymous.

[*At this point a cuckoo began to call, loudly and insistently . . .*]

This is feminine! Now she is saying, "All this Tao is nonsense!" This is just a protest!

THE
TASTE
OF
ETERNITY

The first question:

Bhagwan,
Please explain how I can meditate over some-
thing without using my mind.

Dinesh,

MEDITATION HAS nothing to do with mind; meditation simply means a state of no-mind. The functioning
of the mind is the only disturbance in meditation. If
you are trying to achieve meditation *through* mind
you are bound to fail, doomed to fail. You are trying
to achieve the impossible.

A Zen initiate was meditating for years and whenever he would come to his Master, whatsoever experience he would bring to the Master, the Master would simply reject: "It is all nonsense. You go back and meditate again."

One day the Master came to the hut of the disciple —he was sitting in a Buddha posture. The Master shook him and told him, "What are you doing here? If we needed stone Buddhas we have many in the temple! Just by sitting like a stone Buddha you will not attain to meditation. Do what I have been telling you to do. Just by stilling the body, your mind is not going to disappear, because it is through the mind that you are enforcing a certain discipline on the body. Anything done by the mind is going to strengthen the mind. It is a nourishment for the mind."

A year passed. The Master came again. The disciple was sitting almost in a kind of euphoria, enjoying the morning breeze and sun with closed eyes, thinking that he was meditating. The Master took a brick and started rubbing it on a stone in front of the disciple. It was such a disturbance that finally the disciple had to shout, "What are you doing? Are you trying to drive me crazy?"

The Master said, "I am trying to make a mirror out of this brick. If one goes on rubbing it enough I think it will become a mirror."

The disciple laughed. He said, "I always suspected that you were a little mad—now it is proved! The brick can never become a mirror. You can go on rubbing it on the stone for lives together; the brick will remain a brick."

The Master said, "That shows some intelligence! Then what are you doing? For years you have been trying to make meditation out of the mind; it is like trying to make a mirror out of a brick."

And the Master threw the brick in the pond at the side of the tree the disciple was sitting under. The brick made a great splash in the pond, and the very sound of it was enough to do the miracle. Something awakened in the disciple. A sleep was broken, a dream was shattered: he became alert. For the first time he tasted something of meditation.

And the Master immediately said, "This is it!"

It happened so unexpectedly—the disciple was taken unawares. He was not waiting for this to happen, that the Master would suddenly throw the brick into the pond, and the splash . . .

Basho has a beautiful haiku:

> The ancient pond.
> The frog jumps in.
> The sound . . .

That's all. The sound can awaken you.

Meditation is not a question of effort because all effort is going to be through the mind, of the mind, by the mind. How can it take you beyond the mind? You will go round and round *in* the mind. You have to wake up! Mind is sleep. Mind is a constant process of dreaming, desiring, thoughts, memories.

Dinesh, you ask me: *Please explain how I can meditate over something without using my mind.*

Can't you see something just with your eyes? Can't you watch something without bringing your mind in? The birds chirping, this silence . . . What need is there of the mind? It is a question of watchfulness not of concentration.

But it is not only your problem, it is the problem of millions of people who become interested in meditation all over the world. They all mistake concentration for meditation. Concentration is something of the mind. It is being taught in the schools, colleges, universities. It has its uses—I am not saying it is useless. It is focusing on a certain object.

In science it is needed. You have to focus your mind on a particular object totally so that you can observe deeply. You have to exclude everything else, you have to break it out of everything else. You have to narrow down your consciousness; you almost have to make a pinpoint of it. That's a scientific way as far as the objective world is concerned.

But as far as the subjective world is concerned it is of no help, not at all. There you are not to focus your mind on anything—on the idea of God or on some inner light, flame, love, compassion—you are not to concentrate at all; you have to be simply aware of all that is.

The man of concentration can be distracted easily; anything can become a distraction because he is trying to do something unnatural. Just a child crying, and he will be distracted; the traffic noise, and he will be distracted; an airplane passing by, and he will be distracted; a dog starts barking, and he will be distracted. Anything can distract him. And of course, when he is distracted he will feel miserable, frustrated—he has failed again. The man of meditation cannot be distracted for the simple reason that he is not concentrating in the first place.

Existence is not linear, it is simultaneous. For example, I am speaking here, the birds are chirping, the traffic noise is there, the train is passing by—all these things are happening together. You have to be simple, silent, watchful, witnessing all that is—no need to exclude anything because the excluded thing will try to distract you. If nothing is excluded, if your awareness is all-inclusive, then what can distract you? Can this bird distract you? In fact, it will enhance your silence. Nothing can distract you because you are not in a tense state.

Concentration is tension, hence the word "attention". It comes from the same root, "tension". Awareness is not attention; awareness is relaxation, it is rest.

So rest silently. Thoughts will pass; there is no need to be worried—what can they do? Desires will come and go. Watch them coming and going. Don't have any evaluation. Don't say, "This is good, this is bad." Don't say, "Aha! This is something great, spiritual, far out!" Some sensation in the spine—it may be just an ant crawling up and you start feeling your kundalini is rising, or just imagination—you see some light inside, which is not difficult . . . You can see light, you can see colors, psychedelic colors. You can experience beautiful things, but it is all imagination, howsoever colorful, howsoever beautiful.

Don't start saying that this is good that Jesus is standing in front of you or Krishna or Buddha and that now you are starting to feel you are coming closer and closer to the ultimate realization. Buddha says, "If you meet me on the way, kill me immediately!" He means: If I come in your meditation, don't start feeling very good about it, because if you start feeling good about it you will start clinging to the idea—and it is only an idea. Just watch it with no preference, with no choice. If you can be choicelessly aware of everything outside and inside, meditation will happen one day. It is nothing that you have to do.

You can do only one thing and that is to learn the art of watching, watching without any judgment. Then one day you simply relax, and in that total relaxation there is pure awareness. All thoughts disappear, all desires disappear; the mind is found no more. When mind is not found, this is meditation. A state of no-mind is meditation.

So you have been misunderstanding me. When I say "Meditate", I mean "Watch". If I say "Meditate on the songs of the birds", I am simply saying "Watch". I am not saying "Concentrate"—I am against concentration. And because I am for watchfulness you can watch anything. You can sit in the marketplace and watch people and that will be meditation. You can sit in the railway station and you can watch all kinds of noises: the trains coming and the passengers getting down and the coolies shouting and the vendors, and then the train goes away and a silence falls over the station. You simply watch, you don't do anything.

And slowly slowly you start relaxing, your tensions disappear. Then insight opens up like a bud opening and becoming a flower. Great fragrance is released. In that silence is truth, is bliss, is benediction.

The second question:

Bhagwan,
Is knowledge absolutely useless?

Dharma,

KNOWLEDGE HAS ITS USES, it is not absolutely useless. But if you are going inwards it becomes more and more useless; the deeper you go the more useless it is. If you are going outwards, the farther you go into the world the more useful it becomes. The world respects the knowledgeable person. It needs experts; it needs all kinds of people carrying information, knowledge, expertise. But in the inner world the question does not arise: in the inner world the same knowledge becomes a hindrance. That which is useful in the outside world becomes a barrier to the inner. It is a bridge to the world; it is a barrier to the inner exploration.

Whenever I say anything against knowledge I simply mean that for those who are pilgrims, explorers of their subjectivity, it is utterly useless. There, something else is needed: not knowledge but wisdom. Knowledge is information; wisdom is transformation. Knowledge is borrowed; wisdom is your own. Knowledge is ego-fulfilling; wisdom happens only when the ego is dropped, utterly dropped, totally dropped. Knowledge gives you the feeling that you are higher than others; it is a certain kind of power, just like money. Knowledge *is* power. So if you have a postgraduate degree you feel better than those who don't have postgraduate degrees. If you have a Ph.D. you feel a little more egoistic. If you carry a D. Litt. of course you become very special. If you have many degrees, then you start feeling that you are not an ordinary person.

Once in Varanasi a man came to see me; he was known all over the world because he had twenty M.A.s. He was the only person in the whole world who had twenty postgraduate degrees, but I have never come across such a stupid man. He was utterly stupid, obviously; he had wasted his whole life in acquiring knowledge. And he was moving from one subject to another; his whole effort was to have as many M.A.s as possible. When he came to see me he was almost sixty-five years old; he was preparing for still another examination. When he died he had acquired thirty M.A.s. But when I talked to the man he was very childish, very mediocre—no sign of intelligence, but very egoistic.

In fact, an intelligent person cannot be egoistic; it is impossible. If your intelligence cannot show you the simple thing that ego is a false phenomenon then you don't have intelligence at all. But people love to brag about their knowledge.

In the inner world humbleness helps, simplicity helps. In the outer world these certificates and degrees are certainly of some use.

A distinguished man enters Harrod's in London, asks for a hippopotamus and insists that the animal should be delivered that same afternoon.

"You see," he explains, "I terribly need this animal . . . if I don't have it by this afternoon I'll go crazy!"

Curious, the clerk asks, "And where should we put it?"

"In my bathtub," replies the man.

Even more curious, the clerk exclaims, "You mean, sir, that you want a hippopotamus in your bathtub?"

"Yes! You see, it's for my wife. Whenever I say something she invariably replies, 'Yes, I know it already.' And so tonight when she comes to me saying, 'There's a hippopotamus in the bathtub!' I will finally be able to reply, 'Yes, I know it already!' "

Dharma, if you want that kind of stupid ego to be fulfilled, knowledge has a use; otherwise it is useless. But the outside knowledge has even corrupted religions. I can understand a scientist acquiring knowledge, because he cannot function without it. Science depends on tradition, remember. Religion does not depend on tradition, although people think just the reverse. They think religion depends on tradition and science is a rebellion against tradition. That is not so, not at all.

Science is traditional. Without Newton there would have been no Edison. Without Edison there would have been no Albert Einstein. That's what I mean when I say science depends on tradition: it depends on the past, and you have to be well informed about the past, otherwise no work is possible in scientific inquiry. First you have to know whatsoever is known already, only then can you proceed to discover something which is not known. If you don't know what is already known you may be trying to discover something which has been already discovered and you may come to know it only later on. Then all your effort has been a waste.

But religion is non-traditional. It is rebellion, it is pure rebellion! There is no need for Krishna to be for Buddha to happen; Buddha can happen without Krishna. Christ can happen without Moses, Mohammed can happen without Christ, Ramakrishna can happen without Buddha. Religion is individual; science is collective. Because science is collective it has to depend on knowledge. Religion is individual; you have to make the whole discovery again. You cannot depend on Buddha, you cannot depend on Christ, you cannot depend on anybody else. You always have to start from abc; you cannot take things for granted. You cannot say, "This has been discovered by Buddha so what is the need for me to discover it again?" Yes, Columbus discovered America, now there is no need for you to discover it. Even if you go to America you cannot call it your discovery. People have reached the moon; now even if you go to the moon it won't be of any great value—you won't be a pioneer. But the same is not true about your inner being.

Your inner being has not been discovered yet. Buddha discovered *his* being; that is not *your* being. If you believe in him you will remain only knowledgeable, and the knowledgeable person is always false as far as the inner is concerned.

And my whole concern is the inner. I am not teaching you chemistry, physics or mathematics here, I am teaching you only one single thing: how to discover yourself. That's why I condemn knowledge.

A rabbi and a cantor are praying together in the synagogue, beating their breasts and crying, "O Lord, I am nothing, nothing, nothing!"

The synagogue janitor, hearing them, puts down his broom and joins them, beating his breast and crying, "O Lord, I am nothing, nothing, nothing!"

The cantor turns to the rabbi and says, "Look who thinks he's nothing!"

Just a janitor, just a nobody—and thinking he is nothing? Even to be nothing you have to be somebody special. You see the stupidity of it?

Borrowed knowledge is of no help at all.

A thief and a theologian decided to escape from the prison.

As the thief climbed over the wall, the guard heard some rattling. "Who's there?"

"Meow," said the thief, imitating a cat, and passed safely.

Up came the theologian and again the guard heard some noise. "Who's there?"

"It's nothing," answered the theologian. "Just another cat!"

Knowledge is of no help at all in the inner world. You will have to know yourself. Unless you know yourself, all your beliefs will create a burden; they will not help you to be unburdened, they will not help you to be liberated. They will create new bondages, beautiful bondages.

The bride-to-be is taken by her mother to the chicken roost where she is shown the rooster "doing his work".

"It is going to be something more or less like that, my dear!" exclaims the mother.

On the wedding night the young husband comes into the bedroom wearing pajamas, and is surprised by the scene he sees: the young bride is lying on the bed naked, with a helmet on her head.

"What is this all about, baby?" he asks.

"You can do whatever you like with me, but you are not going to peck my head!" she answers.

Borrowed knowledge is always going to create that kind of state in you. You can repeat Jesus, you can repeat Krishna, you can repeat Moses, Zarathustra, Lao Tzu, but repetitions won't help; you have to learn on your own. Yes, imbibe the spirit of the Masters, of the awakened ones, but remember it is not knowledge that is going to help you but wisdom. And wisdom comes when all knowledge has been put aside. Call it knowledge or call it mind, it is the same thing. Mind *is* knowledge. When you have put aside all knowledge you have put aside the mind itself; you are in a state of not-knowing. And to be in a state of not-knowing is the most beautiful experience because it is innocence. You will be full of wonder and awe. You will be a child again. This will be a rebirth. Only this rebirth can release the hidden splendor of your being.

You are carrying within you a great light, a great treasure, the very kingdom of God, but you are clinging to borrowed things. Rather than clinging to borrowed things, Dharma, go in and discover your own center. Knowledge keeps you on the circumference. Jump from the circumference. Renouncing knowledge is the greatest renunciation.

I don't tell you to renounce your money, your house, your family, because they are not the problem. Renounce your knowledge, your mind; that is the real problem, because that is something that is hindering the path. It is blocking your way in reaching your own center.

Renounce knowledge and rejoice in the state of not-knowing, and great wisdom will be released in you. The Buddha within you will be awakened. Only that can give you the taste of eternity—not words, not scriptures, not beliefs, not knowledge.

The third question:

Bhagwan,
You have said that to be together one must know how to be alone. But I can be alone: the problem comes with being together, because then comes the wanting and the expectation. Is it that one must know how to be alone together?
It seems the path of love must be taken with tremendous awareness.

Krishna Gopa,

YES, I HAVE BEEN telling you again and again that you can be together only when you know how to be alone, but by "alone" I don't mean "lonely". You must have misunderstood me. Everybody can be lonely, but to be alone is a tremendous achievement, it is a great realization. Loneliness is very ordinary. People suffer from loneliness. You can manage not to suffer: you can put up a face, a facade, you can cultivate certain things so that you don't feel the pain of loneliness, but that is not the art of being alone.

It is not just a question of avoiding suffering while you are lonely. Aloneness means positively enjoying it, being positively ecstatic about it, being positively blissful about it, so much so that if you are never together with anybody again no question arises, no problem arises, not even the desire, not even a lurking desire somewhere in the unconscious. When you are so contented—not just satisfied, remember . . . these words are totally different. One can create satisfaction without being contented.

Satisfaction is a kind of "accepting the inevitable". What else can one do? If one is lonely one is lonely; one has to live with it. And man is capable of adjusting to any situation. Even if you are thrown alone somewhere in a desert or on an island you will adjust to the life there; you will still survive. You may even create certain satisfactions there.

I have heard about a man, a Christian priest. His ship was drowned; somehow he survived. He reached a small island—there was nobody on the island. After twenty years another ship passed by. He waved, shouted—the captain heard. The captain saw the man; he stopped the ship and made arrangements to bring the man on board. He himself came in a small boat to take him to the ship.

The lonely priest told the captain, "Before we leave this island I would like to show you my work of twenty years."

He was also an architect; before he had become a priest he had been an architect. He had planned almost a small city, a miniature city.

The captain was delighted. He said, "Wait! let all the passengers of my ship come and see. This is a miracle! You have done something beautiful. Small houses, just like playthings, but beautifully designed. How did you manage this?"

He said, "I had to do something to keep myself engaged, occupied, to remain satisfied. And I was really satisfied. After a few years I completely forgot about the world. Even the desire to reach the world again left me—at least I thought it had left me. Seeing your ship, suddenly I realized that no, it had not left me; otherwise I was very satisfied. This island has everything that I needed to create these small houses." All kinds of houses . . .

And then he said, "The most beautiful thing is . . . I will show you." He took him to a church, he showed him the church, the Catholic church. He had made it a little bigger—you could enter it—because he used to worship there. Of course, he was alone, but the old habit . . .

When they came out the captain was puzzled and all other passengers were also puzzled, because just in front of the church there was another church, a Protestant church.

They asked the priest, "Isn't one church enough for one man? Why did you make another church?"

He said, "That is the church I don't go to, and this is the church I go to!"

Old habits . . . but he was perfectly satisfied. He said, "Nobody goes there; it is always deserted. I have never seen anybody go there."

There was nobody there in the first place except him and he was going to the Catholic church because he was a Catholic priest, but he was very happy and satisfied that the Protestant church was almost deserted. He had made it very ugly too, but he had made it—he himself had made it.

One can be satisfied with any situation. Man is immensely adaptable; that is one of the great qualities of man. That's why man can survive any kind of climate, any kind of temperature: extreme cold, extreme hot, too much rain, no rain. Man can survive everywhere, anywhere. Why?—because man *is* capable of it; he is liquid.

So you can be lonely and you can think yourself satisfied, but when you are together that is the test whether you were really contented. If you were contented in your loneliness it was not loneliness, it was aloneness. If being together brings no disturbance, no wanting, no desiring, no expectation, no jealousy, no possessiveness, no unconscious hankering to dominate the other, then it was aloneness. Otherwise it was only loneliness covered, disguised by a certain false sense of satisfaction.

Krishna Gopa, you have not yet been able to be alone, because if you are alone then this question will not arise at all. Then whether you are alone *or* together you are alone, and your aloneness is so immensely beautiful that who bothers to dominate? Why? For what? You are so full of joy that there is no need to possess anybody; it will be so ugly. You will be able to see the ugliness of it.

But if when you are together all these ugly desires start moving again, rising again, raising their heads again, if all these snakes and these scorpions start

crawling upwards towards the conscious from the unconscious, that simply means they were waiting for
the right opportunity. Now the opportunity is there.
Only the opportunity proves where you are.

That's why I don't tell my sannyasins to leave the
world and go to the mountains, because there you
will simply be leaving the opportunities behind. You
will start living in a cave, and you can deceive yourself
your whole life thinking that you have known what
aloneness is, what solitude is. You will only be lonely
and solitary and you will start thinking that you are
contented and blissful. And you will only be satisfied
and not miserable, but not blissful. Just being not
miserable is not equivalent to being blissful.

Not being ill is not equivalent to being healthy and
whole. Health has something more to it than just not
being ill: it has a certain well-being. There are many
people who are not ill, but they are not healthy.
Sometimes it can happen that a person may be ill and
yet healthy because health has a totally different con-
notation. Health is not only a medical concept, it is
something far bigger, far more comprehensive than
medical science.

For example, Prem Chinmaya was utterly ill. What
more illness can you have? He was suffering from
cancer. The cancer was spreading every day, but he
was healthy; he had a certain well-being. His illness
was only in the body, it was not reaching to his consciousness; he remained floating above it.

His nurse, Puja, wrote just the other day:
"Bhagwan, I am immensely blessed that I served
Chinmaya. I have watched many people die in my life,
but this death was totally different, qualitatively different. I have never seen any man die with such
beauty, with such silence, with such meditativeness."

At the last moment, when he was hearing my last
discourse . . . Puja has written to me—she was there:

"He was in deep pain as far as the body was concerned. The pain was so great that even injections of morphia were not of any help. Even double, treble doses of morphia were not helping at all. The pain was so great that nothing seemed to help him. But when he heard the joke about Jesus and the cancer patient," Puja writes to me, "he smiled."

And she writes also: "I could see that that smile was not only of the body, because the body was not in a state at all to smile; it was coming from somewhere deep. And I could see and feel that deep down he was laughing. That smile was just a little bit of that laughter which had come up to the body."

He was healthy in a totally different sense, in a non-medical sense. There are many people who are healthy in a medical sense, perfectly fit medically, but utterly unhealthy. Deep down there is nothing but turmoil, emptiness, anguish. One can hide it, one can repress it, and one can not only deceive others, man is so capable of cunningness that he can deceive himself.

Krishna Gopa, you say: *You have said that to be together one must know how to be alone.*

I repeat it again: yes, unless you know how to be alone your togetherness will become troublesome, your togetherness will create misery, because your togetherness will bring out everything that remains asleep in you while you are lonely. When you are together the other provokes it, the other becomes a challenge. You become a challenge for the other, the other becomes a challenge for you.

A man/woman relationship brings their unconscious to the surface; they come into their true colors. Of course, in the beginning it is not so. In the beginning it cannot be so because in the beginning you keep the facade. When you meet only for a few hours on the sea beach or in the full-moon night you keep the facade because you still are not certain, the other is also not yet certain whether he can expose his reality to you. But once the honeymoon is over everything is over.

In fact, almost every marriage ends with the end of the honeymoon; then the reality starts. Then the mirage of marriage is over. Now both can take it for granted that the other cannot escape easily. Now you need not be afraid; now you can come into your true colors. And both start exploding. They have been repressive for so long that all their repressions start coming up and togetherness becomes ugly.

That's why for centuries people have escaped into the forests, into the monasteries, into the mountains, just to escape from togetherness. But that is not the true way of spirituality, that is not the true way of growth. That is escapist, that is out of fear, that is cowardly.

I would like you to be in the world. I insist: Be in the world and yet remain alert, aware, watchful. Don't be repressive. If you are not repressive in your aloneness, your aloneness will become a blissful, beautiful experience. Meet with the other person out of your bliss, not out of your misery. And then togetherness does not only double your bliss, it multiplies it. Togetherness always multiplies whatsoever you bring to it. If you bring misery to it, it multiplies misery. Two miserable persons together is not only a double misery, it is multiplied. Two persons blissfully together, the bliss not only doubles, it multiplies. Then togetherness is beautiful, but one should learn to be alone first.

And if you know how to be alone you will know how to be alone together, because it is not a question of learning it again in a different way; it is the same phenomenon. If you know how to be alone you will know it everywhere, whether in relationship or not in relationship. To be alone . . . Then togetherness helps spiritual growth, integrity, tremendously, because it gives you an opportunity, a great challenge. It exposes you to the full light and you can see yourself. The other becomes the mirror.

Relationship is a mirror. You cannot see your face without a mirror. You cannot see your reality without the other. The other becomes a mirror—mirrors are good.

I have heard about an ugly woman who was against mirrors—naturally—because her idea was that mirrors made her look ugly, that mirrors were in a conspiracy against her. Because this was her logic: "Whenever there is no mirror I don't feel any ugliness, I am perfectly okay. It is only when there is a mirror that I immediately become ugly. The mirror must be doing something."

She was so against the mirrors that she used to break mirrors. Wherever she would come across a mirror she would immediately destroy it because mirrors were enemies.

Her logic is not different from your monks and nuns; they are doing the same. Going into a monastery means escaping from the mirrors—condemning relationship, condemning love, condemning the world. All your saints are afraid of mirrors, that's all. But to be afraid of mirrors simply shows you are afraid of your own ugliness; you don't want to see it. And without mirrors of course you will not see it, but that does not mean that it has disappeared—it is there. Any time, anything . . . if not a mirror then maybe just a silent lake, and you will see it. And whether *you* see it or not, others will see it.

You can see your saints' faces, your so-called mahatmas. They are all sad, they don't seem to be blissful. They don't seem to be like lotus flowers; they look like rocks—almost dead, utterly dull, mediocre.

There seems to be no sharpness of intelligence, because they have escaped from where they could sharpen their intelligence. Their intelligence goes on gathering dust, but they think they have achieved satisfaction, they have achieved what God meant them to achieve. They have simply missed the opportunity.

God will ask them, "I had given you life and you escaped from life. You rejected my life, you rejected my gift. You were against me."

George Gurdjieff used to make a very strange statement—but only a man like Gurdjieff can tell the utterly naked truth—he used to say that "All your saints are against God." When you come across such a statement for the first time you cannot believe it. saints, and against God? But Gurdjieff is right. He really means it, he is not joking! Your saints are against God because they are against life.

I am *not* against life. I am in tremendous love with life.

Krishna Gopa, learn to be alone—and that will happen only through meditation—and then allow mirrors into your life so that you can see where you are, what you are, how much you have grown.

In this commune we are doing something new which has never happened ever before. There are growth centers in the world, particularly in the West, where therapy groups are run. There are meditation centers, particularly in the East, where people meditate. This is the only place where people meditate and go through groups, go through groups and meditate—together. On the surface it will look contradictory because meditation means learning how to be alone and group therapies mean learning how to be together. But this is my fundamental approach; you have to learn both.

And you are right, Gopa, that: *the path of love must be taken with tremendous awareness.*

And the same is true about the path of awareness: it must be taken with tremendous love. In fact, love and awareness are two aspects of the same coin.

The fourth question:

Bhagwan,
Instead of giving philosophical lessons, why don't you just tell jokes for a while? I think your sannyasins would appreciate it.

Swami Buddhaprem,

THE QUESTION SHOWS that you are not my sannyasin.

You say: *I think your sannyasins would appreciate it.*

You have fallen into wrong company, it seems. You are not meant to be here. You must have come with a wrong notion. You must have come here to learn philosophy. You must be a serious person—and seriousness is pathological.

Philosophy is all bullshit! I am not interested in philosophy; of course my sannyasins are not interested in philosophy either. Those who belong to me are interested in life, not in philosophy. Life is the real thing; philosophy is the false thing. But philosophy has been praised for centuries and we live with this conditioning. Nobody tells you that philosophy is a false thing.

Buddha is not a philosopher: he loved to tell parables. Jesus is not a philosopher: he used so many parables.

My jokes are New Age parables—because to me laughter is one of the most significant things in life. People who are not capable of laughing become incapable of living.

But it happens. Many times—in fact, more often than not—you come here for the wrong reasons, thinking that you are going to some oriental philosopher. I am neither oriental nor a philosopher! I am not even religious in the old sense: I am not a saint nor a mahatma. In fact, you can't put me in any category. You will have to create a new category for me because no existing category will be adequate. I won't fit in it, and I don't want to fit in any category. *Things* fit in categories, not people, not *real* people.

A lady enters a clothing store and asks if they have falsies.

"Certainly, lady," answers the formal salesman.

"What I want to know," she continues, "is if you have the best quality falsies."

"Of course!" exclaims the salesman "in this store we don't sell imitations!"

All philosophies are false and all philosophies are imitations. I am existential. But you are certainly in the wrong place. Either you will have to change or you will have to leave—I don't leave any other alternative. If you want to be with me you have to understand what is happening here and you have to become part of it. If you feel that that is not possible, that you already know what is right, then this is not the place for you, then this is not the right company for you.

Do you know about the two scientists who first discovered the flying machine, the airplane, which could not leave the ground? Do you know their name? Their name was the Wrong brothers.

And these are Wrong brothers, and you seem to be a very right and righteous person. Either you have to become part of this strange company . . . This is a Noah's Ark—all kinds of animals are here! In the new commune I am not going to call it Buddha Hall again, it will be Noah's Ark!

But if you are interested in philosophy you can go to any university; there are thousands of universities in the world. If you are interested in something false it is very cheap. But remember, all the time that you waste will simply be wasted and one day you will repent.

A tourist threw a coin into the wishing well at Disneyland. He had just expressed a sinful wish when a beautiful girl tapped his shoulder and told him to follow her. She took him to a luxurious flat, gave him silk pajamas, and after she put on some music and lit some candles, she handed him a martini. Then she started undressing.

She took off her long blonde hair, which was a wig, she took off her false eyelashes, and then her beautiful false breasts. Then the tourist saw that she was not even a woman, and in despair he exclaimed, "What does all this mean?"

And the boy replied, "Now you will learn not to throw false coins in the wishing well, you darling little cheater!"

Buddhaprem, you ask me: *Instead of giving philosophical lessons, why don't you just tell jokes for a while?*

And what have I been doing here all along? Do you think I have been giving philosophical lessons? Then you have not heard me at all. It is not the philosophical lessons that I am interested in, I am interested in the jokes. It is not to illustrate philosophy that I use jokes, just the contrary: to illustrate the jokes I use philosophy!

You think that I look at your questions? Nonsense! First I look at my jokes and then at your questions. If your question fits with my jokes, okay, otherwise it goes into the waste basket. Those who really want their questions to be answered, they have learned the trick: first they send the jokes, then they send the question. Then they can be certain their question will be answered. But first, the jokes!

I am much more interested in your laughter . . .

You say: *I think your sannyasins would appreciate it.*

They love it! But for that they have to be my sannyasins. You are not yet a sannyasin, otherwise you would have said, "We would appreciate it." You say "your sannyasins". You are keeping yourself apart, you are excluding yourself from my sannyasins.

What, in fact, is philosophy? It is thinking about things which are unthinkable. It is trying to comprehend something which is incomprehensible. It is an absurd activity. The philosophers know it, but they enjoy the activity. It is like a game, like chess. Just as people enjoy chess there are people who enjoy philosophy.

A philosopher wanted to change the world. He thought that God had made many mistakes and that he should have thought a little longer before creating the world in seven days.

One day, as he was lying in the grass contemplating, some birds flew overhead, while a grazing cow passed slowly by his side.

"Look," he said to himself, "another mistake of nature! Cows, which are very utilitarian to humanity, must drag themselves down the road, while birds, which have no utility at all, can fly and move very easily!"

At that very moment, one of the birds overhead shat on his head.

The philosopher, stunned, contemplated for a few moments and then said out loud, "Excuse me, God, I really didn't mean that cows should fly!"

What is philosophy? It is just contemplating about useless things. For example, just the other day I was saying to you, "In the beginning was darkness and spaghetti." Now, if you are a philosopher you will torture yourself with the question: Who made spaghetti? From where did it come? And I know this is true because I know my Italian sannyasins. I know my medium, Radha. Whenever I touch her third eye there is no third eye . . . layers and layers of spaghetti. I go on, go on . . . It has been years now! But still I like and love to touch her third eye—it is very soft! So I know the story is true.

But philosophers have been asking such questions: "God created the world. Then who created God?" And whatsoever answer you give will create another question. If you say xyz, or anybody, then they will ask, "Who created x? Who created y? Who created z?" It will go on and on; somewhere it has to stop.

So when Kuthumi shouted at me and said, "Shut up!" I immediately understood—he is right, because somewhere one has to shut up!

I am very existential. Rather than bothering about who created spaghetti I looked into Radha and found that it is true. The Akashic records are saying something absolutely right. And everybody should be jealous of it because to be full of spaghetti is far better than being full of cow dung. Indians are full of holy cow dung! They used to drink cow's urine, and now much progress has happened: Morarji Desai drinks his own urine. This is progress! This is evolution! Nobody can deny this is evolution, moving from cow's urine to your own urine. It is a lesson in independence.

Buddhaprem, formally you are my sannyasin—*really* become my sannyasin. Enjoy this great opportunity of being non-serious, of taking life as fun, of enjoying it. Life consists of small things, but if you learn how to enjoy those small things the ordinary becomes extraordinary, the mundane becomes sacred, the profane becomes profound.

Religion is not something that disconnects you from life and its joys, it deepens your joys. In fact, only a really religious person can eat, drink and be merry. It has been said *against* the irreligious; it has been said that it is the materialist philosophy, to eat, drink and be merry. But I tell you that the materialist cannot eat, drink and be merry, only the spiritualist, because he can think deeper. Then spaghetti becomes spiritual. Who bothers about the third eye? What is the need for the third eye? Even the two are creating so much trouble! And three eyes will create more trouble; they will create a triangle in you!

But you must be here almost unconscious.

A philosopher enters a bar and asks for ten glasses of whisky.

"Ten?" exclaims the surprised bartender.

"Ten!" answers the philosopher.

So the bartender brings him all ten drinks, and to his surprise the philosopher drinks them all.

Next he asks for nine glasses of whisky. After drinking them he asks for eight, then seven, and so forth, until he finally asks for just one glass of whisky.

After finishing the last glass he somehow manages to mumble to the bartender, "T-t-tell me, br-bro-brother, w-why is it th-th-that the l-l-less I dr-dr-drink, the mo-more dr-dr-drunk I g-g-get?"

The last question:

Bhagwan,
When more of the existential happens in a person than can be absorbed and digested at one time, is it not then wise to repress until trust and innocence grow? My body is in bad shape because of repression but it feels as though I have bought much needed time.

Anand Tilopa,

IF YOU REPRESS and resist, how out of repression and resistance can trust and innocence grow? You will be making it more and more impossible. Innocence means a state of total nudity, of utter non-repressiveness. Repressed persons become complex, they cannot become innocent. Everything in them becomes crippled, paralyzed, devious. They start becoming split; in fact they become many, not just two. They have one door to show themselves to the world and another door, a back door, through which they live. They say something, they do something—and they think something else. They are always in a chaos, they cannot be innocent.

Innocence does not need repression, it needs spontaneity, it needs naturalness. Whatsoever you repress will become your problem. If you repress anger, anger will become your problem. Then in everything anger will be hiding. In fact, if there is too much repressed anger you will be angry twenty-four hours a day for no reason at all, because now it is not a question of having any valid reason for being angry, you are just boiling within—any excuse will do, or if there are no excuses to be found you will start inventing excuses.

A group of nuns were traveling to a convent in the interior of Africa when they were kidnapped by a ferocious tribe of Africans. The United Nations was immediately informed and some days later a military troop was sent by plane to the heart of the black continent.

It was a successful operation. The soldiers surrounded the tribe, rescued the nuns, and brought them to the plane.

All the nuns boarded the plane with torn clothes, swollen lips, hair a mess, and with their breasts exposed.

"It's so good that you came!" they said, "We couldn't bear it any longer. All those blacks with those enormous 'things' and all day long fucking, fucking, fucking!"

The soldiers tried to console them, one by one. Finally the last nun came on board. She was very pretty, with her habit in perfect condition. She was clean, combed and composed.

One soldier said to her, "What a pity, sister; how you ladies suffered . . . all those blacks with those big

'things' all day long fucking, fucking, fucking.''
And the pretty one answered, ''No, not with me.''
''Why not?'' he asked.
''I wasn't into it!'' she said.

If you repress you will find some way. If you repress sex you will find some way to be raped so that the responsibility is not on you, so that you can feel completely free of the responsibility. It is out of repression that there is rape. It is out of repression that there are crimes of all kinds. It cannot lead you into innocence.

No, Tilopa, if you want to be innocent you don't need time, you need understanding, you need insight. Time won't help, because what will you be doing meanwhile? You will continue your old habits: you will go on repressing. You need immediate insight. You have already repressed for many lives—enough is enough. Now see the point and drop all your repressions. And this is the place! If you cannot drop your repressions here you cannot drop them anywhere in the whole world.

That's why I am condemned so much—obviously, because all the societies in the world exist on repression. And my whole approach is that of non-repressive spontaneity; only then can innocence come back to you. It is your nature. Innocence is not something that has to be achieved; it has only been repressed deep down in you. If all the repressions are removed it will start surfacing. You will become a child again.

And Jesus is right when he says: Unless you are a child again, unless you are reborn, you will not enter into my kingdom of God.

INTO
THE
OPEN
SKY

The first question:

Bhagwan,
Are children really so intelligent as you always
say they are?

Gautami,

INTELLIGENCE IS not something that is acquired, it is inbuilt, it is inborn, it is intrinsic to life itself. Not only children are intelligent, animals are intelligent in their own way, trees are intelligent in their own way. Of course they all have different kinds of intelligences because their needs differ, but now it is an established fact that all that lives is intelligent. Life cannot be without intelligence; to be alive and to be intelligent are synonymous.

But man is in a dilemma for the simple reason that he is not only intelligent, he is also aware of his intelligence. That is something unique about man, his privilege, his prerogative, his glory, but it can turn very easily into his agony. Man is conscious that he is intelligent; that consciousness brings its own problems. The first problem is that it creates ego.

Ego does not exist anywhere else except in human beings, and ego starts growing as the child grows. The parents, the schools, colleges, university, they all help to strengthen the ego for the simple reason that for centuries man had to struggle to survive and the idea has become a fixation, a deep unconscious conditioning, that only strong egos can survive in the struggle of life. Life has become just a struggle to survive. And scientists have made it even more convincing with the theory of the survival of the fittest. So we help every child to become more and more strong in the ego, and it is there that the problem arises.

As the ego becomes strong it starts surrounding intelligence like a thick layer of darkness. Intelligence is light, ego is darkness. Intelligence is very delicate, ego is very hard. Intelligence is like a rose flower, ego is like a rock. And if you want to survive, they say—the so-called knowers—then you have to become rock-like, you have to be strong, invulnerable. You have to become a citadel, a closed citadel, so you cannot be attacked from outside. You have to become impenetrable.

But then you become closed. Then you start dying as far as your intelligence is concerned because intelligence needs the open sky, the wind, the air, the sun in order to grow, to expand, to flow. To remain alive it needs a constant flow; if it becomes stagnant it becomes slowly slowly a dead phenomenon.

We don't allow children to remain intelligent. The first thing is that if they are intelligent they will be vulnerable, they will be delicate, they will be open. If they are intelligent they will be able to see many falsities in the society, in the state, in the church, in the educational system. They will become rebellious. They will be individuals; they will not be cowed easily. You can crush them, but you cannot enslave them. You can destroy them, but you cannot force them to compromise.

In one sense intelligence is very soft, like a rose flower, in another sense it has its own strength. But that strength is subtle, not gross. That strength is the strength of rebellion, of a non-compromising attitude. One is ready to die, one is ready to suffer, but one is not ready to sell one's soul.

And the whole society needs slaves; it needs people who function like robots, machines. It does not want people, it wants efficient mechanisms. Hence the whole conditioning is: make the ego strong. It serves a double purpose. First: it gives the person the feeling that now he can struggle in life. And secondly: it serves the purposes of all the vested interests. They can exploit him; they can use him as a means to their own ends.

Hence the whole educational system rotates around the idea of ambition; it creates ambitiousness. Ambitiousness is nothing but ego. "Become the first, become the most famous. Become a prime minister or a president. Become world known. Leave your name in history." It does not teach you to live totally, it does not teach you to love totally, it does not teach you to live gracefully, it teaches you how to exploit others for your own purposes. And we think that the people who are clever are the ones who succeed. They are cunning, but we call them clever. They are not intelligent people.

An intelligent person can never use another person as a means; he will respect the other. An intelligent person will be able to see the equality of all. Yes, he will see the differences too, but differences make no difference as far as equality is concerned. He will have tremendous respect for others' freedom—he cannot exploit them, he cannot reduce them into things, he cannot make them stepping stones to the fulfillment of some absurd desire to be the first. Hence we go on conditioning children, and the question arises . . .

Your question *is* relevant, Gautami, because it is not only I who am saying that children are intelligent, it has been said by Buddha, by Lao Tzu, by Jesus, by all the awakened ones. Jesus says: Unless you are like a small child there is no hope for you. Again he says: Unless you become like small children you cannot enter into my kingdom of God. Again and again he repeats one of his most famous beatitudes: Blessed are those who are the last in this world, because they will be the first in my kingdom of God. He is teaching non-ambitiousness—to be the last. He says: Blessed are the meek, for theirs is the kingdom of God—the meek, the humble, the people who are standing last in the queue. It was natural, very natural that the society he was born in was against him because he was destroying the very roots of their ambitiousness.

And Jews have always been very ambitious people, so much so that for centuries, against all hazards, they have carried the idea in their minds that they are the chosen people of God. A thousand and one calamities have happened because of this stupid idea; if they can drop it they will be more acceptable in the world. But they cannot drop it—their whole ego is involved in it. And it is an ancient ego, at least three thousand years old. Since Moses they have been carrying the idea that they are the chosen people of God.

And here comes this man who says, "Be the last"! "We are meant to be the first, and he says, 'Be humble and meek'! And we are the chosen people; if we are humble and meek then those who are not chosen will become the first!" And Jews are earthly people; they don't bother much about the other world. They are worldly. "Who knows about the other world? He is saying, 'If you are the last here you will be the first in my kingdom of God.' But where is your kingdom of God? It may be just a fiction, just a dream."

Jesus looks like a dreamer, a poet maybe, but he is destroying their very foundation. They cannot forgive him; they have not even forgiven him yet. They still carry the idea that "we are the chosen people." They have suffered much for it; the more they have suffered the stronger the idea has become—because if you have to face suffering you have to become more and more egoistic, more rock-like so that you can fight, struggle, so that nobody can destroy you. But they have also become very closed.

Jesus was creating an opening for them; they refused him. He was telling them to come into the open sky. He was telling them to be just ordinary: "Drop this nonsense of being special." If they had listened to Jesus their whole history would have been different, but they could not listen.

Hindus have not listened to Buddha for the simple reason—the same reason—that Hindus are also carrying the idea they are the holiest people in the world and their land is the holiest land. Even gods long to be born in India! No other country is so holy. And Buddha said, "This is all nonsense!" They had to reject

187

him. Buddhism was thrown out of this country. No society can tolerate such people, who are telling the truth, because they seem to sabotage the very structure.

But now the time has come when we have suffered enough. All over the world, in different ways, people have suffered much, and it is time to have a look at history and its stupidity and its ridiculousness and drop the whole idea of these egoistic patterns.

Watch small children, Gautami, and then you will not ask me—you will see their intelligence. Yes, they are not knowledgeable. If you want them to be knowledgeable, then you will not think that they are intelligent. If you ask them questions which depend on information, then they will look not intelligent. But ask them real questions which have nothing to do with information, which need an immediate response, and see—they are far more intelligent than you are. Of course your ego won't allow you to accept it, but if you can accept it it will help tremendously. It will help you, it will help your children, because if you can see their intelligence you can learn much from them.

A Sufi mystic, Hasan, was dying. When he was dying a man asked him, "Hasan, you have never told us who your Master was. We have asked again and again; you always somehow managed not to answer it. Now you are leaving the world. Please tell us who your Master was. We are very curious."

Hasan said, "I never answered the question for the simple reason that there has not been just a single Master in my life, I have learned from many people. My first teacher was a small child."

They were puzzled. They said, "A small child! What are you saying? Have you lost your senses because you are dying? Have you gone mad, crazy?"

He said, "No, listen to the story. I went into a town. Although I had not known the truth up to that time, I was very knowledgeable. I was a scholar. I was well known all over the country; even outside the country my name was spreading. People had started coming to me thinking that I knew it. I was pretending that I knew it, and I was pretending without knowing that I was pretending—I was almost unconscious. Because people believed that I knew they convinced me that I must be right, I must be knowing, otherwise why should so many people be coming to me? I had become a teacher. Without knowing, without experiencing anything of truth, without ever entering into my own inner world, I was talking about great things. I knew all the scriptures; they were on the tip of my tongue.

"But for three days I was moving in a country where nobody knew me and I was very much hankering to find somebody to ask me something so that I could show my knowledge."

Knowledgeable people become very exhibitionistic; that is their whole joy. If a knowledgeable person has to remain silent he would rather commit suicide. Then what is the point of living in the world? He has to exhibit his knowledge. Only a wise man can be silent. For the wise man to speak is almost a burden; he speaks because he has to speak. The knowledgeable person speaks because he cannot remain silent. There is a vast difference; you may not be able to know it from the outside because both speak. The Buddha speaks, Jesus speaks, and Hasan was also speaking. And they all say beautiful things. Sometimes the knowledgeable people say wiser things than the wise people because the wise persons may speak in contradictions, in paradoxes, but the knowledgeable person is always logical, consistent; he has all the proofs and arguments, he has all the scriptures to support him.

But for three days he had to keep silent. It was almost like fasting, and he was feeling hungry—hungry for an audience, hungry for somebody. But he had not come across anybody who knew him so nobody asked anything.

He entered this town. It was just getting a little dark, the sun had just set. A small child was carrying an earthen lamp, and he asked the child, "My son, can I ask you a question? Where are you taking this earthen lamp?"

And the child said, "I am going to the temple. My mother has told me to put this lamp there because the temple is dark. And this has been my mother's habit: to always put a lamp there in the night so at least the god of the temple does not have to live in darkness."

Hasan asked the child, "You seem to be very intelligent. Can you tell me one thing—did you light this lamp yourself?"

The child said, "Yes."

Then Hasan said, "A third question, the last question I want to ask you: if you lit the lamp yourself, can you tell me where the flame came from? You must have seen it coming from somewhere."

The child laughed and he said, "I will do one thing—just see!" And he blew the flame out and he said, "The flame has gone just in front of you. Can you tell me where it has gone? You must have seen!"

And Hasan was utterly dumb; he could not answer. The child had shown him that his question, although it looked very relevant, meaningful, was absurd. He bowed down to the child, touched his feet.

He said to the inquirer, "That child was my first Master. That very moment I realized all my metaphysics, all my philosophy was meaningless. I didn't know a thing on my own. I didn't even know from where the light comes into a lamp, where it goes to when the light has been put out—and I have been talking about who made the world, how he made the world, when he made the world! For that moment I have always remembered the child. He may have forgotten me, he may not even recognize me, but I cannot forget that incident.

"And since then thousands of people have taught me. I have avoided the question again and again because there is not a single person I can call my Master. Many have been my Masters, I have learned from many sources, and from each source I have learned one thing: that unless you know through your own experience, all knowledge is futile.

"Then I dropped all my learning, all my knowing; all my scriptures I burned. I dropped the idea of being a scholar, I forgot all my fame. I started moving like a beggar, absolutely unknown to anybody. And slowly slowly, going deeper into meditation, I discovered my own intelligence."

Even though the society destroys your intelligence it cannot destroy it totally; it only covers it with many layers of information.

And that's the whole function of meditation: to take you deeper into yourself. It is a method of digging into your own being to the point when you come to the living waters of your own intelligence, when you discover the springs of your own intelligence. When you have discovered your child again, when you are reborn, then, only then will you understand what I have been meaning by emphasizing again and again that children are really intelligent.

But start watching children, their responses—not their answers but their responses. Don't ask them foolish questions, ask them something immediate which does not depend on information and see their response.

The mother was preparing little Pedro to go to a party. When she finished combing his hair she straightened his shirt collar and said, "Go now, son. Have a good time . . . and behave yourself!"

"Come on, mother!" said Pedro. "Please decide before I leave which it is going to be!"

You see the point? The mother was saying, "Have a good time . . . and behave yourself." Now, both things cannot be done together. And the child's response is really of tremendous value. He says, "Please decide before I leave which it is going to be. If you allow me to have a good time, then I cannot behave; if you want me to behave, then I cannot have a good time." The child can see the contradiction so clearly; it may not have been apparent to the mother.

A passerby asks a boy, "Son, can you please tell me what time it is?"

"Yes, of course," replies the boy, "but what do you need it for? It changes continuously!"

A new transit sign was put in front of the school. It read: "Drive Slowly. Do Not Kill a Student!"

The following day there was another sign under it scribbled in a childish writing: "Wait for the Teacher!"

Little Pierino comes home from school with a big smile on his face.

"Well, dear, you look very happy. So you like school, do you?"

"Don't be silly, mom," replies the boy. "We must not confuse the going with the coming back!"

While slowly walking to school the little boy prays, "Dear God, please do not let me arrive at school late. I pray you, God, let me arrive at school on time . . ."

At this moment he slips on a banana peel and slides on the path for a few meters. Pulling himself up he looks at the sky annoyed and says, "Okay, okay, God, there is no need to push!"

A little boy is having a test with a psychologist. "What do you want to do when you grow up?" asks the shrink.

"I want to become a doctor or a painter or a window washer!" replies the boy.

Puzzled, the psychologist asks, "But . . . you aren't very clear, are you?"

"Why not? I'm very clear. I want to see naked women!"

The father was telling stories to his sons in the living room after dinner. "My great-grandfather fought in the war against Rosas, my uncle fought in the war against the Kaiser, my grandfather fought in the war of Spain against the Republicans and my father fought in the Second World War against the Germans."

To which the smallest son replied, "Shit! What's wrong with this family? They can't relate to anybody!"

The second question:

Bhagwan,
Who are you?

Deben,

I AM JUST A MIRROR —nothing more, nothing less. If you come close to me you can see your face as it is. Many people will see ugly faces and they will become angry at me. They will think that this ugliness is part of me. Many people will see beautiful faces; they will become infatuated with me. They will think that this beauty is part of me. Both are wrong.

Just a few days ago *The Sunday Statesman* published an article about me. The title of the article is: "Rajneesh—Sage or Satyr?" The writer is a famous Bengali scholar, a follower of Sri Aurobindo. He has written many books, particularly on Aurobindo's philosophy. He cannot come to a conclusion; he wavers. I enjoyed his article. One moment he thinks I am a saint, another moment he thinks I am a sinner. One moment he feels I am divine, another moment he thinks I am just the devil incarnate. The whole article is an exercise in utter confusion! That shows *his* face: he must be a man living in confusion. The confusion may have surfaced through reading my book because he must have been reading Sri Aurobindo his whole life.

I don't see anything important in Sir Aurobindo's philosophy because it is only a philosophy. He was a great scholar, a man of great intellectual talents, a genius, but not a Master, not a Buddha. He has written a great system of thought, very logical. His approach is as it should be: academic, scholarly, logical. And he tried to live according to the Indian ideal of the sage, and he managed to live it as far as it is possible to manage it from the outside. He cultivated a great character around himself, but it was only a character without any consciousness in it, it was a conscience without any consciousness in it. He was simply following the Hindu ideal of the sage.

This writer also has a certain idea of the sage. I don't fit into that category. I cannot fit into any category—

Hindu, Christian, Mohammedan, Jaina, Buddhist. I don't belong to the past, I belong to the future. I am creating a new category of my own; in future there will be people who will fit *my* category. It is a new phenomenon, hence it has no history behind it. It has a future but no past. Because he cannot make me fit according to the Hindu ideal of a sage—obviously, the logical mind thinks in terms of either/or—then I must be a devil! But he cannot fit me into that category either; about that too he seems to be shaky and wavering. That too is not possible because the sage and the devil are polar opposites to each other. They both belong to the past—I don't belong to the past at all. So he goes on moving continuously from one point to the other and he ends in confusion, inconclusively.

But if he can see the point . . . the point is that he has come face to face with a mirror in which he can see his own conflict, in which he can see his conflict between the past and the future, in which he can see his conflict between his own conscious and unconscious, between his conscience and consciousness, between his character and his reality. But he may not be aware of that at all. He thinks that he is thinking about me—he is simply looking at his own face.

Deben, you ask me: *Who are you?*

But *you* can understand it—you who are here, who are with me. You can understand this fact: I am just a mirror. Sometimes you become angry. Remember it, that anger has something to do with you, it has nothing to do with me. Sometimes you become very happy and very blissful; that too belongs to you, it has nothing to do with me. I don't take any credit. If you become enlightened that is up to you; I will not take the credit for it. You need not even feel any thankfulness to me. I don't expect even a thank you from you; on the contrary, I will be thankful to you because now you will not need my mirror and my mirror can become available to others. You will become a mirror yourself and you will start mirroring others' faces, their realities.

I want all my sannyasins to become mirrors so they can help millions of people in the world. If you can remember this, great things will start happening to you; otherwise you will go on blaming me because each time I assert something it is going to hurt you. If you have carried a certain idea for a long time and it has become deep-rooted in you and I start hitting . . . And I can do only that. Anything wrong, and the mirror is bound to show it to you. The mirror is not at fault. If your face is looking sad the mirror will show it. Don't destroy the mirror.

That's what the poor man was doing here who threw the knife to kill me. He could not tolerate the mirror. He had listened to me for only three, four days, but he became so agitated because what I was saying showed his fanaticism, showed his Hindu chauvinistic attitude, and it became intolerable for him.

Jesus became intolerable to the Jews for the simple reason that he was showing their faces.

People are carrying ugly faces and without mirrors they cannot see their faces so they remain perfectly contented. When you can't see your face you think you are beautiful. And people are polite, nobody says anything to you. That's why they have to say things when you are not there, they have to talk about you behind your back. They gossip, but they never gossip when you are present. They gossip about others with you and with others about you—and you do the same.

Psychologists say that if every person in the world decides to be absolutely authentic and true for twenty-four hours—just for twenty-four hours the whole world decides: "We will not be polite and we will not tell lies and we will not be formal; we will simply say the truth as it is, as it appears to us"—then there will no longer be any friendship in the world, no more husbands, no more wives, no more lovers. All will be finished!

That's why to my sannyasins I always suggest that if you want to continue your relationship with somebody it is best not to live together, because if you start living together, how long you can be polite? How long you can be formal? Sooner or later the truth starts surfacing.

Just a few days ago Vasumati wanted to live with Krishna Prem. Their relationship has lasted for almost one and a half years. It is such a long long time in this commune—almost impossible!—for the simple reason that they are not living together so they meet only once in a while. They cannot even meet every day because Vasumati is sharing with other people, Krishna Prem is sharing with somebody else. So only once in a while, when they can manage some privacy, they can meet—only for a few hours per week, twice or thrice per week. So it remains a love affair; it has not yet become a marriage. Otherwise it would have been finished long ago!

But when she wanted, I told Vivek . . . Vivek came to me and said, "Vasumati wants to live with Krishna Prem." I said, "That's what every woman wants and that's how every woman destroys. And the man cannot say no because if he says no that means it is immediately finished! But," I said, "if she wants to, then we will manage it in some way."

There was one opportunity—I inquired of Krishna Prem. He proved to be really wise. He wrote a letter, he said to me, "Bhagwan, you decide, because I don't know what is right. My desires say, 'Be together,' but I am an unconscious person—I don't know what will happen out of it. I can't see very far into the future, but you can see so you decide."

So I decided that they live separately.

Just a few weeks ago Radha went to Italy with her lover, Amito, just for four weeks. And immediately I told Vivek, "This relationship is finished!" I told her not to say such things to anybody because let them enjoy at least four weeks, but this is finished. Four weeks together, and in Italy . . . there is no hope, no future for this relationship.

And that's what has happened. Just the other day Radha wrote a letter saying that now she wants to move with Asang. I knew that this was going to happen, it was as absolutely clear as things can be, because when you live together for twenty-four hours a day you have to put aside your masks. At least sometimes, when you go to sleep, you have to put the masks aside; your real face starts showing. And for one, two, three days you can somehow manage: you can act nice, good, beautiful, but for how long? One cannot act twenty-four hours a day for many days; it becomes tiring, it becomes boring. One has to say the real thing.

And I can perfectly understand the psychologists' idea that if we decide to be true, absolutely true, only for twenty-four hours, everything on earth will fall apart. Every relationship will fall apart because truth is truth and there are very few people who can absorb truth; they have become so accustomed to lies. That's why so much gossiping goes on all around, because you have to say the truth somewhere, otherwise it becomes a burden on you. You have to unburden yourself. So when you have told somebody you feel unburdened, you feel better. And the other person can unburden himself to you, and this goes on and on.

everybody is helping as a psychoanalyst to everybody else.

In the West psychoanalysis is needed, not in the East, for the simple reason that in the East people have enough time to listen to each other. In the West nobody has time to listen to anyone—you have to pay for it. The psychoanalyst does nothing; his whole art consists of pretending to be attentive to you.

One psychoanalyst went to a pet shop. He wanted a parrot which did not talk. The owner was puzzled. He said, "You are the first customer who wants a parrot which does not talk. Everybody comes for a parrot which talks!"

He said, "I am tired of talking parrots!"

The owner said, "Have you got many talking parrots?"

He said, "No, many talking patients, but they are parrots. They almost all repeat the same thing. Every husband is talking about his wife and every wife is talking about her husband. Every parent is talking about his children and every child is talking about his parents. I am tired! And I have to pretend that I am listening attentively because that's what they are paying for—and they are really paying too much."

Now it is one of the best professions in the West, one of the most profitable businesses—and with no investment. You just need a couch . . . And Freud was very inventive about the couch, because if you are facing the patient your face may start showing boredom, you may start yawning. Who is concerned with all that nonsense and rubbish about their lives that people go on talking? And the psychoanalyst has been listening to so many people and the story is almost the same. It is always the same because it is the story of the unconscious mind; it can't be much different.

Only conscious people have uniqueness. One Buddha absolutely differs from another Buddha. If you have to listen to the story of Jesus it is going to be tremendously different from the story of Gautam the Buddha or the story of Lao Tzu. They are unique people. But unconscious people, what is their story? The same sexuality, the same repression, the same greed, the same anger, the same hatred, destructiveness, suicidalness, possessiveness, jealousy. It is almost the same story. Only persons differ, but the role they play is the same. The same triangles—two women and one man or two men and one woman—the same triangles. One is bound to get tired.

Freud invented one of the great things of this century: the couch. The patient has to lie down on the couch and the therapist sits behind him so that the patient cannot see his face. The therapist can go on smoking, yawning or reading or he can plug his ears and there is no need to bother about what the person is saying—let him talk. But the person feels immensely relieved. When after one hour's analysis he comes out, he looks fresh, unburdened, younger, less tense, more at ease, collected, calm. He has said many stupid things which he cannot say to anybody else because people will think he is mad. And here you are supposed to be mad so there is no problem!

This psychoanalyst said, "I want a parrot which does not talk."

The pet shop owner was in a little difficulty because he had all kinds of parrots but they were all talking parrots; this was the first customer who had asked for a non-talking parrot. But he went in and brought out a dumb crow.

The psychotherapist said, "Is this a parrot?"

He said, "Yes, it is an African parrot. It is a nigger! And he cannot talk because he knows no English."

So he said, "That's perfectly all right," and took the crow.

After a month the pet owner met the psychotherapist in the park one morning and he asked him, "How are things going? How is the parrot?"

And the psychoanalyst said, "You have given me really a beautiful parrot. He never says a single word and whatsoever I say he listens so attentively that I talk to him for hours! I am feeling so unburdened, so free. I rejoice in him! The whole day I am looking forward to the evening. I rush home.

"There are many people who suspect that it is not a parrot—my wife says, 'You are a fool! This is not a parrot!'—but it doesn't matter whether it is a parrot or not. He pays attention, he listens so attentively! That's the only thing, that is the quality I was looking for!"

In the East psychoanalysis is still not part of the style of life and I think it will take a long time for it to become part of life, because everybody is functioning as a psychoanalyst to everybody else. People can talk to each other and unburden themselves. In the West there is no time. Nobody is ready to listen to you; you have to pay professional listeners.

A Master is not a psychoanalyst, he is a mirror. He simply reflects you with all your burdens, tensions, anxieties, anguish, with all your problems, with all your miseries. And naturally you can become offended.

One sannyasin has just written to me: "Bhagwan, whenever you talk about differences between man and woman I become very resistant." But why should you become resistant? What can I do if there are differences? The rose is different from the marigold. If somebody becomes resistant that means something is wrong in his inner world; something is repressed and that repression starts uncoiling itself. Maybe you have been carrying the idea that man and woman are not different; maybe that has become your fixation. There are many people who think men and women are not different and they find a thousand and one rationalizations to explain why they are not different: that it is only psychological conditioning that makes them different, otherwise they are not different. They *are* different. Psychological conditioning can reduce their differences or can enhance their differences, but differences are there, basic differences are there, and those basic differences should not be overlooked.

A kind of unisex is being born in the world. This sannyasin must be a believer in unisex. Men and women are wearing almost the same clothes, trying to look alike. And of course if psychologically you become conditioned, your biology also, your physiology also follows suit.

In the East the differences have been always accepted, not only accepted but strengthened. There is great wisdom in it because the farther away they are, the more attraction there is between them; if they become alike the attraction will be lost. And in the West it is happening: for the first time in the history of humanity sex is losing its appeal. And once sex loses its appeal you are at a loss—what to do? Where to go?

Sex is a natural phenomenon which gives you glimpses of meditation. From sex you can go to meditation, but if sex loses its appeal the doors for meditation are closed because you won't have any glimpses of meditation. It is only in sexual orgasm that you melt, merge, disappear. And those few moments of disappearance, dissolution, give you the first taste of what it will be to dissolve forever. Those drops of nectar can give you some idea of the ocean that a Buddha carries in his being. But if sex loses its appeal, then even those drops become impossible. And a person who has not even tasted a drop of nectar cannot conceive that there is a possibility of any oceanic experience. For him Buddha will become a fiction.

Try to understand my approach. I want you to transcend sex—but through sex, not by becoming indifferent to it, not by dropping it in an immature way.

The East has always emphasized the difference between man and woman for the simple reason that the East knows the immense value of orgasmic experience. It gives you a glimpse of meditation and then from there you can move on; that can become a jumping board. But in the West sex is losing its appeal, and one of the causes of its losing its appeal is that the differences are being reduced to zero. And it is affecting the physiology also.

In the East you will see women and men have more prominent physiological differences than in the West. Western women are becoming more and more flat-chested; their breasts are becoming smaller and smaller. There is a possibility in the future that they may almost disappear! In the East you can see it very clearly, very prominently, that the women have bigger breasts than western women. The same is the case with the buttocks too. Western women are becoming almost straight lines with no curves; all the curves are disappearing. And then if you are wearing the same clothes, pants and shirt, it becomes almost difficult.

Even for me sometimes it is difficult. Every evening Mukta has to go on looking to see what I am writing, "swami" or "ma", because she has to correct me many times: "Bhagwan, this is a ma! This is a swami!" I don't think any Buddha had this problem before. I must be the first one who is encountering this problem. I also feel puzzled, sometimes utterly puzzled. No spiritual insight helps! I have to depend on Mukta: if she misses, then almost every day there will be at least one case: a ma will become a swami, a swami will become a ma.

But this sannyasin who has written to me: "There is great resistance whenever you talk about differences . . ." The resistance must be coming out of the idea that men and women are equal. I am not saying that they are not equal, I am simply saying they are not similar. Never confuse equality with similarity. They are perfectly equal but they are absolutely dissimilar—and that is their beauty. If you have this wrong notion that similarity means equality then you will be feeling a resistance.

I am just a mirror—don't be angry with me. And there will be ninety percent of cases when you will feel anger against me because I will have to bring out much pus in you; I will have to open your wounds. You may have forgotten about them, completely forgotten; you may have started believing that they no longer exist. And I will have to reopen them to show you where you are, because unless you know where you are you cannot move a single inch, you cannot grow. You can move only from where you are.

And there will be ten percent of cases when you will feel ecstatic. Then don't think that I am giving this ecstasy to you—nobody can give truth to you. I can inspire you, I can challenge you, I can invite you, I can seduce you into the journey, but I cannot give the truth to you. You have to find it yourself; I can only show your face.

I am simply a mirror, Deben.

Fanfani is on an official visit to France and he is taken to the Louvre. The museum director shows him around and they stop in front of a painting.

"Cezanne?" Fanfani asks.

"No," replies the director, "Renoir."

They come to another painting and again Fanfani asks, "Pizarro?"

"No, Your Excellence, Degas."

After walking around a little more he stops in front of another one and asks, "Is this a self-portrait of Toulouse-Lautrec?"

"No, Your Excellence, this is a mirror!"

My sannyasins have to remember always that you are here to discover your real faces, your original faces. And the Master not only reflects your so-called face, he reflects your original face too. But he begins by reflecting your mask, and it hurts to know that you are wearing a mask. And you are not wearing only one mask, you are wearing many masks—masks upon masks. You have to be peeled like an onion and it hurts. But unless your original face is discovered the work that I want to do will remain incomplete. God will recognize you by your original face, not by any artificial mask, howsoever beautiful it is.

Three Cambridge dons were walking by the river one beautiful hot summer day. Coming to a secluded spot, they could not resist the temptation to have a dip. Not having costumes with them, they went in the buff.

Unfortunately just as they came out, a punt full of pretty female undergrads came round the bend, whereupon in some consternation, two of the dons grabbed some clothes around their middles while the third threw something over his head. After the girls had gone the two who had covered their middles turned on the other and said, "Why on earth did you do that?"

Whereupon he answered, "Where I come from, we recognize people by their faces!"

God will recognize you by your original face; nothing else will be recognized there. No degrees, no fame, no money, no power, no prestige, nothing else will be recognized there but your original face; and you will have to stand utterly naked before him.

The Master simply represents God on the earth. You have to be utterly naked before the Master, only then will you be capable one day of facing your God. If you are capable of facing your Master you will certainly be able to face your God.

The third question:

Bhagwan,
What is it to meditate?

Amrito,

WHAT, AGAIN? Just the other day I was talking about meditation. Where have you been?—must have been fast asleep! In fact, whenever I talk about meditation, many of you go into sleep—you think you are going into meditation. You wake up only when I am telling a joke! Then I don't see a single person asleep.

Amrito, meditation is a member of the Tate family.

In a church bulletin the following was read:

"Do you know how many members of the Tate family belong to your parish? There is old man Dic Tate who wants to run everything, while Uncle Ro Tate tries to change everything. Their sister Agi Tate stirs up plenty of trouble, with help from her husband Irri Tate.

Whenever new projects are suggested, Hesi Tate and his wife Vege Tate want to wait until next year. Then there is Aunt Imi Tate who wants our church to be like. all others. Devas Tate provides the voice of doom, while Poten Tate wants to be a big shot.

But not all members of the family are bad. Brother Facili Tate is quite helpful in church matters. And a delightful, happy member of the family is Miss Felici Tate. Cousins Cogi Tate and Medi Tate always think things over and lend a helpful, steadying hand.

And, of course, there is the black sheep of the family, Ampu Tate, who has completely cut himself off from the church."

The last question:

Bhagwan,
I would like to know if there is anything that I should be serious about.

Atulyo,

EXCEPT MY JOKES, don't be serious about anything else. But about jokes I am not joking!

Having come from a small village, Giovanni had never seen a train in his life. So one day he decided to go and see one. Standing on the rail he heard the train whistle, "Tooo-tooo!" Before he knew what hit him, the train was upon him and knocked him off the rail. The last thing he could remember was flying through the air.

207

When he gained consciousness, Giovanni found himself laid up in the hospital for several months. During this time his wife used their accident insurance money to buy a well-equipped, modern flat in the city.

Once fully recovered, Giovanni went to his new home. His wife made a cake to celebrate his recovery and put the new kettle on the stove to make some coffee to go with the cake. As the water boiled, the kettle whispered, "Tooo-tooo!" Startled, Giovanni jumped up, rushed to the kitchen, grabbed the new kettle and smashed it on the floor, kicking it several times.

"What the hell are you doing?" cried out his wife.

"These things!" shouted Giovanni, "You've got to kill them while they're young!"

Atulyo, it is good that in the very beginning you have asked this question that "*I would like to know if there is anything that I should be serious about.*"

Only be serious about jokes; about everything else, from the very beginning, beware, don't get serious. Whatsoever I say, all the sutras have to be forgotten. And you have to forgive me for all the sutras. Just remember me for my jokes, but take them very seriously. They will help you immensely.

A drunk sat alone at one end of the bar watching the well-dressed playboy smoothly talking to one woman after another. Finally he slithered over to the man: "Hey, mister, how come you get to talk to all these women?"

"Well," said the man, "I have a special technique I figured out. It works every time. Look!"

They waited for a buxom redhead to walk by.

"Tickle your ass with a feather?" whispered the playboy.

The woman wheeled around, "What! What did you say to me?" she stormed.

"Particularly nice weather," said the man coolly. "Won't you join us for a drink?" The woman sat down and before she left the man had her phone number and a date.

Then a pretty brunette came along. Again the man said, "Tickle your ass with a feather?"

"I beg your pardon!" exclaimed the lady.

"Particularly nice weather!" cooed the man.

Charmed, the lady joined them for a while. When she left, Mr. Suave-and-Debonair said, "So you see how it works now?"

"Yeah, I get it," slobbered the drunk.

"Now you try it on the next broad," said the playboy.

So when a gorgeous blonde walked in, the drunk gathered up his courage and yelled, "Hey, lady, stick a feather up your ass?"

"What!" she raged. "What did you say?"

"Pretty fuckin' nice out, ain't it?" replied the drunk.

I know you are absolutely in a drunken state. Everything is upside down in you, everything is in a mess. You don't know what you are doing, why you are doing it. You don't know why you are here in the first place! But I know perfectly well why I am here and what I am doing. I am trying to wake you up—you are fast asleep.

Just take one thing seriously and that is to become more and more alert of your sleepiness. And all my efforts here, sutras or jokes, are nothing but means to wake you. Sometimes a joke can wake you up more easily than a serious sutra because listening to a serious sutra you tend to fall deeper into sleep; it is so serious that you can't be awakened by it. But a joke is so light that you don't want to miss it; you listen attentively.

And between the jokes I go on dropping a few dangerous things into your head—just small bombs, between the jokes! Just remember to take the jokes seriously and the remainder you leave to me; the remainder I will do. If you are just awake between two jokes, between the two jokes I am there to drop a bomb inside you which will explode sooner or later. And the moment it explodes you are finished!

NOW
HERE

The first question:

Bhagwan,
I am a judge. Have I any chance of ever enter-
ing nirvana? If your answer is no, then I can
change my profession; I can become a doctor. I
am also trained as a homeopath.

Jagdit Singh,

THERE IS NO RECORD of any judge ever entering nirvana. Just because of you, the whole night I had to
look in the Akashic records again! I could only find
one thing in them:

Satan and St. Peter decided to hold a soccer game in
paradise. It was to be hell versus heaven.

When everything had been arranged, St. Peter said to Satan, "Look, I can't be dishonest with you. There is no way that your side can win. All soccer players are simple, pure people and when they die, they all go to heaven. Heaven is full of soccer players."

"I thank you for your sincerity," replied Satan "but don't worry, we can defend outselves."

When St. Peter had left, Satan's secretary said, "St. Peter is right—we will lose the game. All the good soccer players go to heaven."

"Don't worry," said Satan. "Where do you think all the judges go?"

Jagdit Singh, changing your profession from judge to doctor is not going to help you either! About that also there is a reference in the Akashic records.

A doctor came to heaven's door. St. Peter looked at the guy, asked his profession and said, "Wrong door, son. Please go to hell."

The doctor was puzzled, looked very confused and said, "But I went there first and they said, 'Go to the other door.' "

"I know," said St. Peter, "they meant the back door."

"But why?" asked the doctor.

St. Peter said, "That is the entrance for the suppliers."

This is not going to help, Jagdit Singh. Why don't you become a sannyasin? Then there will be no need to bother about nirvana because you will enter it immediately. Then it will not be a question of tomorrow. You can look at my sannyasins. Nobody is worried about nirvana—they are already in it. To be a sannyasin means to be in nirvana. A sannyasin does not need to enter into nirvana; nirvana enters into him. Hence wherever he is nirvana is. You can throw him into hell, but he will be in nirvana; it will not make any difference at all. If your nirvana depends upon certain conditions it is not much of a nirvana.

Nirvana is a state of unconditional acceptance. Wherever you are, if you can accept your life with totality, with joy, with gratitude, if you can see your life as a gift, then nirvana is never a problem. The problem arises only because you don't accept your life, you reject life. And the moment you reject life you start looking for some other life and you become worried about whether it is going to be better than this life or not. It may be worse. That's what hell is: the fear of a worse life than this. And that is nirvana: the greed for a better life than this. But there is no other life; there is no hell, no heaven. Only fools are interested in such things.

But you being an Indian are brought up with the idea of a geographical concept of heaven somewhere above and hell somewhere below. In fact, there is no below and no above. Existence is unlimited, unbounded; there is no bottom to it and no roof either. Something can be above the roof of Buddha Hall—for example, this plane passing by; this is "above" the roof. You are below the roof and the ground, the floor, is below you and the earth is below the floor. But existence has no roof, no bottom; it is unbounded on all sides.

What Indian scriptures say about hell is nothing but talk about America! If right now you dig a hole wherever you are sitting here and go on digging you will reach to America, because the earth is round. But the Americans also think in the same geographical way, that hell is below. If they look into the hole, you will be in hell. You will think they are in hell and they will think you are in hell. And only my sannyasins will laugh at the whole affair. Who is above and who is below?

These heaven/hell concepts have nothing to do with geography or space, and they don't have anything to do with time either. So it is not a question of tomorrows, not a question of something after death; it is a question of understanding, it is a question of meditation, it is question of becoming utterly silent, herenow. There is no other space than the here and no other time than the now. These two words contain the whole existence: "now", "here".

Swami Rama Teertha used to tell a beautiful parable:

There was a great philosopher; he was an absolute atheist, continuously arguing against God. Twenty-four hours a day he was concerned with destroying the idea of God. Whosoever came to him he would try to convince.

On the wall of his sitting room in big letters he had written "God is nowhere" just to start an argument with anybody. Whosoever the visitor was he was bound to ask him, "What do you mean by writing this?" It was impossible to overlook it—such big, bold letters. The whole wall was covered with big letters: "God is nowhere." Everybody was bound to ask, "God is nowhere? What do you mean? Are you an atheist?" And that was enough to start the argument. And he was really very skillful at arguing.

Atheists are always more skillful as far as argumentation is concerned than the theists. Theists are believers; they are gullible people. Atheists believe in logic and nothing else, and logic knows only how to deny. Logic has no idea of how to say yes. The word "yes" does not exist in the logicians's mind, only "no".

Then a child was born to the great atheist, and the child was learning language. It was difficult for him to read the whole word "nowhere"; it was such a big word. One day he was trying to read "God is nowhere." Seeing that the word was too big, he divided it in two; he read instead "God is now here." "Nowhere" turned into "now here"! And he must have been in a certain beautiful space, in a certain silent space; he started thinking about now and here, he became interested in the phenomenon of now and here. "What is 'now'? What does it mean?" He had never experienced now and he had never experienced here.

And that is the case with millions of people in the world: they think of the yesterdays and the tomorrows; they never experience the now. They think of every other place; they never think, they never experience, they never taste what it means to be here.

This child opened some doors of the greatest mystery of life. The philosopher forgot about God, he forgot about arguing against God; his whole interest started revolving around now and here.

And there is only one way to know what is now and what is here, and that is meditation. One has to become utterly silent, because mind is always going either backwards or forwards; either it moves into memories or into imagination. It never stays here, it never remains in the now, for the simple reason that to be in the now means the death of the mind. It is afraid of the now, it is afraid of the present.

Slowly slowly he learned the art of being now and here. And the day he succeeded in being now and here he experienced God.

Jagdit Singh, my suggestion to you is forget about nirvana. Nirvana means something that will happen after this life—don't be concerned about it. Be concerned about this moment, because this is the only true moment there is, and enter into it. And that very entrance is the entrance into nirvana. And once you have found it, nobody can take it away from you.

Then you can remain a judge, you can become a doctor, you can be whatsoever you want to be; it does not matter. There are great stories . . .

One Chinese parable says:

Lao Tzu used to send his disciples to learn the art of meditation from a butcher. The disciples were very puzzled—why the butcher? And Lao Tzu would say, "You go and see. The man lives exactly the way one should live, always herenow. It does not matter what he is doing. He is not the doer at all; he is just a watcher, he is a witness. It is a role that he is playing —he is acting as a butcher."

And he was no ordinary butcher; he had been especially appointed by the Emperor of China to his own kitchen.

The Emperor asked Lao Tzu, "How to learn to be herenow?—because you are always talking about herenow."

Lao Tzu said, "You need not ask me; your butcher is the right person. Even I send many of my disciples to watch him."

The Emperor was shocked. He said, "My butcher! What does he know about it?"

Lao Tzu said, "You watch him work."

And the Emperor watched. And it was really a tremendously ecstatic experience even to watch him working. His instrument, his knife, was so sharp, so shining, as if it was absolutely new, as if he had brought it for the first time.

The King asked—he was very interested in weapons—he asked, "From where did you get this beautiful knife?"

He said, "This knife was given to me by my father who died forty years ago. For forty years I have been working with this knife, cutting animals with this knife."

"Forty years!" the King said. "And the knife looks so new, so fresh!"

The butcher said, "There is an art to it. If you are doing everything watchfully, alert, conscious, then no rust gathers—not only in you, not only on the inside, but even on the outside no rust gathers. I am fresh, my knife is fresh. I am young, my knife is young. And I am working as a meditation. This is just a role that I am playing."

A Zen master used to tell his disciples the story of a master thief who became enlightened . . .

So don't be worried about being a judge or a doctor—even a thief can become enlightened. The question is not what you do, the question is how you do it. The question is not about the act but the consciousness out of which that act arises.

This is one of the most famous Zen stories. I love it tremendously.

The thief was known as a master thief—no ordinary thief. Even the king respected him because never in his life was he caught. And everybody knew that he was the greatest thief in the country. In fact, his fame was such that people used to brag that "Last night the master thief entered our house," that "Our treasure has been stolen by the master thief." It was a privilege because the entry of the master thief meant you were really rich, because he would not go to any ordinary person, only kings and very rich people had the privilege of the master thief visiting them.

The thief was becoming old. His son said to him, "Now you are old and soon you will die. Teach me your art!"

The master thief said, "I was also thinking about it. But it is not an art, it is rather a knack. I cannot teach you, it cannot be taught, but it can be caught."

That's how religion is: it cannot be taught, it can only be caught. That's the difference between a teacher and a Master: the teacher teaches, the Master only makes himself available to be caught. You have to imbibe his spirit. If you only listen to his words you will miss him; if you start tasting his wine, only then will you understand him.

The thief said, "It is a knack; if you can catch it, I am ready to help you, I will make myself available to you. I had been wondering myself, but it is such a great skill—like poets, real thieves are born not made. But one never knows unless one tries. You come along with me tonight."

The son followed. The son was young, healthy, very strong. The old man was really old, more than eighty. The old man arrived at a rich house. He broke the wall, he removed the bricks—but the way he was doing it! And the young man was just watching, standing there and trembling. It was a cold night and the young man was perspiring and trembling. And he was so afraid: he was looking all around—somebody might be coming. "And what kind of man is my father? He is doing everything so silently, so gracefully, as if this was our own house! No hurry, no worry."

The father did not even look around even a single time. He entered the house, gestured to the son to follow. He followed trembling, perspiring, his whole body was just bathed in perspiration; it was flowing like water. He had never experienced this kind of perspiration even on hot summer days—and it was a cold winter night, ice cold! And the old man was moving in the house, in the darkness, as if he had always lived there. He didn't stumble against anything.

He reached inside the house, he opened the inner-most room. Then he opened a closet and told the son to enter the closet. The son entered the closet . . . and what the father did was unimaginable to the son. The father locked the closet—the son was inside!—shouted loudly, "Thief! Thief!" and escaped.

The whole house was awake, the neighborhood was awake. People rushed here and there; they look-ed all around inside the house. You can imagine the situation of the son! He thought, "This is the end. Finished! My father is mad! I should not have asked —this is not for me. He was right to say that thieves are born not made. But is this a way to teach? If I stay alive I will kill this old man! I will go home and cut his head off immediately!"

He was really angry—anybody would have been in his situation—but there was no point in being angry. Right now something had to done and he could not think of anything. The mind simply stopped.

That's what meditation is: the mind simply stops. It cannot figure out what it is all about, what to do, because all that it knows is useless; it has never been in such a situation before. And mind can only move again and again in the world of the known. Whenever anything unknown is encountered, mind stops. It is a machine. If you have not fed it the right information before, it cannot work, it cannot function.

Now this was such a new situation, the young man could not conceive what to do. There was nothing to do. And then a woman servant came with a candle in her hand looking around for the thief. A thief had cer-tainly entered the house: the wall was broken, the door had been opened—all the doors had been opened. The thief had entered the innermost room— he must be hiding somewhere.

She opened the closet door to look in—maybe he was hiding inside. She would not have opened the

TAO: THE GOLDEN GATE

door of the closet, but something happened inside the closet, which was why she opened it. She heard some noise, some scratching noise as if a rat were biting clothes. She opened the door to look for the rat really. This was the young man making this scratching noise, he was doing it. And it had come to him spontaneously, it was not out of the mind. Seeing somebody entering with a light . . . he could see that somebody was inside the room, he could hear the footsteps, he could see the light outside; suddenly it was not so dark. The only way to get the doors opened was to do something. What to do? Out of nowhere, intuitively —this is not out of intellect but out of intuition—he started scratching like a rat and the door was opened. The woman looked inside with her candle. Again, out of intuition, out of the moment, he blew out the candle, pushed the woman aside and ran away.

The people followed—almost a dozen people were following him carrying torches and lamps—and it was certain he would be caught. Suddenly he came across a well. He took a rock and threw the rock into the well, then stood by the side of a tree to watch what happened. It was all *happening*, he was not doing it. All the people surrounded the well—they thought the thief had jumped into the well. "Now there is no point in bothering about him on this cold night. In the morning we can see. If he is alive we will put him in the jail; if he is dead he is punished already." They went back.

The young man reached home. The father was fast asleep, snoring. He pulled his blanket aside and he said, "Are you mad or something?"

The father looked at him, smiled and said, "So you are back—that's enough! No need to tell the whole story. You are a born thief! From tomorrow you start on your own. You have caught the spirit of it. I am not mad—I gambled. Either you would be finished or you would come out of it proving that you have the intuitive insight—and you have come out of it. No need to bother me at this moment in the night. Go to sleep. In the morning, if you feel like telling me, you can tell me. But I know what has happened—if not the details, then the essence of it, and that's enough. That's my whole art, my son; you have learned it. And if I die tomorrow I will be dying happily because I will know I am leaving somebody who knows the art. This is how *my* father taught me—this is the only way. One has to risk."

Even a thief can become enlightened. Even a thief can live in the moment, can drop out of the mind.

So I am not too concerned about what you are doing. That's why I never ask anybody, "What profession do you belong to? What you are doing?" Whosoever comes to me to be initiated I initiate, irrespective of his profession. Sometimes people themselves say, "Bhagwan, before you initiate me let me tell you that I am a drunkard," that "I am a thief," that "I am a murderer"—this and that—that "I have just come out of the jail." I say to them, "Don't bother me with all these details. Whatsoever you have done in your sleep is all the same. Whether you have been virtuous or a sinner, whether you have been a saint or a devil incarnate, it does not matter."

Unconscious acts are unconscious acts; they are all the same. One man can dream that he is a sinner, a murderer; another can dream he is a great saint. In the morning both will find that they were dreaming—all dreams are the same. So don't bother me at all.

Not only that, people have taken sannnyas who are imprisoned. From their jails they write to me: "We are imprisoned for life. Can *we* become sannyasins?" I say, "Why not?—because everybody is imprisoned for life! A few are imprisoned outside, a few are imprisoned inside the prison; it is the same. You are in a smaller prison, others are in a bigger prison; it does not matter. But if you want to become a sannyasin, the only thing is you will have to learn the knack of being herenow. You can become a sannyasin."

There are many prisoners who have taken sannyas, from almost all countries. I have given them sannyas. Of course, they cannot wear orange; they write to me; "It is impossible because of the prison rules; we have to wear a certain dress." I say, "No need to worry about it."

One prisoner wrote to me from Germany: "I will carry an orange handkerchief; that much is possible. I will keep your mala in my pocket. I cannot wear it—it wouldn't be allowed." But I can understand; that's okay. He writes: "But I will meditate every day." And he has been meditating; for these two years he has been meditating regularly, again and again writing to me that "I am immensely happy. In fact, I feel it a great blessing that I have been imprisoned; if I was not imprisoned I may not have become your sannyasin. It is in the prison library that I came across one of your books."

Now the prison has become his door to nirvana.

Jagdit Singh, don't be worried. Don't be concerned about those Akashic records and the stories that I was telling you. There is no need to change your profession. If you want to change it there is no need to find any excuse, you can change it. You can become a doctor, you can become anything you want, but don't make it something great, don't make it an ego trip. But start meditating.

If you can take a jump into sannyas you will have proved yourself a man of courage. Then right now you will be in nirvana. And I believe in nirvana now or never!

The second question:

Bhagwan,

You are teaching us to believe in nothing. But why should I try to drop my ego without believing that life is better without an ego? Before I drop my ego I cannot know how life is without an ego. Therefore I have to believe that life is better without an ego before I try to drop the ego. But I can't believe it, because I suppose that life without an ego is life without a will of my own. The idea of giving up my own will is horrible to me. I cannot imagine that anybody would do this of his own free will, because my ego is all I have.

Bhagwan, please talk to us about this.

Bernd Schweiger.

IT HAPPENS ALL THE TIME that I say one thing and you understand something else for the simple reason that I am talking from a state of no-mind and you are listening *through* the mind. It is as if a person who is awake is talking to a person who is fast asleep. Yes, even in sleep you can hear a few words, fragments of words, maybe even fragments of sentences, but you will not be able to understand exactly what is being said to you. You are bound to misunderstand.

That is one of the problems faced by all those people who have experienced something of the beyond. The beyond cannot be put into words. It remains inexpressible for the simple reason that you can understand only that which you have experienced.

I am not saying drop the ego; that is impossible. Even if you want to drop it you cannot drop it. It is impossible because the ego does not exist. How can you drop something which does not exist? You can only drop something which exists in the first place. But the ego is a false phenomenon; nobody has ever been able to drop it.

Then what do I mean when I say learn the secret of being egoless? I do not mean that you have to drop it but that you have to understand it. There is no question of belief.

Now the whole question has come out of your misunderstanding, but you are making it look so logical that anybody looking at your question will think, "Of course, how can you drop the ego without believing that life will be better without the ego?" And I say don't believe in anything. I repeat again: don't believe in anything. I am not saying that you should believe me and become egoless, I am simply saying— sharing my own experience—that the more I tried to understand the ego the more I became aware that it is non-existential. When I became fully conscious of it, it disappeared.

It disappears of its own accord. You don't drop it. If you drop it, then who will drop it? Then the ego will survive; then it will be the ego dropping another ego, dropping the gross ego. And the gross is not dangerous, the subtle ego is more dangerous. Then you will become a pious egoist, you will become a humble egoist, you will become a spiritual egoist. Then you will become an "egoless" egoist. And that is getting into more trouble because that is getting into more contradictions.

All that I am saying to you is very simple. Try to understand what this ego is. Just look at it, watch it. Become aware of all its subtle ways, how it comes in. And there are moments when it is not—watch those moments also. Even *you* have those moments when it is not. It needs constant pedaling—it is like a bicycle. If you go on pedaling it, it can go on moving; if you stop pedaling it . . . how far can it go without pedaling? Maybe a few feet, maybe one furlong, two furlongs, but then it is bound to fall.

The ego needs to be constantly nourished. There are moments when you forget to nourish it and it disappears. For example, seeing a beautiful sunset it disappears because the sunset possesses you so totally. It is so beautiful, it is so extraordinary, so exquisite, it fills you with wonder and awe; for a moment you forget completely that you are, only the sunset is, and the clouds and the luminous colors on the clouds, and the birds coming back to their nests, and the day ending, entering into a silent night; as the sun starts disappearing below the horizon, something in you stops.

It happened to Ramakrishna—his first experience of egolessness. He was only thirteen. He was coming home from the field—he was a poor man's son and he lived in a small village. He was passing by the lake. A silent evening, the sunset, and there was nobody on the lake; his coming to the lake . . . There was a big crowd of white cranes sitting by the side of the lake. They suddenly flew up—it was so sudden, as if out of nowhere—and against the backdrop of a black cloud which was shining like velvet against the setting sun, those white cranes in a row flashed before his eyes like lightning. It was a moment, a tremendous moment!

He fell on the ground. He was so possessed by the beauty of it he became unconscious. He had to be carried home by others. After one hour somebody found him lying down there on the shore of the lake. It took six hours for him to be brought back to consciousness. When he came back to consciousness he started crying. And they asked, "Why are you crying? You should be happy—you have come back to consciousness."

He said, "No, I am crying because I have come back to the ordinary world. I was not unconscious. I had moved to a higher plane of consciousness, I had moved to some new plane. I don't know what it was, but *I* was not there and still there was great joy. I have never tasted such joy!"

That was his first experience, his first *satori*: a moment of egolessness. Then he started seeking and searching for it deliberately, consciously. He would go to the lake again and again in the morning, in the evening, in the night, and it started happening again and again more easily.

It happens to you too; it has happened to everybody. God comes to everybody. You may have forgotten him; he has not forgotten you—he cannot. It is not only that you are searching for him; he is also groping for you, he is also searching for you.

I am not telling you to drop the ego, I am telling you to understand it, to see it. Seeing it, it disappears. And see and become aware of those moments when it disappears of its own accord. Making love, it disappears. In a deep orgasm, it disappears; you melt, merge into existence. The wave again becomes the ocean; it is no more separate, it falls back into the ocean. It is only for a moment. Remain conscious of that moment and you will see the beauty of it. Once you have seen the beauty of egoless moments, then it will be easy for you to see the ugliness of the ego, the misery of the ego.

You need not believe me, I am simply inviting you to experience it. I am utterly against belief—belief is the cause of destroying religion on the earth. It is belief that has made religions false and pseudo.

Now listen to your question again, Schweiger.

You say: *Bhagwan, you are teaching us to believe in nothing.*

Absolutely true.

But why should I try to drop my ego . . .?

Who has said this? You must have heard it, that I can understand, but I have not said it.

A young man went to a sex therapist for advice about his staying power. "Ah yes, " said the therapist. "Premature ejaculation is quite a common problem for many young men. It is entirely due to overeagerness and there is a definite cure."

"What is that, doctor?" asked the young man.

"Next time you go to bed with a woman, imagine that you are about to eat a delicious meal in a gourmet restaurant. Imagine every aspect of the meal, from the soup to the coffee.

"Begin with the soup . . . imagine it steaming in the bowl . . . taste each spoonful. Next, order the wine, perhaps a rose . . . smell the bouquet of the wine, look at it sparkling with each sip. Imagine the main course . . . perhaps a mushroom-garnished steak with a baked potato, sour cream and chives and a fresh green salad. Eat it very slowly, tasting each bite. After the main course order dessert . . . perhaps a chocolate mousse or a pecan pie with whipped cream. And then . . . you are ready for your coffee . . . Brazilian, French roast, or maybe cappuccino. Then you can relax and feel the contentment of having enjoyed a very satisfying meal.

"By the time you have enjoyed such a banquet in your imagination your problem will disappear. You will have such an orgasm, such fulfillment—together!"

The young man thanked the therapist and went away, delighted. That same evening in bed with his woman friend, they began making love. So he started to fantasize. He pictured the restaurant in his mind, sat down at the table, and called out, "Hey, waiter, we'll have the tomato soup . . . and a cup of coffee!"

You may have heard it, but I have not said it!

You say: *Before I drop my ego I cannot know how life is without an ego.*

You have known it many times already. Nobody is so poor . . . I have never come across a man who has never known a few moments of it. Just try to remember. Or now, if you cannot remember, just try every day to watch. Soon you will be able to see a few moments which are without ego. Even this moment, if you are not too concerned about your question, this moment can be without ego; it is so for everybody else. It may not be for you because you will be so disturbed that I am destroying such a logical question of yours, that I am avoiding the real question, that I am trying to evade it, that I am not being logical. I never am, because what I am trying to indicate is basically supra-logical.

If you just try to listen to me as if this were not Schweiger's question but some other fool's—some idiot has asked this, not you—then even this moment can be of tremendous beauty and you can experience egolessness. And then you can compare. Only your own experience and comparison will make it possible for you to decide. Who am I to decide for you? I never decide for anybody else.

The third question:

Bhagwan,
I am going back to the West. Please tell me a few jokes about therapists.

Prem Elli,

[At this point there was a power failure and the lights went out in Buddha Hall.]

IT IS NIGHT . . . You see how miracles happen!

A therapist is walking down the street when a woman with a basket filled with flowers comes to him and says, "Do you want to buy flowers, sir?"

"No, thank you."

"But don't you want to take flowers to the woman you love?"

"Stop this, lady. I'm a married man!"

An old therapist visits another therapist. "Friend," he says, "I have a problem. I am eighty years old and I still run after young girls."

"Well, your case is quite common. It happens to almost everyone at your age," replies the other shrink.

"But, you see, I have forgotten why I'm after them!"

In his study a psychotherapist is laughing.

"What are you laughing at?" asks his wife.

"Oh, nothing special, dear. It is just that I love to tell jokes to myself, and this last one was new!"

And the last:

A very old shrink comes to a prostitute. They agree on the price and the old man starts undressing himself. He takes off his jacket, tie and shirt, and throws them all out of the window. As he holds his trousers in his hand, ready to throw them out of the window, the prostitute grabs him by the arm and says, "Why are you doing that? When we are finished you cannot go naked on the street!"

231

"Well," answers the old shrink, "you see, darling, by the time I come, these clothes will be out of fashion!"

The fourth question:

Bhagwan,
First a joke:

Two madmen went into a pub and while look-
ing around for a place to sit they saw
themselves in a big mirror on the opposite wall.
One madman said to the other, "Hey, look at
those two guys over there. They look so familiar
to me. Let's go over and say hello to them."
As they start moving, however, the other mad-
man says, "Never mind, they are already com-
ing to see us!"

This joke says a lot about how I have been feel-
ing since I started work two months ago. The
closer I come to you, the closer I come to myself,
and vice versa. Yet when I feel close to you
sometimes great fear arises. Could I be too
much afraid of love?
Please comment.

Prem Rajendra.

LOVE CERTAINLY CREATES GREAT FEAR because we have been brought up to hate, not to love. Our whole conditioning is against love, but the strategy is very subtle and very few people become aware of the phenomenon that we are brought up to hate. The Hindu hates the Mohammedan, the Mohammedan hates the Christian, the Christian hates the Jew. The religions all hate each other. The theist hates the atheist, the atheist hates the theist. All political ideologies are based on hatred. Communists hate fascists, fascists hate socialists. All nations are rooted in hatred; they all hate each other. This world is full of hatred. Your blood, your bones, your very marrow are full of hatred. Even if sometimes you seem to be united you are always united *against* something, against the common enemy, never otherwise. It is not a union of love.

Adolf Hitler was aware of this psychology. He writes in his autobiography, *Mein Kampf*, that people are not united because of love—love has no power; all power comes through hatred. Create hatred and they will become united. And I can fully understand his insight. He may have been a lunatic, but sometimes lunatics have great insights. This is a great insight into mob psychology.

He says in another place, "If you want your country to be ready and alert, always keep them full of the fear that they are going to be attacked, that the war is just knocking on the doors, that everybody surrounding the nation is your enemy. Whether they are enemies or not does not matter; if they are, good; if they are not, still, invent, propagate, that they are enemies. Only then will your country be united."

Hindus become united if there is a fear of the Mohammedans. Mohammedans become united if they are afriad that Hindus are going to attack. India becomes united if the fear arises that Pakistan is getting ready for war. Russia goes on piling up more and more atom bombs, hydrogen bombs and whatnot, just out of the fear that America is getting ready for war. And America goes on piling up the same atom bombs, hydrogen bombs, in the fear that Russia is getting ready for war. This whole world seems to live out of fear and hatred.

Love has been destroyed. For centuries, for thousands of years, your love has been paralyzed and poisoned, so whenever love arises in you, your whole conditioning goes against it; it creates trembling in you, it creates fear in you. If it is pseudo then there is no problem, you can manage. But if it is real, if it is authentic, then certainly you are going to be tremendously afraid of it, as if you are being thrown into a fire.

Something very strange has happened to man. Love is man's intrinsic nature and without love nobody ever grows, without love nobody ever blooms, flowers, without love nobody can ever feel fulfilled, contented. Without love there is no God. God is nothing but the ultimate experience of love. Hence, because your love is pseudo—and you can manage only pseudo love because it creates no fear in you—your God is also pseudo. The Christian God, the Hindu God, the Jewish God, these are all false gods. God cannot be Hindu and cannot be Christian and cannot be Jewish. Can love be Hindu? Can love be Christian? Can love be Jewish? But there are many books on "Christian love".

It seems that the whole earth has become a madhouse. Soon you will find books on Christian roses, Hindu marigolds, Buddhist lotuses. If love can be Christian, then why not roses? Everything that is false is manageable. Marriage is manageable, love is not. If you want to remain in control without any fear, than go on playing with toys; then real things are not for you.

But if you have come here, Rajendra, then all toys have to be broken. That's my whole work: to destroy all toys, to make you aware that you have played with toys your whole life, that you are not yet mature, you are still childish. And remember, to be childish is ugly; to be childlike is a totally different phenomenon. To be childish means to be retarded; then one goes on playing with toys, paper boats and sandcastles.

If one is really mature, integrated, then one is childlike, innocent, full of wonder and awe, sensitive to the beauty of existence, so sensitive that his whole life becomes an overflowing of love. You are surrounded by such a beautiful existence and if your heart does not dance with it you can't be said to be alive. You must be dead, you must be living a posthumous existence, you must be already in your grave. And I am trying to pull you out of your grave. I am calling to you, "Lazarus, come out of your grave!" And if you have lived for a long time in the grave . . . Graves are comfortable, very comfortable places; in fact, there is nothing more comfortable than the grave. Nothing ever happens in a grave, no fear, because there is no longer any death possible; no disease, no illness, no old age. You cannot be cheated, you cannot be deceived, you cannot be robbed, you cannot go bankrupt. You are safe, secure.

Life is insecure. Life basically is dangerous. And I teach you how to be alive, how to live dangerously, because that is the only way to live; there is no other way. If you want to live safely, comfortably, that simply means you are desiring death, you are suicidal, you are a coward, escapist.

Your feeling is true. You have come across something immensely significant. Now don't turn back.

You say: . . . *when I feel close to you sometimes great fear arises.*

Let it arise! That means the beginning of life. Accept it. Go through it. And it will not harm you; it will help you—it will make you stronger than ever. If you can go through the fear consciously, fear will disappear and you will come out of the fire of it purer, like pure gold.

Love is the death of the ego, hence the fear. The ego is very much afraid of going into love. It can pretend to, but it cannot go into love. It can come only up to a certain point; beyond that it becomes afraid. Then it starts shrinking back, turning back. Anybody who has ever been in love knows it.

And with me, of course, Rajendra, it is going to be far deeper than it can be with an ordinary love. The love between a disciple and the Master is the greatest love existence has ever known. It is trust, it is trusting the unknowable. It is going with a madman into the uncharted sea, leaving the shore behind where all the security was. Getting into a love relationship with a Master means in the worldly eyes going mad.

Jesus came once in the early morning to a lake. A fisherman has just thrown his net, the sun just on the horizon. A beautiful morning: the birds singing and the silent lake and the silence and the freshness . . . And Jesus put his hand on the shoulder of the fisherman. The fisherman looks back. For a moment no word is uttered by Jesus or by the fisherman. Jesus simply looks into his eyes: the man falls in love. Something has transpired.

Jesus says, "How long are you going to waste your life in catching fish? Come along with me! I will show you the way to catch God."

The man must have been of immense courage. He threw his net in the lake. He didn't even pull the net out. He followed Jesus without asking a single question, without asking, "Who are you and where are you leading me?"

The psychologists will say that he was hypnotized. If it is hypnosis, then it is available only to the very fortunate ones. It is not hypnosis. In fact, he was not hypnotized because the word "hypnosis" comes from a root which means sleep. He was awakened— he was asleep before. His whole life he was just catching fish; that was sleep. Now this man has stirred a new longing in him, a new desire; a new star has risen in his heart. He would like to go with this man. And without any question he followed him.

When they were just going outside the town, a man came running. He told the fisherman, "Where are you going? Have you gone mad? This man is mad! Come home! And, moreover, your father who was ill is dead so we have to make arrangements for his last rites and rituals."

For the first time the fisherman spoke to Jesus. He said, "Can I be allowed to go home just for three days to fulfill my duties as a son to my dead father?"

Jesus said, "Don't be worried. There are so many dead people in the town—they will take care of it. The dead will bury the dead. You come along with me. If you come with me then there is no going back. If you have chosen me then there is no going back. Come along with me!"

And the man followed. The person who had come to inform him stood there amazed. "What is happening? His father is dead and this man is following a madman!"

Jesus was known as being mad. Buddha was known as being mad. Mahavira was known as being mad. And in a way they look mad to people because their ways are so different, so diametrically opposite to the worldly people.

I am a madman and, Rajendra, you have come and fallen in love with me. There is no going back, fear or no fear. Gather courage! You have to come with me; the journey has already started. Even if you go back you will not find the old shore again. Even if you go back, those old toys will not be of any help anymore; you are finished with them, you will know they are toys. Now the real has to be found, has to be inquired into. And it is not very far away either—it is within you.

Falling in love with a Master means really falling in love with your ultimate nature, falling in love with your Tao. Hence your joke is beautiful.

Two madmen went into a pub and while looking around for a place to sit they saw themselves in a big mirror on the opposite wall. One madman said to the other, "Hey, look at those two guys over there. They look so familiar to me. Let's go over and say hello to them."

As they start moving, however, the other madman says, "Never mind, they are already coming to see us!"

The closer you come to me the closer you will be to yourself. The day you are dissolved in me you will be dissolved in yourself. I will disappear immediately. I am just a device, just an excuse to dissolve. Suddenly you will find yourself, you will discover yourself.

The function of the real Master is to help you to discover yourself, to help you to be yourself. And unless you are yourself you are not free and you cannot know what bliss is and you cannot know what truth is and you cannot know what God is.

The last question:

Bhagwan,
A Master
Surrendering to the birds!
Thanks for the lesson.

Prem Prabhati,

THE BIRDS are far more intelligent than the so-called people. The birds are never stupid—they cannot be, because they don't have schools, colleges, universities. The birds are never mediocre—they cannot be, because they are not part of any church, any religion, any sect, any belief, any dogma. They are free of all nonsense; they are very sensitive, they are not foolish. It is only man who falls from Tao.

The whole existence moves according to Tao, except man. And why does man fall?—for the simple reason that man is the only conscious being; it is his privilege to be conscious. Now, consciousness is a double-edged sword. If you use it rightly you will enjoy Tao far more deeply than any bird, than any tree, than any river, than any star. But if you are not conscious you will fall from Tao; you will be miserable— more miserable than any bird, than any tree, than any river, than any star.

The birds are not miserable—they cannot be, because they cannot go against Tao. They have no egos, they simply follow the Tao; it is a natural phenomenon. They cannot understand it, they cannot be conscious of it. Their bliss is unconscious.

Man is conscious, hence either he will be very miserable or he will be very consciously blissful. Either he will become an idiot or he will become a Buddha. And you have to choose between the two, you cannot simply remain in between. You cannot say, "Why can't I remain just like a bird or a flower or a river or a mountain?" You cannot. Either you will be an idiot or you will be a Buddha. Either you have to fall below nature or you have to rise above nature. The birds are really in a beautiful space. You can also be in the same space—and in a far better way, in a far deeper way.

Surrender to nature, that's the lesson. Surrendering to nature means surrendering to Tao.

You cannot believe that you can be Buddhas; because you are living such idiotic lives, it seems impossible. Even Jesus' parents could not believe, Buddha's father and wife could not believe, Mahavira's brother, wife, daughter could not believe that he'd attained. You are living such an idiotic life, in your darkness how can you conceive that there is a possibility of attaining light?

I have heard:

In 1912, after his inauguration, Woodrow Wilson visited an old deaf grand-aunt.

"What are you doing for a living now, Woodrow?" she asked.

"I'm President," he bellowed into her earhorn.

"President of what?"

"President of the United States!"

"Woodrow, don't be silly!"

She cannot believe that this Woodrow can be the President of the United States. But this is not something special—anybody can be the President of the United States. But if Woodrow had said "I have become Jesus Christ!" then she would have really laughed. She would not have even said, "You are silly"; she would have said, "You have gone mad! You just see a psychotherapist or get yourself admitted to a mad asylum. What nonsense you are talking!"

Birds are intelligent people. And here in this Buddhafield they become more and more full of the vibe that sometimes you miss; they go on drinking it. They are not aware, certainly, but they drink to the full.

A family was moving from one house to another in a small city in the interior of Brazil. They were moving by bullock cart. All the furniture was piled high and tied with ropes. On the very top was the parrot in his cage.

As the cart moved along the rough road it occasionally hit a hole in the road. Each time a hole was hit, the parrot's cage fell off and someone would rush to pick it up. Then the cage was placed back on top of the huge pile of furniture.

By the fifth fall, the parrot was very irritated. When he fell again the sixth time he exclaimed in frustration, while frantically arranging his feathers, "Look . . . do something! Give me the fucking address and I'll walk there!"

THE VENERABLE MASTER SAID:

When man attains the power to transcend that which changes, abiding in purity and stillness, heaven and earth are united in him.

The soul of man loves purity, but his mind is often rebellious. The mind of man loves stillness, but his desires draw him into activity. When a man is constantly able to govern his desires, his mind becomes spontaneously still. When the mind is unclouded, the soul is seen to be pure. Then, with certainty the six desires will cease to be begotten and the three poisons will be eliminated and dissolved.

The reason men do not possess the ability to achieve this is because their minds are not clear and their desires are unrestrained.

He who has the power to transcend his desires, looking within and contemplating mind, realizes that in his mind, mind is not; looking without and contemplating form, he realizes that in form, form is not; looking at things still more remote and contemplating matter, he realizes that in matter, matter is not.

TAO
TAKES
CARE

TAO BELIEVES IN SPONTANEITY—not in cultivating virtues, not in creating a character, not even in conscience but only in consciousness. Character, discipline, conscience, they are all ego efforts, and ego is against Tao. Tao is a state of let-go: to be in tune with

243

existence with such totality that there is no separation at all. You are not even the part, you are the whole. You are not the wave but the ocean itself. Hence there is no question of doing. Tao means being.

All other so-called religions insist on doing. They believe in commandments: "Do this, don't do that." They have many shoulds and should nots. The Buddhist scriptures have thirty-three thousand rules for a monk; even to remember them is impossible. People forget even what the Ten Commandments are—how can they remember thirty-three thousand rules? Their whole life will be wasted only in remembering them. When are they going to cultivate these rules? It will take millions of lives.

Maybe because of this the idea of many many lives became so significant in the East, because time is needed to cultivate. One life is not enough—even a thousand lives will not be enough—you need millions of lives to cultivate all this. In fact, the whole approach helps you to go on postponing. The tomorrow becomes bigger and bigger, almost infinite, and the today is so small that you can deceive yourself, you can say to yourself, "Let me remain whatsoever I am today; tomorrow I will change. And today, anyway, is so small, nothing much is possible. I will start tomorrow." Of course the tomorrow never comes; it is there only in the imagination.

Tao believes in this moment; Tao has no idea of future. If you can live this moment in purity, in silence, in spontaneity, then your life is transformed. Not that *you* transform it: Tao transforms it, the whole transforms it. You simply allow the river to take you to the ocean; you need not push the river.

But when such great truths are put into language, difficulties arise beause our language is made by us. It is not made by people like Lao Tzu, Chuang Tzu, Lieh Tzu, Ko Hsuan, it is made by the mediocre people the world is full of. Obviously, language is their invention and it carries their meanings, their attitudes towards life. So whatsoever you say is going to be somewhere inadequate—not only inadequate but deep down wrong also.

This has to be remembered, and even more so about these sutras because these sutras were written originally in Chinese. Chinese is a language totally different from any other language, it is the most difficult language in the world for the simple reason that it has no alphabet, it is a pictorial language. Pictorial languages are the most ancient languages; they must have come from the very dawn of human consciousness, because when man is a child he thinks in pictures, he cannot think in words, so his language is pictorial. That's why in children's books there are so many colored pictures; the text is not much but pictures are many. The child is not interested in the text, he is interested in the pictures. Looking at the picture of the mango, a very juicy colorful mango, he may become interested to know what it is called, how it is written, and he may read the text—only a few words about the mango. Slowly slowly the mango disappears, giving place to language. In the university books pictures disappear completely. The more scholarly a book is, the less is the possibility of pictures; all is language. In your sleep you still dream not in a linguistic way but in a pictorial way because in your sleep you again become a child.

Chinese is a dream language—and we know the difficulty with the dreams. You have dreamed something, but in the morning you cannot figure out what it means. You will need an expert to interpret it, and even experts won't agree. The Freudian will say one thing, the Jungian will say something else, the Adlerian may say just the opposite. And now there are many more new trends, new schools of psychoanalysis, and they all have their interpretations. And whomsoever you are reading will look valid, reasonable, because they can all provide great rationalizations. The dream is yours, but you don't know what it means because a dream can mean many things; a dream is multi-dimensional.

And that's the difficulty with the Chinese language: it is a dream language, a pictorial language—each picture can mean many things. Hence there are translations of Chinese scriptures, many translations, and no two translations ever agree, because a picture can be interpreted in as many ways as there are people to interpret it. The Chinese language is only symbolic; it indicates. It is very poetic, it is not like arithmetic.

If you remember this, only then will you not fall into the trap in which almost all the scholars have fallen.

These sutras were not written in an alphabetical language so whatsoever is being said in these sutras is an interpretation. And I myself don't agree in many places; if *I* were to translate it it would be a totally different translation. I will tell you where I differ and why.

THE VENERABLE MASTER SAID:

When man attains the power to transcend that which changes . . . heaven and earth are united in him.

The first thing that's absolutely wrong is the idea of attainment. Tao does not believe that you have to attain anything or that you *can* attain anything. You are already that which you can be: nothing more can be attained. The very idea of attainment, of achievement is alien to the Taoist approach. There is nothing to attain, nothing to achieve. The idea of attainment and achievement is rooted in our egos. The ego is always ambitious; it can't be otherwise. Either it has to attain worldly things or it, has to attain other-worldly powers, *siddhis*, but something has to be attained. The ego lives by attaining.

And Tao says the ego has to be dissolved, you cannot be allowed to be ambitious—to be ambitious is to go against Tao. Tao teaches non-ambitiousness. You have just to be yourself as you are. You are already perfect; you have never left your perfection for a single moment. You are already in Tao; it is just that you have started dreaming that you have lost it, that you have gone far away.

It is just like as in your sleep you remain in your room, in your bed, but you can dream of faraway places. You can visit the moon and Mars, you can go to the stars, but in the morning you will find you have not left your bed, not even for a single moment.

When one becomes conscious one becomes aware of the whole ridiculousness of all the achievements and failures. It is the idea of achievement that brings failure, frustration in its wake. If you succeed it brings ego. Ego is misery because the more ego you have the more you think that you are separate from the whole, that you have become somebody special, unique, superior, higher, holier, that you don't belong to the ordinary world, that you are a saint, a mahatma. If you fail, then there is frustration; that brings pain, that brings anguish. Whatsoever happens, success or failure, you will suffer. Ego brings suffering; whether it succeeds or fails makes no difference. Hence with the Taoist approach this idea of attainment is totally wrong—remember it.

The translator says:

When man attains the power . . .

Again the word "power" is not right because Tao does not believe in power. It believes, really, in utter powerlessness, because when you are powerful you are fighting against the whole. Adolf Hitler is powerful, Alexander the Great is powerful, Ivan the Terrible is powerful; Genghis Khan, Tamburlaine, these are powerful people, but they are fighting against nature, spontaneity.

Jesus is not powerful, Jesus is utterly powerless. When Jesus was crucified his disciples were waiting: "Now is the time he will show his power." The enemies were waiting, the friends were waiting for the same thing: "Now he is going to show his miraculous power, now he will prove that he is the only begotten son of God." He didn't prove anything, he simply died. He died like any mortal—he died like the two thieves who were crucified with him. He was just in the middle; on either side of him there was a thief. The enemies were frustrated, the friends were frustrated even more. What happened? Where had his power gone? And he was always talking about being the son of God . . . But to be the son of God simply means to be utterly powerless.

How we go on misunderstanding people like Jesus, Lao Tzu, Ko Hsuan! Our misunderstanding is almost infinite. He surrendered to God. Yes, for a moment he himself had become aware of all the expectations. Almost one-hundred thousand people had gathered to see; friends were very few. He must have seen the expectation in people's eyes—they were expecting miracles. Great things were going to happen—something that only happens once in thousands of years. For a moment he may have been impressed, hypnotized by so much attention, by so much expectation. The whole atmosphere must have been charged with only one desire: to see his power.

And he asked God, "Have you forsaken me?" But then immediately he understood—he was a man of intelligence, tremendous intelligence. Immediately he understood that whatsoever he has said is wrong. How can God forsake him? The very idea that God can forsake him is negative, is ugly; it is not trust.

If God shows miracles, then it is very easy to trust. If he is proving your power then it is very easy to trust; anybody will be able to trust. No intelligence is needed to trust, no special understanding is needed to trust; any fool would have trusted.

But nothing was happening and the last moment has arrived. Jesus immediately understood the point —this is the time to understand. He surrendered. He said: Thy kingdom come, thy will be done. Don't listen to me, you simply go on doing whatsoever you want to do. Who am I to suggest? I am no more, I am in your hands.

This was real powerlessness. This is Tao. Ko Hsuan would have understood it; the Jews could not understand it. And the whole gathering was of Jews, friends or enemies. And they had always believed in achievement, in power, in ambition—all their prophets had been doing miracles. If they were angry with Jesus the reason was that he was not coming up to the mark: he was not proving himself to be really a prophet, because the ancient prophets had done so many miracles.

And my feeling is that he never did any miracles. If he had done any miracles, all the Jews would have converted; they would not have crucified him. It is enough proof that he never did any miracles. And all the miracles that are propounded by the Christians are invented. These Christians are also of the same mind, the same desire, the same ambition: "How can Our Lord be without miracles? If ordinary prophets were doing so many things, how can Our Lord be without miracles?" So they have invented even better miracles, greater miracles than those of all the prophets.

But my feeling is that Jesus was a man of Tao. He was really a man who can be called religious.

I have heard a beautiful story. It is not recorded anywhere. It must have gone from one Master to another, just by word of mouth: that Moses, Abraham, Ezekiel, three ancient prophets, were sitting under a tree in heaven talking about great things, talking about the Old Testament. Then suddenly Abraham said, "We know everything about the Old Testament. Had Jesus been here he would have told us something about the New Testament."

Moses laughed and he called a boy who was sitting just by the side of the tree and said, "Jesus, please go and bring three cups of coffee for us."

Abraham was shocked. This is Jesus? And Jesus went to bring three cups of coffee for the old prophets.

But I love this story. Only Jesus can do that—so utterly powerless. His powerlessness is his miracle: he has annihilated himself totally. They were not even aware of his presence, that he is sitting by the side of the tree. He didn't say a single word: that "I am Jesus Christ, the only begotten son of God. And what are you saying? I should go and bring three cups of coffee for you? You go yourself! Is this the way to talk to the son of God?" But he simply went.

Only Jesus can do it, or Lao Tzu or Ko Hsuan or Bodhidharma or Basho. These are people who have dropped the whole power trip, the whole number.

Ko Hsuan cannot mean what the translation will create in your mind. It says:

*When man attains the power to transcend
that which changes . . .*

No. If I were to translate it . . . I don't know Chinese at
all, but who cares? I can still translate, not knowing a
single word of Chinese, because I know the spirit of
Tao; that's my experience. If I were to translate it, I
would say;

*When man surrenders to the power of Tao, he
transcends that which changes.*

When man becomes utterly powerless as a separate
entity, then he transcends that which changes. Then
he abides in purity and stillness. Then the purity that
comes to him is not something cultivated from the
outside.

It is not something that you have to maintain continuously, that you have to guard because otherwise
you will lose it . . . Your saints are continuously on
guard. They know perfectly well that even if they are
relaxed for a single moment they will lose all their
purity. They don't abide in it, it is not natural to them,
it is something artificial, arbitrary; they have imposed
it on themselves.

You don't need to *breathe*, you need not remember
to breathe; otherwise you would have been dead long
before now, because any time you forget about
breathing—a beautiful woman passes by and you
forget about breathing—and finished! There is the full
point. Then you cannot breathe again. But breathing
continues even while you are asleep—not only while
you are deeply asleep, even if you are in a coma
breathing continues; it does not depend on you.

Once I went to see a woman . . . Her husband loved
me very much. He came crying and weeping and he

251

said, "This was my wife's last wish, that she wanted to see you. But for nine months she has been in a coma and the doctors say there is no possibility that she will ever become conscious. But please come with me just to fulfill her last desire. That was her last desire before she became unconscious."

So I went to see the woman. For nine months she had been in a coma, but she was breathing perfectly. To be in a coma means to be almost dead. And she died after three months; after remaining one year in a coma she died. But for one year she continued to breathe; her breathing was perfect, there was no disturbance in it.

Tao takes care of your breathing; it is natural. Your blood circulates continuously, day in, day out, year in, year out. For centuries man used to think that there was no circulation of the blood in the body; blood simply filled the body as water filled a pot. It is only three hundred years ago that it was discovered that blood did not just fill the body; it continuously circulates, it goes on circulating at a very great speed. That keeps your inner world alive, dynamic. Who is circulating your blood?—certainly not you, otherwise you might forget it. Who digests your food?—certainly not you. In fact, if you become very conscious of digestion you will disturb your stomach.

Try a simple experiment for twenty-four hours: when you are eating just become conscious that the food is going into the stomach; now you have to digest it. And troubles will start: you will feel heavy and you will not know what to do, how to digest it. Just remain conscious that the food is in the stomach and it has to be digested, and you are almost incapable of doing anything. Do a few yoga exercises, stand on your head, jog, jump, and within twenty-four hours you will have a bad stomach; you will have disturbed the whole process. It does not need you at all. Once the food has gone below your throat you need not bother about it; Tao takes care of it.

All that is essential is natural, and to live your whole life in a natural way is the only teaching of Tao. It teaches you powerlessness, but there is great power in powerlessness—the power of God, the power of the whole, not your power, not my power, not anybody's power.

Then there arises a purity in you. You are not the author of it, you are not the architect of it; you are simply a witness, a watcher. And there arises a tremendous stillness, not something forced from the outside. That's what your so-called religious people are doing all over the world: they are *forcing* purity. And whenever you force purity on yourself, whenever it becomes a cultivated phenomenon, it is repression and nothing else. And repression only creates ugliness; it creates a split in you, it makes you schizophrenic.

One priest invites another priest to lunch at his house. At the end of the meal, the guest, who is slightly drunk, notices how pretty the maid is.

He turns to his colleague and says, "You are an old friend, you can tell me—do you sleep with the girl?"

The host is very angry. "How dare you speak like this in my house?" he cries. "Please leave immediately!"

After his friend has gone, the priest notices that a beautiful silver spoon has disappeared, so the following morning he sends his friend a note saying, "My dear holy friend, I am not saying that you are a thief, but if you find my silver spoon, please send it back!"

The answer comes quickly:

"My dear holy friend, I am not saying that you are a liar, but if you had slept in your own bed last night, you would have found your silver spoon!"

All cultivated purity creates hypocrisy, it creates a duality in you. It is bound to create it because you have not understood; you have simply denied something. It has not disappeared; it is there waiting to take revenge. And it will find its own way—it will come from the back door. If you don't allow it to come from the front door it will come from the back door.

Tao does not believe in any cultivated character; it believes in a natural purity, in a natural stillness. You must have watched how if you try to become silent then each and every thing becomes a disturbance, a distraction. Just a dog barking, who is not at all aware that you are trying to meditate, who has nothing against meditation, who is not an old enemy, who is not taking any revenge on you for some past karma . . . He is enjoying his barking; that is his meditation. Maybe he is doing Dynamic Meditation! He seems to be more modern and up to date than you—you are doing vipassana and he is doing Dynamic! But you will be disturbed. He is not disturbed by your vipassana and you are disturbed by his Dynamic Meditation for the simple reason that you are forcing something; it is not natural. It is just a very thin layer of stillness that somehow you have painted upon yourself. Deep down a thousand and one dogs are barking, and they immediately understand the dog barking and they start feeling a great urge to bark. The distraction comes from your inner dogs, it is not coming from the outer dog; the outer dog is not responsible at all. If your silence is natural, the dog's barking will not be a distraction; it may even enhance your stillness, it may become a background to your stillness. That's how it happens.

When in the night you see the stars, beautiful stars, have you ever thought what happens to these stars in the day? They don't go away—where can they go? They are there, but because the background is no more there, the darkness is no more there, you cannot see them. In the night the darkness functions as a background: the darker the night, the more shining are the stars. They are not so shining on a full-moon night, but when there is no moon at all the stars are really beautiful.

The same is true about a real silence: everything that ordinarily proves a distraction becomes a background. The dog barking, the traffic noise, somebody shouting, children crying, running, the wife cooking food in the kitchen—everything becomes a background and everything deepens your silence because you are not concentrating, you are not forcing anything; you are simply relaxed. Things go on happening, you remain untouched; you remain absolutely centered, and effortlessly centered.

This thing has to be remembered: Tao teaches you effortless naturalness; it does not believe in effort as Yoga does. Yoga and Tao are totally opposite to each other. That's why Yoga could not penetrate China. Buddha impressed China for the simple reason that he also says that you should be natural, that your meditation should be effortless, that it should not be imposed from the outside, that it should arise from your innermost core. It should not be a plastic flower, it should be a real rose.

When man attains the power to transcend that which changes, abiding in purity and stillness, heaven and earth are united in him.

That's what I call the meeting of the East and the West, the meeting of materialism and spiritualism. That's my idea of Zorba the Buddha: *Heaven and earth are united in him.*

Tao is not other-worldly like Jainism; it is not this-worldly either like Charvakas. It believes in the unity of existence; it does not divide existence in any way.

Its whole vision is that of total unity, organic unity. Heaven and earth are one; in you they are already meeting. Your body is part of the earth, your soul is part of heaven. The meeting is already happening— you are not aware of it. If you relax you will become aware of it, and the meeting is tremendously beautiful. Earth alone is dead. That's why a materialist philosophy of life sooner or later comes to realize that life is meaningless.

That's what has happened in the West. All great thinkers of this century in the West are obsessed only with one problem: the meaning of life. And they all agree on one point at least: that life is meaningless.

In Dostoevsky's famous novel, one of the most important novels ever written . . . If I am asked to name the ten best novels in the world, then this will be one of those ten—not only one of them but the first of those ten: *The Brothers Karamazov*. It is one of the greatest creations.

In *The Brothers Karamazov* one of the characters says to God, "Where are you? I want to meet you— not that I am interested in seeing you, not that I want to know about you; I simply want to give you back the ticket that you gave me to enter into this world. Please take it back! This whole world is absolutely meaningless."

Marcel says in one of his writings that suicide seems to be the most important metaphysical problem. If life is meaningless then of course suicide seems to be the most important metaphysical problem. Why go on living? In the past people used to think that it was only cowards who commit suicide; now the pendulum seems to have moved to the other extreme. The materialists are feeling so meaningless that the idea is arising slowly and gathering force that it is only cowards who go on living; it is the brave people who try to commit suicide. Why go on living if there is no meaning?

But this has happened because only earth was accepted, not the sky, not heaven. Earth is meaningless, barren; without the sky there is no soul—you are just a body, a corpse. And what meaning can a corpse have? When the soul leaves the body, meaning has left the body. And if you don't believe in the soul then you are bound to feel sooner or later that life has no meaning. The West is feeling this great meaninglessness.

And the East believed only in heaven, only in the soul, but that is an abstraction. The body is concrete, the soul is only an abstraction; it is intangible. And when you start running after intangibles, after invisibles, you lose track of all that is concrete. That's why the East is poor, starving, ill, burdened with thousands of problems and seems to have no way of solving them for the simple reason that for centuries we have never bothered about the earth; our eyes were fixed on the sky.

An ancient Greek parable says:

One very famous astrologer was looking at the sky in the night, watching the stars, studying the stars. He lost his way, naturally, because he was not looking at the earth where he was walking, and he fell in a well. Then he became aware, but then it was too late. He started shouting, "Save me!" He was outside the village.

An old woman who lived nearby somehow managed to save him. When he came out he told the woman, "You may not know me, you may not recognize me in this dark night, but I will tell you who I am: I am the king's special astrologer! It is very difficult for people even to approach me, but you can come to me. I will tell you about your future.''

The old woman laughed. She said, "You fool! You don't know even where is the well and where is the road, and you will tell me about my future!"

That's what has happened in the East: the East has fallen into the well, lost track of the concrete, become too metaphysical.

Tao seems to be the only life vision which is total. It does not deny the earth, it does not deny the sky. It accepts both, it accepts the unity of both. It says: The man who has come to know spontaneous purity and stillness, who has become relaxed with the whole, with the law of the ultimate—in him heaven and earth are united.

That's my concept of a sannyasin too. In you I would like this meeting to happen. You will be misunderstood all over the world: in the East people will think you are materialist, in the West people will think you have become metaphysical. That means you have gone crazy, berserk, that you are talking mumbo-jumbo. They will say, "Stop all this nonsense! Be realistic, Be pragmatic." You will be misunderstood everywhere because the East has believed only in half and the West has believed in half.

I believe in the whole. To me to trust the whole is the only way to be holy, and to trust the whole is the only way to be whole. And when you are whole, life is bliss, life is benediction, life is a celebration.

The soul of man loves purity . . . but his desires draw him into activity.

Man has three layers; those three layers have to be understood. The first, the deepest core, is the soul; the soul means your center of being. And the outermost circumference consists of desires. And between the two is another concentric circle, half way from both, from the outer and from the inner. It is neither outer nor inner—that is your mind.

The soul of man loves purity . . .

By purity Ko Hsuan always means innocence, so don't misunderstand it with any moralistic meaning of purity because Tao does not believe in any morality or any immorality: only innocence. That's why the child is innocent, because when he is born he is just the intrinsic center; the two circles have not yet gathered around the center. That's why every child looks so beautiful. Have you ever come across an ugly child? It is impossible. And what happens to all the beautiful children?—because if all children are beautiful then all people should be beautiful because these same children become grown up people. But somewhere on the way they all disappear; something ugly sets in. We give them wrong circumferences; we give them wrong minds, wrong desires. We create such a dichotomy in their being that they become a crowd, not a unity. They are no more integrated beings; they become fragments. And to be fragmentary is to be ugly because you lose all harmony, and without harmony there is no beauty, no grace.

The soul of man loves purity . . .

If you reach to your innermost core you will suddenly find innocence arising in you, roses of innocence flowering.

. . . but his mind is often rebellious.

But the mind is not willing just to be innocent. Innocence says yes, it is trust; the mind says no, it is doubt. The mind always lives through the no, it is negative; the soul is always positive. The soul has no idea of saying no, it knows nothing about the no; and the mind knows nothing about the yes. If the mind sometimes has to say yes, it only says it unwillingly. You can watch it in yourself: whenever your mind says yes it says it unwillingly because it cannot find any way of saying no, that's why it says yes. Yes is not spontaneous for the mind; no is spontaneous.

Watch the truth of this statement. These are not theories, hypotheses, these are simple facts. You can just watch it in yourself: the first thing that happens to your mind is no; it immediately says no—even if there is no reason to say no.

Just the other day I received a letter from a sannyasin: "Bhagwan, when you talked about Prem Chinmaya's coming back, his dying from the sixth center and that he will have to live only one more life, I cannot believe you or trust you."

You may not know anything about reincarnation; you can simply say, "I don't know about it, so how can I believe or disbelieve?" You can remain open. But you will not miss any oportunity of saying no. Now, this sannyasin must be waiting for something to say no to. Do you know what it means to die from the sixth center? Have you any idea of the inner physiology of man?

Ask Puja and Sheela what happened when Chinmaya died. They were surprised—they could not believe what was happening: his whole body became cool, his head became very hot. He complained also that something strange was happening ". . . as if my whole energy is coming into the head. My body is cool and calm, but my head is feeling almost as if it is on fire."

Whenever the soul leaves the body, the center that becomes its leaving center becomes hot—naturally, because the whole energy concentrates there. The energy that is spread all over the body gathers together at one point; that point certainly becomes absolute fire.

You don't know anything about the inner physiology. If you don't know, I am not telling you to believe in it—I am the last person to tell you to believe in anything—but there is no need to say no either; you can simply remain open, you can say, "I will see what happens when I die."

And then he says, "I don't believe you, I don't trust you. Does it matter?" To me it does not matter, not at all, because I don't depend on your belief, but it matters immensely for you. I am not saying force yourself to say yes to me, because a forced yes will be only a disguised no, I am simply saying being here be open. There is no need to say yes or no, you can simply say, "I don't know." Function out of a state of not-knowing so that you remain available to experiment, to experience. If you say no you have become closed, and yes you can say only when you have experienced. So I am not asking you to believe in it, but I will certainly request you not to disbelieve. There is no need for belief and no need for disbelief. But this sannyasin's mind must have been waiting for some opportunity.

It is very rare here because I don't talk about things which you will find difficult to believe—I rarely talk about things which are beyond you, I leave them; I prepare you so that you can experience them one day. But once in a while something happens. For example, Prem Chinmaya's death was such an occasion that I had to say something about death, something about which center he died from. I had to say this, that he will be back here soon. And these things are not

261

beyond your comprehension if you are going deep into meditation, but if you are not going into deep meditation they are beyond comprehension.

The mind wants to say no and if you listen to the mind you stop listening to the Master. If you want to listen to the Master, first you have to be open so that one day yes can surface in you spontaneously. It matters much as far as you are concerned.

Being here and saying no in some way simply means you will be physically here and spiritually absent. It will be a sheer waste of your time; then there is no need to be here.

The whole effort of this Buddhafield, the whole purpose of it, is to help you to go beyond mind, to go beyond no.

Ko Hsuan's sutra says:

> *The soul of man loves purity, but his mind is often rebellious. The mind of man loves stillness, but his desires draw him into activity.*

The soul loves purity, innocence; that's its natural joy. The mind is not interested in purity, in innocence, because innocence needs yes as a foundation and mind lives through no. But because the mind continuously says no it has to suffer much turmoil, hence there is a great need in the mind to be still, to be silent, to be calm and quiet.

> *The mind of man loves stillness . . .*

But then there is another outer circle in your being—the circle of desires which don't even allow you silence; they drag you into activity. The mind drags you into no's, into negativity; that disturbs your purity. Yes is your innocence, no means you have lost your innocence. Then there are desires which don't leave you at the mind, they want some activity; just no won't do. They drag you into a thousand and one activities—the Chinese expression is into "ten thousand things"; they keep you constantly occupied—money, power, prestige; they go on goading you, "Do this. Achieve this. Without achieving this you are not a real man. Prove that you are powerful, prove that you are great, prove that you are special." And to prove it you have to move almost into a state of insanity. That's what politics is.

Politics is the other pole, exactly the opposite pole to religion. Religion takes you to the essence of your being and politics takes you to the accidents of your desires. The desires keep you so occupied with the mundane, with the futile, that you start forgetting everything that is intrinsic, that is really valuable. Running after money, you forget all about the inner treasure. Running after power, you forget all about the power of Tao, which is the supreme power. Running after name and fame, you forget completely that name and fame are just momentary. But they go on goading you; they won't leave you for a single moment. In the night you will dream about desires, in the day you will run after desires. And all desires are mirages, like the horizon that looks so close that if you just go, within an hour you will be able to reach it. But you never reach it because it does not really exist.

You go on forgetting everything: you forget the soul, the heaven; you even forget the body, the earth. You become almost mad. All your politicians are mad. All your people who are running after money are mad, who are running after fame are mad. But because they are in the majority, they appear to be absolutely right. In fact, the person who is not interested in name and fame, power and prestige seems to be a little out of his senses. What has happened to this man?

You will be asked again and again, "What has happened to you? Why are you not interested in accumulating more money? What do you do just by sit-

ting silently looking inwards?" You will be condemned by the world because the world consists of
extroverts. They will call you introverts, they will tell
you that introversion is a kind of perversion, they will
tell you that you are selfish, that you are narcissistic,
that you are only interested in your own joy, that you
should be concerned with others, that you should live
like everybody else, that you should be part of the
crowd. Of course, they are many and you will be very
alone.

Jesus has said to his disciples, "I am sending you
amongst wolves." And I know what he means. When
I send you into the world I also know I am sending
you amongst wolves. You are trying to be silent, innocent, childlike, and the world is trying to achieve just
the opposite ends.

*When a man is constantly able to govern his
desires, his mind becomes spontaneously still.*

Again wrong words have been used.

*When a man is constantly able to govern his
desires . . .*

No, Ko Hsuan cannot say "to govern his desires"
because that means repression, that means control. He
can only say:

When a man is constantly able to understand *his
desires, his mind becomes spontaneously still.*

Only understanding is needed; nothing else ever
helps. If you understand a desire it disappears. Desires
are like darkness: you bring light and darkness disappears. You need not throw it out, you need not
repress it, you need not close doors to keep it
out—you cannot do anything directly with darkness-
—you just have to bring light in. A small candle will
do, and all darkness disappears. Just a little light of

understanding and desires start disappearing. Then arises spontaneous stillness.

Remember this word "spontaneous"; that is the key word as far as Tao is concerned.

When the mind is unclouded, the soul is seen to be pure.

And when there are no desires, thoughts automatically disappear, because thoughts are servants of desires. When there are desires, your mind is full of thoughts, full of plans—what to do, how to do, how to fulfill these desires. When desires disappear you have cut the tree from the very root. Then leaves start disappearing, branches disappear, the tree itself disappears of its own accord, and the mind is unclouded. In that unclouded state of mind, in that thoughtless state of mind you will be able to see the purity of your inner being.

Then, with certainty the six desires will cease to be begotten and the three poisons will be eliminated and dissolved.

This is something very significant to remember.

All the religions have talked only about five senses; it is only Tao that talks about six senses. All the religions have talked about five desires because man consists of five senses; Tao talks about six desires. The insight is tremendous because just recently, just in this century, science has discovered the sixth sense; otherwise the sixth sense was not known. Your ear has two senses; your ear is not a single sense—hidden inside it is another sense: the sense that keeps your body balanced.

That's why when you see a drunkard walking you can see that he cannot walk straight; zigzag he goes. His steps are not in harmony for the simple reason that alcohol affects the sixth sense, that which keeps your body balanced. It has been a Taoist insight for five thousand years that there are six senses. Through the eye the desire for beauty arises, through the ear the desire for music arises, from the nose the desire for nice smells arises, from the tongue the desire for taste, and from the whole skin the desire to touch—these are the five traditional senses—and from the sixth sense the desire to remain in control, balanced. If somebody hits your ear hard you will lose balance; you will see stars in the day.

These six desires no longer arise. Not that the eyes go blind; in fact, now they can see beauty more truly, but there is no desire to possess beauty. Not that you become deaf to music, but now there is no desire to possess anything. You enjoy more because your energy is free and your senses are more clear, more transparent.

Nobody can see beauty more clearly than a Buddha, nobody can hear music more deeply than a Lao Tzu, nobody can taste better than Jesus. All their senses become truly sensitive, they are real senses. Your senses are dull. Your society helps you to keep them dull because the society is afraid: if your senses are really very keen and very sensitive then you can be a dangerous person because of your desire to possess. You see a beautiful woman: she is somebody else's wife, and if your eyes are really able to see the beauty and you have the desire to possess also then you will grab the woman, you will escape with the woman, you will rape the woman. Something criminal is bound to happen.

Nature allows you total sensitivity only when you become capable of dropping all possessiveness, all idea of possessing. Then you can touch, and then even rocks feel velvety. Then everything starts having a divine quality, everything is transformed.

. . . and the three poisons will be eliminated and dissolved.

What are the three poisons? The first is sexuality—not sex, remember, but sexuality. Sex is natural. Tao is not against sex, it is the only religious approach which is in total agreement with sex. Tao has its own science of sex, it has its own Tantra, which really goes far deeper than Indian Tantra. But sexuality is a totally different phenomenon; sexuality means a perverted state of sex energy. Then it becomes poisonous.

The second poison is anger and the third poison is greed. Sexuality, anger, greed: these three poisons combined together, this unholy trinity, creates your ego. And all these three can be dissolved, eliminated. If sexuality disappears you will be surprised that anger disappears—without any effort on your part. Anger simply means that your sexuality is hindered. Anybody who hinders your sexuality creates anger in you; he is your enemy. And sexuality creates greed; greed is a form of sexuality, it is a perverted form. Money becomes your object of love because the society does not allow any other kind of love. It allows money, power; they can become your objects of love. It helps to change your object of love. First it changes your sex into sexuality . . .

See the difference. Sex is a natural phenomenon; it is your capacity to reproduce. Sexuality means your mind is continuously occupied by sex; it is no more a natural phenomenon, it has become cerebral. It is no more confined to the sex center, it has gone to the head. Now you are constantly thinking.

Just watch for one hour how many times you think of sex—you will be surprised. Psychologists say that you are in for a great surprise if you watch your mind to see how many times in an hour you think about sex. Men think about it twice as much as women do; that may be one of the causes of conflict between them. They have a different kind of sexuality. Man's sexuality is more repressed than woman's for the simple reason that man has to earn money, has to become famous, has to be a prime minister or a politician. Naturally, from where is he going to get all this energy to be the president? There is only one energy; you don't have many energies in you, mind you, you have only one kind of energy. Whatsoever name you want to give to it you can give, "xyz", but you have only one kind of energy. Sigmund Freud has called it libido, but it simply means sex. Now if you want to have more money or more power, you want to be the president of the country or the prime minister of the country, then you have to take your sexuality and channelize it.

I have heard:

One day Carter and Brezhnev met for a long meeting. The two wives waited outside the meeting room for so many hours, they eventually struck up a conversation. Soon they were finding they liked each other and were sharing intimacies.

Rosalyn Carter confessed, "You won't believe this, my dear Brezhnova, but Jimmy just isn't the same man I married. For such a long time now he hasn't even looked at me. He comes home so tired he immediately goes to bed and falls asleep."

"With me it is the same," said Brezhnova. "I just don't know what to do."

"The other night," explained Rosalyn Carter, "I finally decided to tempt Jimmy. I put on my transparent black negligee and some expensive perfume, turned down the lights, put some sexy French music on the stereo and piled pillows on the bed. And then I waited for him in the bedroom.

TAO TAKES CARE

"He came into the bedroom already talking about all the problems in the Middle East, the dollar going down, et cetera, et cetera, and I threw him down on the pile of pillows, took off his shirt, opened up my negligee to show him my bare breasts and asked him, 'Jimmy, does this remind you of anything?'

"He looked at my tits, put his hand to his forehead and said, 'Of course . . . I must call Moshe Dayan!' "

"That's nothing," said Brezhnova. "With me it was worse. I did everything you did, except I didn't bother with the negligee. As soon as he lay down on the bed I jumped on him and put my cunt right in front of his face and said, 'Look at this, Brezy . . . does it remind you of something?' And he replied, 'Oh yes! I forgot to call Fidel Castro!' "

It is bound to happen. You have to divert your sexual energy; then money, power, prestige, they become your sexual objects. And these people can talk about morality and discipline easily; they can teach others how to control their sexuality very easily, but in fact what they are doing is nothing but a perversion of sex. And these people become very violent; they are violent—they keep the whole world always on the brink of war.

When sex becomes perverted, love becomes hatred. Nothing is wrong with sex, but everything is wrong with sexuality. Sex should be allowed a natural flow. Yes, one day, if you live it naturally, transcendence happens; but it is spontaneous, it is not celibacy. It comes through celebration.

Just as at the age of fourteen you become mature sexually, at the age of forty-two, if you have lived your sex naturally, you will go beyond it. But it is a strange world. Children become sexual, children who are not sexually mature, because the whole atmosphere is poisoned. Small children start thinking of sex. Seeing films, reading novels, looking at obscene magazines, they start thinking about sex.

Italian Piero comes to a village. He asks a farmer, "Do you know where little children come-a from?"

"They grow out of cabbages!" the farmer answers.

Piero walks a little further and meets the milkman. "Hey!" says Piero. "Do ya know where little children come-a from!"

"Sure," answers the milkman, "the stork brings them."

Piero continues on his way a little despondent, then . . . "Ah!" he thinks, "here comes-a the right-a man to ask-a! Vicar! Do ya know where little children come-a from?"

"Yes, my son," responds the Vicar. "God sends them from heaven."

"Shit-a!' exclaims Piero. "Isn't there anyone in this-a village who fucks-a?"

Children become sexual before their time, and then you will find eighty year-old men running after women. Both are in an unnatural state.

Tao believes in total naturalness. It is not against sex, it is against sexuality, because it knows that if sexuality does not enter in your life—that means if perversion does not enter in your life—if nobody teaches you to be against sex there will be no perversion. It is because of your saints and moralists and puritans that you all have become perverted—children and old men, all. If sex is left alone without interference from any moral teaching, then one day the child will become sexually mature nearabout fourteen, and one day nearabout forty-two he will transcend it. He will have seen by that time that it is child's play and enough is enough. And that transcendence is beautiful. Anything that happens on its own is beautiful because it comes through Tao. And then anger will not be there in your mind, neither will greed.

The reason men do not possess the ability to achieve this is because their minds are not clear and their desires are unrestrained.

Meditation brings both clarity and a certain inner discipline. And by "meditation" Tao simply means watching your mind and its functions.

He who has the power to transcend his desires, looking within and contemplating mind . . .

That is the definition of meditation according to Ko Hsuan:

. . . looking within and contemplating mind . . .

Just silently watching all the processes of the mind—thoughts, memories, imagination, dreams, desires—a realization happens, a realization that:

. . . in his mind, mind is not . . .

This sutra is immensely significant. When you watch the mind clearly, silently, the mind starts disappearing. More watchfulness, less mind. One percent watchfulness, ninety-nine percent mind. Ninety-nine percent watchfulness, one percent mind. One hundred percent watchfulness and there is no mind in the mind. All thoughts have gone, the mind is absolutely empty. And in that emptiness Tao comes in, rushes in. You have created the right space for it.

. . . looking without and contemplating form . . .

Then you are capable of looking without. First look within, let the mind disappear, attain to clarity, then look without.

. . . looking without and contemplating form . . .

Then meditate on the forms outside: the trees, the clouds, the stars, the moon . . .

. . . he realizes that in form, form is not . . .

Then you will be surprised to see that the waves are not there, only the ocean. In the form there is no form. The trees are not there but only life expressing itself in millions of forms but not confined to any form; it is formless.

. . . looking at things still more remote and contemplating matter, he realizes that in matter, matter is not.

That too is of great significance. It is only now that modern physicists have said that matter does not exist, but Tao has been saying for five thousand years that:

. . . in matter, matter is not.

If you can meditate, start from within, then look around and then look into things at their deepest core. First mind disappears, then form disappears, then matter disappears. Then what is left? That which is left is Tao, is nature. And to live in that nature is to live in freedom, is to live in eternal bliss.

"Tao" is the word of Ko Hsuan for God. "Dhamma" is the word of Buddha for Tao. Buddha says: *Ais Dhammo sanantano*—this is the eternal law. Once you have seen the eternal law you become part of eternity. Time is transcended, space is transcended. You are no more and for the first time you are. You are no more as a separate entity, but for the first time you are the whole.

This is my vision too. My agreement with Tao is absolute. I cannot say that about other religions; with Tao I can say it without any hesitation. Tao is the most profound insight that has ever been achieved on the earth.

SAYING
YES
TO
LIFE

The first question:

Bhagwan,
Why can't I say yes to myself? I have the feeling
that all my misery is rooted in this incapacity.

Anand Renata,

IT IS ONE of the greatest problems. Every human being has to face it, because the whole society up to now
has been based on self-condemnation. All the
religions, all the societies, all the cultures create a
tremendous guilt in you that you are not what you

should be. They give you perfectionist ideals to fulfill which are impossible. They simply drive you crazy.

Perfectionism is the root cause of all neurosis. Nobody can be perfect—nobody *need* be perfect; life is beautiful because everything is imperfect. Perfection is death; imperfection is life. It is because of imperfection that growth is possible. If you are perfect then there is no growth, no movement. Then nothing can happen to you; all has already happened. You will be utterly dead.

Hence I say God is the most imperfect phenomenon because God is the most evolving factor in existence, and evolution and perfection are against each other. It is because of this that all the religions have been against the idea of evolution. Christianity condemned Darwin and his philosophy as much as possible. The reason was this: Christianity believed in a perfect God, and a perfect God can create only a perfect world. How can imperfection come out of a perfect creator? Then there is no possibility of evolution. If the possibility of evolution is accepted, then the world, the creation, is imperfect and ultimately it will lead to the logical conclusion that the creator is imperfect.

No religion has dared to declare that God is imperfect, but I declare that God is imperfect because imperfection means evolution, imperfection means life, imperfection means flow, growth. And God is infinitely imperfect; he will never become perfect. The moment he becomes perfect the whole existence will disappear into nonexistence.

But because of this idea of a perfect God we have all been trying for centuries to be perfect, and there are two outcomes of it. One is: if you are simple, innocent, you will start *trying* to be perfect and you will go neurotic. And you can never become perfect, hence you will carry a mountainous burden of guilt. It will crush you, it will destroy all your joy in life, it will poison you. It won't allow you to celebrate, to sing, to dance. It is suicidal. Or if you are not innocent and simple, if you are cunning and clever, then you will become a hypocrite. You will talk about perfection; that will be just a facade, a mask, and hidden behind the mask you will go on being whatsoever you are.

Both are ugly phenomena. Going crazy, becoming, neurotic, guilt-ridden is ugly; becoming a hypocrite is ugly. But your so-called religions leave you no other alternative: they all talk about saying yes, but they all teach you saying no. They all think they are theistic—they are all atheistic, because to me atheism means a deep-rooted no and theism means a fundamental yes to life. Theism has nothing to do with God, nor has atheism anything to do with the denial of God. Theism is saying yes to life with all its imperfections, as it is, saying yes to it with no conditions, with no strings attached. And atheism to me means saying no to life as it is and trying to make it better, trying to make it perfect.

Renata, you say: *Why can't I say yes to myself?*

Because you have been told you are all wrong, you are nothing but a sinner. Everything that you do is wrong, everything that you think is wrong, everything that you are is wrong—how can you say yes to yourself? You have been given ideas, great ideals, shoulds: "You should be like this, like that . . ." And you go on comparing yourself with those stupid ideals. Of course, you fall very short, and when you fall very short you start feeling a deep no to yourself, you want to destroy yourself; you cannot love yourself.

You have been told to love others, but you have never been told to love yourself. And you can love others only if you have loved yourself in the first place: if you don't love yourself you cannot love anybody else in the world. Loving yourself, you learn the art of love. And if you can love yourself with all your imperfections you will be able to love other human beings with all their imperfections. If you cannot love yourself with your imperfections, how are you going to love others with their imperfections? You will hate them!

Parents hate their children, children hate their parents, wives hate their husbands, husbands hate their wives, for the simple reason that they can see the imperfections. Everybody is in search of a perfect person and you will not find a perfect person anywhere, except some fools who go on claiming that they are infallible, perfect. Pope John Paul the Polack, he is infallible! Popes are infallible. They represent God—how can they be fallible? In India Satya Sai Baba claims to be infallible. Now, to me these are utter idiots! They have no sense of any manners, of any etiquette even; they don't have any intelligence. Otherwise they could see—it is so simple. But it is a traditional thing.

Jainas in India have claimed that Mahavira is all-knowing. Buddha laughed at the whole idea. He was an intelligent man, a really penetrating intelligence, but he never claimed that he was infallible. No intelligent person can do that. He laughed at the whole idea that Mahavira was infallible. We don't know what was Mahavira's own statement about it because according to the Jaina tradition he remained silent, he never said a single word. There were interpreters of his silence who were telling people what he meant. I cannot conceive that he would have ever meant that he was infallible. A man of such intelligence as Mahavira could not do that.

Buddha says, "I have heard: Mahavira going for a morning walk steps on a dog's tail, and when the dog barks then he comes to know that there is a dog—because it is still dark in the morning. And this is the all-knowing man who knows past, present, future, and he does not know that he is stepping on the tail of a dog!''

Buddha has said, ''I know that Mahavira has many times stood begging in front of a house where nobody lives; the house has been empty for years. Only when people say to him that 'This house is empty, nobody lives here,' will he move to another house to beg.''

And the followers claim that he knows past, present and future, that he knows everything, that he is omniscient, that he is omnipotent, that he is all-powerful. But he suffered throughout his life from stomach diseases, he died of stomach diseases—it may have been something like a stomach cancer, the word ''cancer'' was not known in those days—and he is thought to be omnipotent and he is thought to be omnipresent: all the qualities of God. But these are the claims of the followers. That I can understand: followers are stupid people, otherwise why should they follow?

I don't have any followers here. You are all my friends. I don't want any followers because I don't want to live surrounded by fools!

But Satya Sai Baba declares that he is infallible, that he knows all, that he has never committed a mistake, that he cannot commit a mistake. Now these are all maniacs. Ego cannot be more mad.

Perfection is not possible. You are imperfect, and there is nothing wrong in being imperfect; this is the only way to be. Once you accept your imperfection you have accepted your humanity, and in that acceptance the yes arises. And then you can love yourself and you can love others too, because they are as imperfect as you are.

Renata, you are still trying to live according to the ideas given by your parents to you. In that way all parents have poisoned their children for thousands of years; that poisoning still continues. And once a child is poisoned, from the very beginning he starts thinking it is his own idea. It gets so deep-rooted—it goes to the very guts—that you completely forget that it has been implanted from the outside. And then you try to live it out. You cannot manage it, and it will mess up your whole life.

One Indian friend has asked: "Bhagwan, nothing moves without the will of God, not even a single blade of grass . . ." These are his actual words:

> *Bhagwan,*
> *When you say that not a single blade of grass moves but by his will, why is there a metal detector and so many security arrangements here?*

The questioner is Prakash Singh Madhuban. It is because of his will! If not a single blade of grass moves, how can the metal detector move? It is so simple! If not a single blade of grass moves, how can so many guards move? But he thinks he is asking a very wise question. He must be thinking he is asking something which is unanswerable.

You know nothing of God nor of his will, but you go on repeating cliches. You have heard these things and you start repeating them like gramophone records. You don't see the absurdity of it. If it is your understanding, the question cannot arise. The question is absolutely meaningless if it is your understanding. But it is not *your* understanding; somebody else has planted it in you. And all parents are doing it. and I am not saying that they are doing it knowingly; they are as unconscious as you are. These ideas have been planted in them by others, their parents, and so on and so forth. But you have to jump out of this vicious circle.

Renata, your name is so beautiful—it means rebirth. Being here with me you have to go through a process of being reborn, and the first step will be to drop all the ideas that have been imposed upon you. The roses are beautiful because they are not carrying the idea that they have to be as big as the lotus flowers; otherwise they will be miserable, they will stop growing—they will shrink in shame, ashamed of themselves. They are beautiful, fragrant, for the simple reason that whatsoever they are, they are. The marigold flowers are not worried why they are not roses. Even the blades of grass are not at all ashamed of not being big trees like the cedars of Lebanon. They are perfectly happy as they are.

A man came to a Zen monk and he asked, "Why are you always so blissful? Why am *I* not so blissful?"

The Master said, "Wait. When everybody else has left, then I will answer your question."

The man waited and waited because people were coming and going and there was not a single moment of aloneness. He was getting tired and impatient and many times he thought to leave, because "When is this thing going to stop? People are still coming."

But by the evening when the sun was setting, everybody had left and he was alone with the Master. He reminded him, "Now please tell me."

He said, "Look outside the window. You see this big tree?"

He said, "Yes, I see it."

And he said, "You see that small bush by the side?"

He said, "Yes, I see that too."

The Master said, "I have never heard the bush saying to the big tree, 'Why are you so big and I am so

281

TAO: THE GOLDEN GATE

small?' That's why both are happy. The tree is big and
the bush is small, but so what? Both are unique. They
don't compare themselves—and they are standing
side by side. And for fifteen years I have been trying to
find out why they don't compare themselves. They
are perfectly happy; *both* are happy.

"You are unhappy because you are comparing, you
are living in comparison. And I am happy because I
have dropped all comparison; I have simply accepted
myself as I am. That is my simple secret."

And you are constantly comparing. Somebody else
is more beautiful than you, somebody else has more
beautiful eyes than you, somebody else has more
beautiful hair than you, somebody else is more strong
than you, somebody else seems to be more intelligent
than you, somebody else has something else, and so
on and so forth . . . there is no end to it! You will
become more and more miserable.

And you have been told: "Become like Jesus."
"Become like Buddha." "Become like Krishna." You
will be miserable. Buddha never tried to become like
Krishna, that's why he was happy. Krishna never tried
to become like anybody else, that's why he was
happy. Krishna never tried to become like anybody
else, that's why he was happy. Jesus never tried to
become like Moses, that's why he was happy—even
on the cross he was happy. And you are constantly
trying to be somebody else.

These ideals have to be dropped; they have to be
destroyed completely. And then, Renata, a deep and
profound yes will arise from the depths of your being.
It will fill you with tremendous fulfillment.

And, to me, this is religion. This yes filling your
whole being, overflowing you, is religion. Right now
you are full of of no's, thousand and one no's; about
everything there is a no, and that's what is making

your life a hell. You have to be alert because you have to get rid of all this rubbish that has been poured upon you by your parents, by your society, by your church. And it hurts if something is taken away because you have believed in it for a long time; it has become almost part of your blood, your bone, your marrow. It hurts, although it is just pus and nothing else; but to take it away hurts.

One old woman took sannyas in America; she must have taken sannyas for wrong reasons. Many people take sannyas for wrong reasons. They become aware of it only later on when there arises some clash between their idea of sannyas and my vision of sannyas. And she was writing beautiful letters, very poetic. The reason deep down that she became a sannyasin was because she was reading my books on Jesus; *The Mustard Seed* was the thing that moved her deeply. But it was not me; it was because of Jesus. She became convinced of Jesus' truth, and because I had helped her, she became a lover of me.

Then just yesterday her letter arrived. She is very disturbed: what to do now? Because in some tapes she has heard that I have said that in old days there were records, there are written records, about Jesus' physical appearance saying that he was an ugly man, that his height was only four feet five inches, and not only that, he was a hunchback and his face was disgusting. Now she is shocked. Now she says, "I want to go back to my old Master, Jesus. I don't want to remain a sannyasin anymore." Now this was the time for her to get free of a conditioning. She missed the opportunity. Going back she will be the same as she has always been. A moment had come when a door opened, but she turned away.

Many of you are here for wrong reasons, and if you are here for wrong reasons you will be in trouble sooner or later. I am going to disturb you, disturb all

283

your dreams, disturb all your ideals. I am going to put dynamite inside you! My whole work consists in sabotage. Once I can destroy all your ideals that you have carried all along, once I can make you free of all the jargon that you have learned from others, once I am able to uncondition you, then you will be able to say yes to yourself.

Every tree says yes to itself; every animal, every bird says yes. Nobody is needed to teach it. The no is taught; yes is natural. Yes is part of Tao; no is a conditioning.

Renata, you have felt rightly that: *I have the feeling that all my misery is rooted in this incapacity.*

That is true. That is the beginning of a tremendous journey; you have felt the right direction. Now go on moving into it. It will take time and it will take effort and it will be an agony; before the ecstasy can happen you will have to pass through many agonies. That is the price we have to pay. But once you have gathered courage enough to drop your whole past—Christian, Hindu, Mohammedan, Jaina, Buddhist—once you are unconditioned, your life becomes a flow, a beautiful flow. And then the ocean is not far away. Every river reaches to it with no maps, with no guides. Every river reaches to it naturally, spontaneously. That is the way of Tao.

The second question:

Bhagwan,
I don't want to take sannyas because I believe in the philosophy of do-it-yourself. What have you to say about it?

Angelo,

WHY ARE YOU ASKING ME? Do it yourself! What is the need to know my opinion? And if you don't want to take sannyas, why the question at all in the first place? There must be some deep hidden desire in you to take sannyas; otherwise, the question is irrelevant—it cannot arise at all. The very question shows that some longing has arisen in you to take the jump. But you are afraid to accept the longing, you are trying to rationalize that you can do it yourself, you are trying to repress a certain desire that must be becoming more and more strong every day.

Sannyas simply means a quantum leap into the unknown. The mind lives in the known; it moves within the known. It goes in circles, round and round; it is repetitive. It cannot enter into any communion with the new, with the unknown, with the unknowable. Sannyas is a jump. It is like a snake slipping out of its old skin. You must be getting tired of your old skin, you must be dragging it. And you must be seeing people here rejoicing in their new birth. And the longing must be arising in you too: why not take the jump?

But the courage is lacking. The desire is there, the courage is not there. But you want to deny the desire because nobody wants to accept that he is a coward. It is better to deny the desire itself; then you can avoid the idea of being a coward. Everybody wants at least to pretend to others, and to himself too, if possible, that one is a courageous man—if one wants to do something one will do it: "But I don't want to do it in the first place. That's what is preventing me, otherwise nobody can prevent me."

But why are you asking? From where does the question arise? I have not asked you to become a sannyasin. I didn't even know that you were here. You could have gone without making yourself known, without asking the question. And if you cannot gather enough courage, at least be honest enough to accept that you are a coward.

The desire is there. Don't repress the desire, because the first act of courage is to accept your cowardice. Once you accept it, it starts dying. It can remain only if it is not accepted. Once it is brought into the light of acceptance it can't exist for long; it becomes impossible for it to exist for long.

You say: *I believe in the philosophy of do-it-yourself.*

How will you do it? What will you do? You don't know anything about sannyas. It is an absolutely new concept. Nothing like it has ever existed in the whole history of humanity. Yes, there have been Hindu monks, Buddhist monks, Christian monks, Jaina monks, but they were all life-negative.

My sannyas is life-affirmative. Nothing like this has ever flowered on the earth. It is a totally new phenomenon. All the old ideas about sannyas were based on escapism, on renunciation. My sannyas has nothing to do with escape, it is *against* escape, because to me God and life are synonymous. It has never been said that God and life are synonymous. God has always been put *against* life: you have to drop life to attain God. And I say to you, you have to live as totally as possible, as intensely as possible, as passionately as possible if you want to know God at all, because there is no other God than life.

God to me is not a person; it is another name for life energy. This distant call of the cuckoo, this is God. Your silence, this is God. The birds chirping, this is God. God is not "somewhere", God is everywhere. In fact, "God" is not the right word; but all our languages are addicted to nouns—they always change verbs into nouns.

My effort here is to do just the opposite: to change every noun into a verb. There is no God as a person, but there is godliness—a quality, a certain flavor, a certain experiencing; alive, flowing, not confined within boundaries.

You don't know what it is. How are you going to do it? Yes, I have heard about the philosophy of doing-it-yourself . . .

The main trend of the fifties was to do-it-yourself.

Around Easter time, an ad appeared in The New York Times: "Do Easter at home for only five thousand dollars!"

Mr. Jones sent the five thousand dollars and recived a parcel with: a box of nails, two wooden beams, one measuring three meters and the other measuring one meter and eighty centimeters, and a blonde Jew, thirty-three years old.

Angelo, what will you do by yourself? You don't know even the abc of it. You will need to become part of a Buddhafield. You will need to become part of a place where many many people are growing. Alone in a desert you cannot bloom; you will need to become part of a garden.

This is the garden of a Master where many trees are growing, here many trees are coming to a flowering, to fruition. The seed in you will start having a tremendous confidence in itself that "If it can happen to other seeds, if this miracle is possible, then it is possible for me too."

It is possible only in a certain commune. That's why all the awakened ones have always created communes, simply so that you can see what *is* possible and you can see people in all kinds of stages: the beginners, the people who have gone a little ahead, the people who have gone far, the people who are almost reaching the climax, and the people who have blossomed.

When the seed sees all this it becomes confident. Otherwise there persists a self-doubt. "Who knows whether I have the potential or not?"

To be a sannyasin simply means to fall into a kind of synchronicity. Musicians are aware of it. You can do a small experiment. In an empty room, close the room completely. In one corner of the room, an absolutely empty room, put one sitar, and you sit exactly in the opposite corner and start playing on another sitar. And you will be surprised that as you start playing on your sitar, the other sitar, which is just resting against the wall in a corner—and there is nobody to play it—starts falling into a certain synchronicity. Its strings start vibrating; it starts creating certain sounds. This is a well known fact. And if the musician is really great he can almost create music on the other sitar also, which he has not even touched. But what happens to the other sitar? The vibration that is filling the whole room is caught by it.

When a commune gathers around a Master, a certain vibration is there—very tangible to those who are sensitive, aware, loving, surrendered, committed; who are not just outsiders, observers; who are not just standing by and trying to see what is happening but who are courageous enough to become part of it. Then your heart starts falling in tune with the heart of the Master. And where thousands of hearts are functioning in the same rhythm, beating in the same rhythm, you cannot resist the temptation. That's the only way to grow towards the unknown. Sannyas is a mysterious journey.

And, Angelo, in your ordinary, unconscious state you will not be able to do it by yourself.

Four drunken Italians stumbled into a funeral parlor. After bumbling around for a half hour, one of them fell over a piano.

"Here's the coffin," he advised his friends.

One of them peered at the piano.

"Do you recognize him?" the first one asked.

"No," admitted the other drunk, "but he sure has a good set of teeth!"

Angelo, you are an Italian . . . forget all about doing it by yourself!

Two Italians were going home after a night full of wine to discover that the last bus to Rome had left. For a few moments they staggered around the big hall in which all the buses were parked and then one of them said, "Why don't-a you get-a inside and-a steal a bus. I'll keep-a an eye on-a the street to see if-a the police is-a coming."

The first one agreed and disappeared in the hall. Soon an awful screeching, bumping and crashing was heard. This lasted for half an hour, when the doors swung open and a bus drove out.

"What the hell-a took you so long-a?" exclaimed the one who had been waiting outside.

"Well," replied the other, "the bus-a to Roma was all-a the way in the back!"

The third question:

Bhagwan,
Why did you never get married?

Dheerendra,

JUST BECAUSE I AM NOT MAD!

Jesus was standing in front of a full-length mirror, admiring his complexion and clear eyes. He brushed his long hair, oiled it and arranged it in a braid. Then he plucked his eyebrows and combed his blonde moustache.

Mary was watching him. "My son," she sighed, "you are so handsome . . . you should really get married!"

"Me! Married?" cried Jesus. "I would rather be nailed to a cross!"

The fourth question:

Bhagwan,
Your jokes make me afraid and confused.
Please tell me one of Buddha's sutras about
God.
P.S. I'm leaving for Italy tomorrow. Thank you.

Anand Satyam,

I CAN UNDERSTAND—jokes are dangerous. That's why no Master before me has ever touched them. But I love danger. Jokes have a tremendous beauty if you can allow them to enter into your very innermost core. No sutras can reach there, because when you are hearing a sutra you start falling asleep. It is very difficult to keep oneself awake hearing sutras for the simple reason that sutras are serious, dry, like the desert. How long can you look at the desert? Sooner or later you will start yawning, because it is the same desert going up to the very horizon—on all sides it is all sand and sand and sand, and the scene is exactly the same. The sutras are exactly the same; they are desertlike.

SAYING YES TO LIFE

They create sleep: they function like lullabies. If you suffer from sleeplessness, then reading a few sutras of Buddha or Patanjali will be very helpful. Just read a few sutras—you are bound to fall asleep. When all tranquilizers fail, sutras work.

That's what the hypnotists go on doing: they simply repeat a certain sutra. Anything repeated again and again creates such boredom that you have to escape from it. And the easiest escape is into sleep.

Mulla Nasruddin suffered very much from sleeplessness. All efforts failed—all the tranquilizers, the sleeping pills; nothing worked. His sons were getting very worried. Finally they found a hypnotist who said, "Don't worry, I will come tonight." And he came, and he started simply repeating: "You are falling asleep . . ."

Nasruddin was lying down on the bed with closed eyes, the lights were out, and the hypnotist was repeating again and again, "You are falling asleep . . . your eyelids are becoming heavier, heavier, heavier . . . you are falling asleep, falling asleep, falling asleep . . . a deep sleep is taking over . . ."

Nasruddin started snoring. The hypnotist tiptoed out of the room.

The sons were very happy. They handed him double his fees, thanked him very much. They went in to see. Nasruddin opened one of his eyes and said, "Has that idiot left yet or not? He would have killed me, hence I had to pretend! That snoring was just false. I was faking it so that he would leave me!"

Sutras are boring. That's why only old people who are already dead go to religious discourses. You can see them in all the churches and temples.

When people come to visit this ashram they are surprised to see so many young people. It is unbelievable because young people are not supposed to be in such places. Only old people, dead, rotten, leading some kind of posthumous existence, are supposed to be in such places. So many young people—what are these young people doing here? They are not here for the sutras, Satyam. *I* am here for the sutras, they are not here for the sutras. So we have made a compromise: they have to listen to a few sutras and I have to tell a few jokes. They will be here for the jokes, I am here for the sutras! If I stop telling jokes, they will disappear. If I have to tell only jokes, I will not be needed. I can leave a big collection of jokes and Teertha can read the jokes; there will be no need for me to be here. If you want me to be here you will have to hear a few sutras, and if I want you to be here, I have to tell a few jokes too. This is understood, this is a contract.

Jokes are tremendously important in a way. Jokes are not simple phenomena; they are really mysterious, their mechanism is mysterious. You don't know how a joke works, how it goes deep into your depths, how it brings laughter to you, how it brings wakefulness to you. The mechanism *is* mysterious.

A joke functions almost like a sexual orgasm. It is not accidental that many jokes *are* concerned with sex. Jokes as such are basically sexual for the simple reason that the joke creates a build-up of energy in you, a great curiosity about what is going to happen, because a joke is a joke only when something unexpected happens, when it takes such a sudden turn that logically you could not have conceived it; it was inconceivable. And it takes the turn so quickly and so suddenly that it does not give you time enough to think about it. Because there is no time to think . . . Mind needs time. The joke goes on towards the south and then suddenly turns towards the north: your mind goes on moving towards the south, but the joke has taken a turn towards the north so suddenly that the mind halts. In that very halt there is an experience of silence, of meditation.

The same happens in sexual orgasm: a certain energy is built up in you, a certain tension is built up in you. You go on moving upwards, upwards, upwards, and then comes a sudden relaxation, a sudden release. It is so sudden—it happens in a single moment—the mind stops, the mind disappears for a moment. It is not conceivable for the mind. The mind needs time.

If you understand the joke you will miss the whole point. If you can understand where it is going, what the logical end of it will be, then it will not be a joke for you. Whatsoever you understand from the very beginning is not going to be the end; the end is going to be absolutely unpredictable.

That's the beauty of a joke; it shocks you, shakes you, it wakes you up. It is impossible to remain asleep when a beautiful joke is being told.

Buddha goes on telling his disciples, "Wake up!" What is the need? I simply tell a joke and they wake up! And that is far more existential.

An aircraft bound for Florida with two hundred and forty passengers on board ran into some engine problem. The plane was sure to crash so the pilot alerted all the crew members about this sad state of affairs and told them all to get hold of a parachute each and jump off the plane.

A young steward asked the captain, "What about the passengers, sir?"

"Fuck the passengers!" the captain replied.

Said the steward, "What! Do we have time for that?"

You say, Satyam: *Your jokes make me afraid . . .*

293

Because they must be shattering many things in you. You must be thinking religion is serious. It is not—at least my vision of religion is not serious at all. My religion is rooted in playfulness, in non-seriousness; sincere, of course, but serious, never. My religion is laughter, love. It is not renunciation, it is rejoicing.

I am not concerned with God at all, and you are asking me for one of Buddha's sutras about God. In fact, Buddha never believed in God; he has no sutra about God. Buddha is absolutely atheistic in that sense: he never believed in God. Buddha was not so childish as to believe in God the Father who created the world and who lives in heaven. These are all fictions, fairy tales.

Every month St. Peter and Lucifer meet to divide the newly arrived souls between them.

"What is your name?" St. Peter asks.

"Karl Marx," replies a white-bearded soul.

"Ah! You are an atheist. Therefore you will be going to hell."

The next month, to St. Peter's great amazement, Lucifer is late. This had never happened before. After a few hours Lucifer arrives in a horrible state—one of his horns is broken, his tail is burnt, his complexion is pale.

"What is the matter with you?" St. Peter asks.

"Oh my God! That Marx, you know? He has created fucking hell! He began by complaining that it was too hot, and then that there was not enough air, and then that the place was unhealthy. To make a long story short, after a few strikes, protests and demonstrations, I had to allow air conditioning, massages in the breaks between torture sessions, thermostats to keep the heating system under control! Peter, I am at a loss. Help me! Could you take care of him for the next month to give me some peace?"

"What! Marx in heaven! Have you gone crazy or what?"

"Do it for my sake, Peter! Remember, we have been friends for eternity!"

"But I just cannot!" replies St. Peter. "Marx amongst all the angels and saints! Can you imagine it?"

"One month only, Peter, please."

"Well, okay. Just because you are my friend I will keep him—but for one month only!"

Next month St. Peter and Lucifer are both punctual. Lucifer eagerly asks, "So, Peter, how are things going?"

"Oh, fine thanks, Lucifer."

"Fine? What about Marx?"

"Oh, that Marx! Nice chap!"

"You mean he did not raise any protest?"

"Oh never! We had many pleasant discussions together. He is a cultured man."

"Indeed? But what does God say?"

"Oh, come on, Lucifer! You know God doesn't exist!"

Satyam, Buddha has no sutras about God. He was the first mature religious person in the whole world. He talks in terms of maturity, not in terms of childishness.

And you say: *I am leaving for Italy tomorrow . . .*

Then it will be good if you take this joke with you:

Two village boys from Sicily go to visit their cousin in New York. On the third day of being shown around downtown New York they somehow get separated from the cousin. After looking for him for a few hours they finally end up in a police station.

"Please-a, sir, can-a you find-a our cousin?"

"What's his name?" the police officer asks.

"Gino."

"Gino who?"

"Don't-a know-a"

"Where does he live?"

"In New York-a."

"What does he look like?"

"A man-a."

"Where did you lose him?"

"Don't-a know-a."

"Is there anything special about his features? A flat nose? One eye? Something like that?"

The two boys think hard but sadly shake their heads. Then the face of one brightens slowly and he says "Ah, yes-a sir, he has-a two assholes!"

"Two assholes!" exclaims the policeman "Are you sure? How do you know?"

"Well-a," replies the boy, "every time we go to eat-a spaghetti or dance-a at the disco, his friends say-a, 'Look! There's Gino with-a the two-a assholes!' "

Satyam, go to Italy, but come back soon, because the whole of Italy has come here! All the juicy people have disappeared from Italy; they are here.

Just the other day I was reading a newspaper report from Italy about so many young people, young men and women, having disappeared from Italy that the government has become concerned about what is happening to them. They need not be concerned, they need not go anywhere to look for them, they can come here—they are all here! Either they have come or they are on the way, but they are all going to end up here. What will you be doing there Satyam? Come back soon—as soon as possible!

Italy will look very non-Italian to you. We have made a compact Italy here, and far more juicy! Slowly slowly my jokes will help you to come to your senses;

they will help you to come out of your confusion. There is nothing more healthy than a good laughter, there is nothing more sane than a good laughter. Laughter is very vital.

I would like my sannyasins to be laughing sannyasins. I would like the world to know my people as the most laughing, dancing, singing people. I don't want any sad, serious-looking people here. I don't want any long faces here. Yes, when you come you come with a long face, but then I have to hit you and sooner or later you lose your mask—because that is only a mask.

No child is born with a long face; every child is born with laughter, with a great joy which is ready to explode. We destroy his joy. My effort here is to release that joy again, to bring your childhood back to you.

The fifth question:

Bhagwan,
I think I know
That if I knew
How much you give
The agony of the ecstasy
Would kill me.

Dharma Chetana,

IT IS TOO LATE! You have been killed already, but the recognition comes always too late, when the work is finished. I do my surgery in such a way that you become aware only when you start missing your appendix, tonsils, and head, and everything . . . when you are just a hollow bamboo!

297

Now Dharma Chetana is a hollow bamboo. Now she is ready. Now the whole can sing any song through her. The only way to be reborn is to be crucified.

The eastern scriptures say the Master is death, and they are right. The Master *is* a death, but that is only a half-statement. The other half is that the Master is also a resurrection.

The sixth question:

Bhagwan,
Where is my heart?

Prem Pankaja,

IT IS THE SAME QUESTION. I have taken it out! Now you will never find it. Everything has to be taken out because all that you are carrying inside—your mind, your heart—is just junk! You call it antique furniture, maybe; I call it simply junk. I am not interested in antiques at all, no; my whole interest is in the absolutely new.

Mukta wanted to bring an antique Rolls Royce for me. I said, "Mukta, I am not interested in antiques at all!"

She said, "Bhagwan, it is very beautiful! It is a 1939 model, with gold," et cetera.

I said, "Forget all about it! I am interested only in the latest."

Now Sheela is bringing a Lincoln Continental for me. I told her, "Bring a 1981 model."

She said, "Bhagwan, where will I find a 1981 model? It is 1980!"

I said, "You try! By the time you find it it will be 1981!"

And the last question:

Bhagwan,
I am very impatient, I want to know God, but I
don't want to waste my time in search of him.
Can you show me a short cut?

Dharmesh,

A YOUNG MAN once came to a venerable Master and asked, "How long will it take to reach enlightenment?"

The Master said, "Ten years."

The young man blurted, "So long?"

The Master said, "No, I was mistaken. It will take twenty years."

The young man asked, "Why do you keep adding to it?"

And the Master answered, "Come to think of it, in your case it will probably be thirty!"

Dharmesh, there are no shortcuts. And if you are impatient you will never find. Patience is the only way, and if you are absolutely patient you can find right now. This is the ultimate paradox of religious inquiry, of the seach for truth, for God, for *nirvana*: if you are impatient you will have to wait for eternity. That venerable Master must have been a very polite man; he said only thirty years. But to tell you the truth, if you are impatient you will have to wait forever and forever. If you are patient, totally patient, then it is possible even now—*this very moment, here and now!*

Don't ask for any shortcut, Dharmesh. There has never been any shortcut; there cannot be any shortcut to truth. You cannot have it cheap. And patience means love because only love can be patient. Love can wait—love knows how to wait. It can wait forever, and because it can wait forever it becomes capable of receiving the gift right now.

Two students were talking to each other. One of them bragged about all the women he got to go to bed with him.

"How do you get so many women do to it? What is your secret?" asked the other student.

"Well, this is how I do it. All I do is paint a white circle on my dashboard. The girl will usually ask about it. Then we'll start talking. I'll start referring to the color white and all the things associated with it—virginity, purity, chastity. Then the conversation will expand. We'll talk about the purity of the saints and Tantra Yoga, et cetera. It all depends on how good you can talk. Just use the white circle and go on from there. You shouldn't have too much trouble getting them to do it."

The friend followed his advice and painted a white circle on his dashboard, then went and picked up his date. When she got into the car she noticed the white circle on the dashboard.

"That's really an interesting circle on your dashboard," she said.

"It sure, is," he replied. "Would you like to screw?"

BOOKS PUBLISHED BY
RAJNEESH FOUNDATION
INTERNATIONAL

For a complete catalog of all the books published by
Rajneesh Foundation International, contact:

Rajneesh Foundation International
P.O. Box 9
Rajneeshpuram, Oregon 97741 USA
(503) 489-3462

THE BAULS
The Beloved (2 volumes)

BUDDHA
The Book of the Books (volume 1 & 2)
the Dhammapada

The Diamond Sutra
the Vajrachchedika Prajnaparamita Sutra

The Discipline of Transcendence (4 volumes)
the Sutra of 42 Chapters

The Heart Sutra
the Prajnaparamita Hridayam Sutra

BUDDHIST MASTERS
The Book of Wisdom (volume 1)
Atisha's Seven Points of Mind Training

The White Lotus
the sayings of Bodhidharma

HASIDISM
The Art of Dying
The True Sage

JESUS
Come Follow Me (4 volumes)
the sayings of Jesus
I Say Unto You (2 volumes)
the sayings of Jesus

KABIR
The Divine Melody
Ecstasy: The Forgotten Language
The Fish in the Sea is Not Thirsty
The Guest
The Path of Love
The Revolution

RESPONSES TO QUESTIONS
Be Still and Know
From Sex to Superconsciousness
The Goose is Out
My Way: The Way of the White Clouds
Walking in Zen, Sitting in Zen
Walk Without Feet, Fly Without Wings
and Think Without Mind
Zen: Zest, Zip, Zap and Zing

SUFISM
Just Like That
The Perfect Master (2 volumes)
The Secret
Sufis: The People of the Path (2 volumes)
Unio Mystica (2 volumes)
the Hadiqa of Hakim Sanai

Until You Die
The Wisdom of the Sands (2 volumes)

TANTRA

The Book of the Secrets (volumes 4 & 5)
Vigyana Bhairava Tantra

Tantra, Spirituality & Sex
Excerpts from The Book of the Secrets

The Tantra Vision (2 volumes)
the Royal Song of Saraha

TAO

The Empty Boat
the stories of Chuang Tzu

The Secret of Secrets (2 volumes)
the Secret of the Golden Flower

Tao: The Golden Gate (volume 1)

Tao: The Pathless Path (2 volumes)
the stories of Lieh Tzu

Tao: The Three Treasures (4 volumes)
the Tao Te Ching of Lao Tzu

When The Shoe Fits
the stories of Chuang Tzu

THE UPANISHADS

The Ultimate Alchemy (2 volumes)
Atma Pooja Upanishad

Vedanta: Seven Steps to Samadhi
Akshya Upanishad

Philosophia Ultima
Mandukya Upanishad

WESTERN MYSTICS

The Hidden Harmony
the fragments of Heraclitus

The New Alchemy: To Turn You On
Mabel Collins' Light on the Path

Philosophia Perennis (2 volumes)
the Golden Verses of Pythagoras

Guida Spirituale
the Desiderata

Theologia Mystica
the treatise of St. Dionysius

YOGA

Yoga: The Alpha and the Omega
(10 volumes)
the Yoga Sutras of Patanjali

ZEN

Ah, This!

Ancient Music in the Pines

And the Flowers Showered

Dang Dang Doko Dang

The First Principle

The Grass Grows By Itself

Nirvana: the Last Nightmare

No Water, No Moon

Returning to the Source

A Sudden Clash of Thunder

The Sun Rises in the Evening

Zen: The Path of Paradox (3 volumes)

ZEN MASTERS

Hsin Hsin Ming: The Book of Nothing
Discourses on the faith-mind of Sosan

The Search
the Ten Bulls of Zen

Take It Easy (2 volumes)
poems of Ikkyu

This Very Body the Buddha
Hakuin's Song of Meditation

INITIATION TALKS
between Master disciple

Hammer On The Rock
(December 10, 1975 - January 15, 1976)

Above All Don't Wobble
(January 16 - February 12, 1976)

Nothing To Lose But Your Head
(February 13 - March 12, 1976)

Be Realistic: Plan For a Miracle
(March 13 - April 6, 1976)

Get Out of Your Own Way
(April 7 - May 2, 1976)

Beloved of My Heart
(May 3 - 28, 1976)

The Cypress in the Courtyard
(May 29 - June 27, 1976)

A Rose is a Rose is a Rose
(June 28 - July 27, 1976)

Dance Your Way to God
(July 28 - August 20, 1976)

The Passion for the Impossible
(August 21 - September 18, 1976)

The Great Nothing
(September 19 - October 11, 1976)

God is Not for Sale
(October 12 - November 7, 1976)

The Shadow of the Whip
(November 8 - December 3, 1976)

Blessed are the Ignorant
(December 4 - 31, 1976)

The Buddha Disease
(January 1977)

What Is, Is, What Ain't, Ain't
(February 1977)

The Zero Experience
(March 1977)

For Madmen Only (Price of Admission: Your Mind)
(April 1977)

This Is It
(May 1977)

The Further Shore
(June 1977)

Far Beyond the Stars
(July 1977)

The No Book (No Buddha, No Teaching, No
Discipline)
(August 1977)

Don't Just Do Something, Sit There
(September 1977)

Only Losers Can Win in this Game
(October 1977)

The Open Secret
(November 1977)

The Open Door
(December 1977)

The Sun Behind the Sun Behind the Sun
(January 1978)

Believing the Impossible Before Breakfast
(February 1978)

Don't Bite My Finger, Look Where I am Pointing
(March 1978)

Let Go!
(April 1978)

The Ninety-Nine Names of Nothingness
(May 1978)

The Madman's Guide to Enlightenment
(June 1978)

Don't Look Before You Leap
(July 1978)

Hallelujah!
(August 1978)

God's Got a Thing About You
(September 1978)

The Tongue-Tip Taste of Tao
(October 1978)

The Sacred Yes
(November 1978)

Turn On, Tune In, and Drop the Lot
(December 1978)

Zorba the Buddha
(January 1979)

Won't You Join the Dance?
(February 1979)

You Ain't Seen Nothin' Yet
(March 1979)

The Sound of One Hand Clapping
(March 1981)

OTHER TITLES

The Book
*an introduction to the teachings of
  Bhagwan Shree Rajneesh
  Series I from A to H
  Series II from I to Q
  Series III from R to Z*

A Cup of Tea
letters to disciples

The Orange Book
*the meditation techniques of
  Bhagwan Shree Rajneesh*

Rajneeshism
*an introduction to Bhagwan Shree Rajneesh and His
  religion*

The Sound of Running Water
*a photobiography of
  Bhagwan Shree Rajneesh and His work*

BOOKS FROM OTHER PUBLISHERS

ENGLISH EDITIONS
UNITED KINGDOM

The Art of Dying
(Sheldon Press)

The Book of the Secrets (volume 1)
(Thames & Hudson)

Dimensions Beyond the Known
(Sheldon Press)

The Hidden Harmony
(Sheldon Press)

Meditation: The Art of Ecstasy
(Sheldon Press)

The Mustard Seed
(Sheldon Press)

Neither This Nor That
(Sheldon Press)

No Water, No Moon
(Sheldon Press)

Roots and Wings
(Routledge & Kegan Paul)

Straight to Freedom (Original title:
Until You Die)
(Sheldon Press)

The Supreme Doctrine
(Routledge & Kegan Paul)

The Supreme Understanding (Original title:
Tantra: The Supreme Understanding)
(Sheldon Press)

Tao: The Three Treasures (volume 1)
(Wildwood House)

UNITED STATES OF AMERICA

The Book of the Secrets (volumes 1-3)
(Harper & Row)

The Great Challenge
(Grove Press)

Hammer on the Rock
(Grove Press)

I Am The Gate
(Harper & Row)

Journey Toward the Heart (Original title:
Until You Die)
(Harper & Row)

Meditation: The Art of Ecstasy
(Harper & Row)

The Mustard Seed
(Harper & Row)

My Way: The Way of the White Clouds
(Grove Press)

Only One Sky (Original title:
Tantra: The Supreme Understanding)
(Dutton)

The Psychology of the Esoteric
(Harper & Row)

Roots and Wings
(Routledge & Kegan Paul)

The Supreme Doctrine
(Routledge & Kegan Paul)

Words Like Fire (Original title:
Come Follow Me, volume 1)
(Harper & Row)

BOOKS ON BHAGWAN

The Awakened One: The Life and Work
of Bhagwan Shree Rajneesh
by Swami Satya Vedant
(Harper & Row)

Death Comes Dancing: Celebrating Life
with Bhagwan Shree Rajneesh
by Ma Satya Bharti
(Routledge & Kegan Paul)

Drunk On The Divine
by Ma Satya Bharti
(Grove Press)

The Ultimate Risk
by Ma Satya Bharti
(Routledge & Kegan Paul)

Dying For Enlightenment
by Bernard Gunther (Swami Deva Amitprem)
(Harper & Row)

Neo-Tantra
by Bernard Gunther (Swami Deva Amitprem)
(Harper & Row)

FOREIGN LANGUAGE EDITIONS
DANISH

TRANSLATIONS

Hemmelighedernes Bog (volume 1)
(Borgens Forlag)

Hu-Meditation Og Kosmisk Orgasme
(Borgens Forlag)

BOOKS ON BHAGWAN

Sjælens Oprør
by Swami Deva Satyarthi
(Borgens Forlag)

DUTCH

TRANSLATIONS

Drink Mij
(Ankh-Hermes)

Het Boek Der Geheimen (volumes 1-4)
(Mirananda)

Geen Water, Geen Maan
(Mirananda)

Gezaaid In Goede Aarde
(Ankh-Hermes)

Ik Ben De Poort
(Ankh-Hermes)

Ik Ben De Zee Die Je Zoekt
(Ankh-Hermes)

Meditatie: De Kunst van Innerlijke Extase
(Mirananda)

Mijn Weg, De Weg van de Witte Wolk
(Arcanum)

Het Mosterdzaad (volumes 1 & 2)
(Mirananda)

Het Oranje Meditatieboek
(Ankh-Hermes)

Psychologie en Evolutie
(Ankh-Hermes)

Tantra: Het Allerhoogste Inzicht
(Ankh-Hermes)

Tantra, Spiritualiteit en Seks
(Ankh-Hermes)

De Tantra Visie (volume 1)
(Arcanum)

Tau
(Ankh-Hermes)

Totdat Je Sterft
(Ankh-Hermes)

De Verborgen Harmonie
(Mirananda)

Volg Mij
(Ankh-Hermes)

Zoeken naar de Stier
(Ankh-Hermes)

BOOKS ON BHAGWAN

Bhagwan: Notities van Een Discipel
by Swami Deva Amrito (Jan Foudraine)
(Ankh-Hermes)

Bhagwan Shree Rajneesh: De Laatste Gok
by Ma Satya Bharti
(Mirananda)

Oorspronkelijk Gezicht,
Een Gang Naar Huis
by Swami Deva Amrito (Jan Foudraine)
(Ambo)

FRENCH

TRANSLATIONS

L'éveil à la Conscience Cosmique
(Dangles)

Je Suis La Porte
(EPI)

Le Livre Des Secrets (volume 1)
(Soleil Orange)

La Meditation Dynamique
(Dangles)

GERMAN

TRANSLATIONS

Auf der Suche
(Sambuddha Verlag)

Das Buch der Geheimnisse
(Heyne Taschenbuch)

Das Orangene Buch
(Sambuddha Verlag)

Der Freund
(Sannyas Verlag)

Reise ins Unbekannte
(Sannyas Verlag)

Ekstase: Die vergessene Sprache
(Herzschlag Verlag, formerly Ki-Buch)

Esoterische Psychologie
(Sannyas Verlag)

Die Rebellion der Seele
(Sannyas Verlag)

Ich bin der Weg
(Rajneesh Verlag)

Intelligenz des Herzens
(Herzschlag Verlag, formerly Ki-Buch)

Jesus aber schwieg
(Sannyas Verlag)

Jesus -der Menschensohn
(Sannyas Verlag)

Kein Wasser, Kein Mond
(Herzschlag Verlag, formerly Ki-Buch)

Komm und folge mir
(Sannyas Verlag)

Meditation: Die Kunst zu sich selbst zu finden
(Heyne Verlag)

Mein Weg: Der Weg der weissen Wolke
(Herzschlag Verlag, formerly Ki-Buch)

Mit Wurzeln und mit Flügeln
(Edition Lotus)

Nicht bevor du stirbst
(Edition Gyandip, Switzerland)

Die Schuhe auf dem Kopf
(Edition Lotus)

Das Klatschen der einen Hand
(Edition Gyandip, Switzerland)

Spirituelle Entwicklung
(Fischer)

Sprengt den Fels der Unbewusstheit
(Fischer)

Tantra: Die höchste Einsicht
(Sambuddha Verlag)

Tantrische Liebeskunst
(Sannyas Verlag)

Die Alchemie der Verwandlung
(Edition Lotus)

Die verborgene Harmonie
(Sannyas Verlag)

Was ist Meditation?
(Sannyas Verlag)

Die Gans ist raus!
(Sannyas Verlag)

BOOKS ON BHAGWAN

Rajneeshismus - Bhagwan Shree Rajneesh und
seine Religion
Eine Einfuhrung
Rajneesh Foundation International

Begegnung mit Niemand
by Mascha Rabben (Ma Hari Chetana)
(Herzschlag Verlag)

Ganz entspannt im Hier und Jetzt
by Swami Satyananda
(Rowohlt)

Im Grunde ist alles ganz einfach
by Swami Satyananda
(Ullstein)

Wagnis Orange
by Ma Satya Bharti
(Fachbuchhandlung fur Psychologie)

Wenn das Herz frei wird
by Ma Prem Gayan (Silvie Winter)
(Herbig)

Der Erwachte
by Vasant Joshi
(Synthesis Verlag)

GREEK

TRANSLATION

I Krifi Armonia (The Hidden Harmony)
(Emmanual Rassouliṣ)

HEBREW

TRANSLATION

Tantra: The Supreme Understanding
(Massada)

ITALIAN

TRANSLATIONS

L'Armonia Nascosta (volumes 1 & 2)
(Re Nudo)

Dieci Storie Zen di Bhagwan Shree Rajneesh
(Né Acqua, Né Luna)
(Il Fiore d'Oro)

La Dottrina Suprema
(Rizzoli)

Dimensioni Oltre il Conosciuto
(Mediterranee)

Io Sono La Soglia
(Mediterranee)

Il Libro Arancione
(Mediterranee)

Il Libro dei Segreti
(Bompiani)

Meditazione Dinamica:
L'Arte dell'Estasi Interiore
(Mediterranee)

La Nuova Alchimia
(Psiche)

La Rivoluzione Interiore
(Armenia)

La Ricerca
(La Salamandra)

Il Seme della Ribellione (volumes 1-3)
(Re Nudo)

Tantra: La Comprensione Suprema
(Bompiani)

Tao: I Tre Tesori (volumes 1-3)
(Re Nudo)

Tecniche di Liberazione
(La Salamandra)

Semi di Saggezza
(SugarCo)

BOOKS ON BHAGWAN

Alla Ricerca del Dio Perduto
by Swami Deva Majid
(SugarCo)

Il Grande Esperimento:
   Meditazioni E Terapie Nell'ashram
Di Bhagwan Shree Rajneesh
by Ma Satya Bharti
(Armenia)

L'Incanto D'Arancio
by Swami Swatantra Sarjano
(Savelli)

JAPANESE

TRANSLATIONS

Dance Your Way to God
(Rajneesh Publications)

The Empty Boat (volumes 1 & 2)
(Rajneesh Publications)

From Sex to Superconsciousness
(Rajneesh Publications)

The Grass Grows by Itself
(Fumikura)

The Heart Sutra
(Merkmal)

Meditation: The Art of Ecstasy
(Merkmal)

The Mustard Seed
(Merkmal)

My Way: The Way of the White Clouds
(Rajneesh Publications)

The Orange Book
(Wholistic Therapy Institute)

The Search
(Merkmal)

The Beloved
(Merkmal)

Take It Easy (volume 1)
(Merkmal)

Tantra: The Supreme Understanding
(Merkmal)

Tao: The Three Treasures (volumes 1-4)
(Merkmal)

Until You Due
(Fumikura)

PORTUGUESE. (BRAZIL)

TRANSLATIONS

O Cipreste No Jardim
(Soma)

Dimensões Além do Conhecido
(Soma)

O Livro Dos Segredos (volume 1)
(Maha Lakshmi Editora)

Eu Sou A Porta
(Pensamento)

A Harmonia Oculta
(Pensamento)

Meditacão: A Arte Do Extase
(Cultrix)

Meu Caminho:
  O Comainho Das Nuvens Brancas
(Tao Livraria & Editora)

Nem Agua, Nem Lua
(Pensamento)

O Livro Orange
(Soma)

Palavras De Fogo
(Global/Ground)

A Psicologia Do Esotérico
(Tao Livraria & Editora)

A Semente De Mostarda (volumes 1 & 2)
(Tao Livraria & Editora)

Tantra: Sexo E Espiritualidade
(Agora)

Tantra: A Supreme Comprensao
(Cultrix)

Antes Que Voce Morra
(Maha Lakshmi Editora)

SPANISH

TRANSLATIONS

Introducción al Mundo del Tantra
(Colección Tantra)

Meditación: El Arte del Extasis
(Colección Tantra)

Psicológia de lo Esotérico:
La Nueva Evolución del Hombre
(Cuatro Vientos Editorial)

¿Qué Es Meditación?
(Koan/Roselló Impresions)

Yo Soy La Puerta
(Editorial Diana)

Sòlo Un Cielo (volumes 1 & 2)
(Colección Tantra)

BOOKS ON BHAGWAN

El Riesgo Supremo
by Ma Satya Bharti
(Martinez Roca)

SWEDISH

TRANSLATION

Den Väldiga Utmaningen
(Livskraft)

RAJNEESH MEDITATION CENTERS, ASHRAMS AND COMMUNES

There are hundreds of Rajneesh meditation centers throughout the world. These are some of the main ones, which can be contacted for the name and address and telephone number of the center nearest you. They can also tell you about the availability of the books of Bhagwan Shree Rajneesh — in English or in foreign language editions. General information is available from Rajneesh Foundation International.

A wide range of meditation and inner growth programs is available throughout the year at Rajneesh International Meditation University.

For further information and a complete listing of programs, write or call:

> Rajneesh International Meditation University
> P.O. Box 5, Rajneeshpuram, OR 97741 USA
> Phone: (503) 489-3328

USA

RAJNEESH FOUNDATION INTERNATIONAL
P.O. Box 9, Rajneeshpuram, Oregon 97741.
Tel: (503) 489-3301

SAMBODHI RAJNEESH NEO-SANNYAS COMMUNE
Conomo Point Road, Essex, MA 01929. Tel: (617) 768-7640

UTSAVA RAJNEESH MEDITATION CENTER
20062 Laguna Canyon Rd., Laguna Beach, CA 92651.
Tel: (714) 497-4877

DEVADEEP RAJNEESH SANNYAS ASHRAM
1430 Longfellow St., N.W., Washington, D.C. 20011.
Tel: (202) 723-2186

CANADA

ARVIND RAJNEESH SANNYAS ASHRAM
2807 W. 16th Ave., Vancouver, B.C. V6K 3C5.
Tel: (604) 734-4681

SHANTI SADAN RAJNEESH MEDITATION CENTER
1817 Rosemont, Montreal, Quebec H2G 1S5.
Tel: (514) 272-4566

AUSTRALIA

PREMDWEEP RAJNEESH MEDITATION CENTER
64 Fullarton Rd., Norwood, S.A. 5067. Tel: 08-423388

SAHAJAM RAJNEESH SANNYAS ASHRAM
6 Collie Street, Fremantle 6160, W.A.
Tel: (09) 336-2422

SATPRAKASH RAJNEESH MEDITATION CENTER
4A Ormond St., Paddington, N.S.W. 2021
Tel: (02) 336570

SVARUP RAJNEESH MEDITATION CENTER
303 Drummond St., Carlton 3053, Victoria. Tel: 347-3388

AUSTRIA

PRADEEP RAJNEESH MEDITATION CENTER
Siebenbrunnenfeldgasse 4, 1050 Vienna. Tel: 542-860

BELGIUM

VADAN RAJNEESH MEDITATION CENTER
Platte-Lo-Straat 65, 3200 Leuven (Kessel-Lo).
Tel: 016/25-1487

BRAZIL

PRASTHAN RAJNEESH MEDITATION CENTER
R. Paulas Matos 121, Rio de Janeiro, R.J. 20251.
Tel: 222-9476

PURNAM RAJNEESH MEDITATION CENTER
Caixa Postal 1946, Porto Alegre, RS 90000.

CHILE

SAGARO RAJNEESH MEDITATION CENTER
Golfo de Darien 10217, Las Condes, Santiago.
Tel: 472476

DENMARK
ANAND NIKETAN RAJNEESH MEDITATION CENTER
Stroget, Frederiksberggade 15, 1459 Copenhagen K.
Tel: (01) 139940, 117909

EAST AFRICA
AMBHOJ RAJNEESH MEDITATION CENTER
P.O. Box 59159, Nairobi, Kenya

FRANCE
PRADIP RAJNEESH MEDITATION CENTER
23 Rue Cecile, Maisons Alfort, 94700 Paris.
Tel: 3531190

GREAT BRITAIN
MEDINA RAJNEESH BODY CENTER
81 Belsize Park Gardens, London NW3.
Tel: (01) 722-8220, 722-6404

MEDINA RAJNEESH NEO-SANNYAS COMMUNE
Herringswell, Bury St. Edmunds, Suffolk 1P28 6SW.
Tel: (0638) 750234

HOLLAND
AMITABH RAJNEESH MEDITATION CENTER
Postbus 3280, 1001 AB Amsterdam
Tel: 020-221296

DE STAD RAJNEESH NEO-SANNYAS COMMUNE
Kamperweg 80-86 8191 KC Heerde. Tel: 05207-1261

GRADA RAJNEESH NEO-SANNYAS COMMUNE
Prins Hendrikstraat 64, 1931 BK Egmond aan Zee.
Tel: 02206-4114

INDIA
RAJNEESHDHAM NEO-SANNYAS COMMUNE
17 Koregaon Park, Poona 411 001, MS. Tel: 28127

RAJ YOGA RAJNEESH MEDITATION CENTER
C5/44 Safdarjang Development Area, New Delhi 100 016.
Tel: 654533

ITALY
MIASTO RAJNEESH NEO-SANNYAS COMMUNE
Podere S. Giorgio, Cotorniano, 53010 Frosini (Siena).
Tel: 0577-960124

VIVEK RAJNEESH MEDITATION CENTER
Via San Marco 40/4, 20121 Milan. Tel: 659-5632

JAPAN
SHANTIYUGA RAJNEESH MEDITATION CENTER
Sky Mansion 2F, 1-34-1 Ookayama, Meguro-ku, Tokyo 152.
Tel: (03) 724-9631

UTSAVA RAJNEESH MEDITATION CENTER
2-9-8 Hattori-Motomachi, Toyonaki-shi, Osaka 561.
Tel: 06-863-4246

NEW ZEALAND
SHANTI NIKETAN RAJNEESH MEDITATION CENTER
119 Symonds Street, Auckland. Tel: 770-326

PUERTO RICO
BHAGWATAM RAJNEESH MEDITATION CENTER
Calle Sebastian 208 (Altos), Viejo San Juan, PR 00905.
Tel: 725-0593

SPAIN
SARVOGEET RAJNEESH MEDITATION CENTER
C. Titania 55, Madrid, 33. Tel: 200-0313

SWEDEN
DEEVA RAJNEESH MEDITATION CENTER
Surbrunnsgatan 60, S11327 Stockholm. Tel: (08) 327788

SWITZERLAND
GYANDIP RAJNEESH MEDITATION CENTER
Baumackerstr. 42, 8050 Zurich. Tel: (01) 312 1600

WEST GERMANY
BAILE RAJNEESH NEO-SANNYAS COMMUNE
Karolinenstr. 7-9, 2000 Hamburg 6. Tel: (040) 432140

DORFCHEN RAJNEESH NEO-SANNYAS
Urbanstr. 64, 1000 Berlin 61. Tel: (030) 324-7758

RAJNEESHSTADT NEO-SANNYAS COMMUNE
Schloss Wolfsbrunnen, 3446 Meinhard-Schwebda.
Tel: (05651) 70044

SATDHARMA RAJNEESH MEDITATION CENTER
Klenzestr. 41, 8000 Munich 5. Tel: (089) 269-077

WIOSKA RAJNEESH SANNYAS ASHRAM
Lutticherstr. 33/35, 5000 Cologne 1. Tel: 0221-517199

Bhagwan Shree Rajneesh

THE BOOK
OF THE SECRETS

Discourses on "Vigyana Bhairava Tantra"

VOLUME V

The last in the series of five volumes on the
112 meditation techniques from the tantric
scripture **Vigyana Bhairava Tantra,** which
form the basis of all meditations the world
has ever known.

"If you really understand me, these 112
techniques will show you that everything can
become a technique . . . Everything can
become a technique if you understand the
quality of mind which brings meditation."

$4.95 paperback   ISBN 0-88050-529-X

Please make payment to:
Rajneesh Foundation International
P.O. Box 9
Rajneeshpuram, OR 97741 U.S.A.